Christmas 1998

DERVLA MURPHY

VISITING
RWANDA

THE LILLIPUT PRESS
DUBLIN

First published 1998 by
THE LILLIPUT PRESS LTD
62-63 Sitric Road, Arbour Hill,
Dublin 7, Ireland.
E-MAIL: lilliput@indigo.ie
Web site: http://indigo.ie/~lilliput

A CIP record for this
title is available from
The British Library.

ISBN 1 901866 11 4

Set by Sheila Stephenson in 10 on 13 Sabon
with display heads in Felix Titling
Map by Timothy O'Neill
Printed in Scotland
by Caledonian International Book Manufacturing Ltd

CONTENTS

ACKNOWLEDGMENTS

Without the advice and support of John Walton my Rwanda visit might never have happened. His colleagues in Kigali offered generous hospitality. So did various NGO workers throughout Rwanda, but they would prefer not to be named. Invaluable documentary backup came from a dear friend who would also prefer not to be named. To my first granddaughter, Rose, a special debt of gratitude is owed; she started the whole thing by migrating to Zaire at the age of three months. On another plane, an equal debt of gratitude is owed to Antony Farrell and Brendan Barrington of The Lilliput Press.

CHRONOLOGY

1885 German Empire given responsibility for Rwanda-Burundi region at Berlin Conference.

1899 Germans set up civil administration.

1916 Belgian troops arrive as Germans withdraw.

1919 Treaty of Versailles entrusts region to Belgium as mandated territory.

1946 League of Nations mandate replaced by United Nations Trusteeship.

1957 The Hutu Manifesto demands independence from both the Belgians and the Tutsi monarchy, which since 1931 has collaborated with the colonial regime.

1959 After death of Mwami (King) Mutara III, some 100,000 Tutsi are killed in a revolt against Tutsi rule and more than 200,000 flee into exile.

1961 The Hutu majority seizes power, abolishes the monarchy and proclaims a republic, recognized by Belgium. Rwanda and Burundi become separate states.

1962 Gregoire Kayibanda becomes first president of the independent Hutu republic and restricts his government to Hutus.

1965 The ruling party, PARMEHUTU, obtains 97 per cent in a general election and Rwanda is declared a one-party state.

1973 In a non-violent coup, Juvenal Habyarimana overcomes Kayibanda, who dies in jail soon after.

1975 The MRND, Habyarimana's party, replaces PARMEHUTU as single ruling party.

1986 Rwandan (mainly Tutsi) refugees contribute significantly to the victory in Uganda of the army of Yoweri Museveni.

1988 In Washington a gathering of Tutsi refugees from all over the world endorses their unconditional repatriation as the only possible solution to their problems.

1990 Fred Rwigyema, formerly a major-general in Museveni's army, leads an RPA invasion of Rwanda from Uganda on 30 September. French, Belgian and Zairean troops help to repulse invasion.

1991 Another invasion from Uganda is repulsed in January. On 8 June Habyarimana promises constitutional reform and a multi-party system.

1992   A transitional government is formed in April to hold power until the 1995 multi-party elections agreed to by MRND, which later rejects agreement. This government never took power.

1993   Three-year war ends when Habyarimana signs peace accord with RPF in Arusha, Tanzania, on 4 August. In June Melchior Ndadaye wins Burundi's presidential election and becomes the first Hutu president. In October his assassination by Tutsi officers in a military coup provokes extreme violence. United Nations Assistance Mission to Rwanda (UNAMIR), a peacekeeping force, deployed in Rwanda.

1994

5 April – UNAMIR's mandate extended to 29 July by the Security Council. Next day Habyarimana and President Cyprien Ntariyamira of Burundi die together in a plane crash and the genocide starts in Kigali.

9 April – Belgian and French paratroopers arrive in Kigali to rescue expatriates.

12 April – Government forces and RPA begin the battle for Kigali. Throughout the country thousands of Tutsi are being massacred every day.

21 April – UNAMIR troops reduced from 2500 to 270 by Security Council Resolution 912.

17 May – Over half a million Tutsi have been slaughtered. Security Council Resolution 918 calls for the end of the massacres and increases the Blue Helmets to 5500 (UNAMIR II). Two months later only a tenth of these have been deployed.

17 June – Number of victims has risen to three-quarters of a million. A French initiative for 'humanitarian' intervention approved by UN Secretary-General Boutros Boutros-Ghali.

30 June – Massacres described as 'genocide' by UN Human Rights Commission Special Rapporteur, in a detailed report.

1 July – UN Security Council Resolution 935 calls for the setting up of a committee of 'impartial experts' to investigate the evidence for 'possible acts of genocide'.

4 July – RPA forces capture Kigali.

14 July – RPA forces take Ruhengeri, the main town in northern Rwanda, and tens of thousands of refugees flee over the border into Zaire.

17 July – RPA forces capture Habyarimana's last bastion, Gisenyi.

18 July – The end of the war is declared and the RPF installs a new 'government of national unity' with a Hutu president and Hutu prime minister.

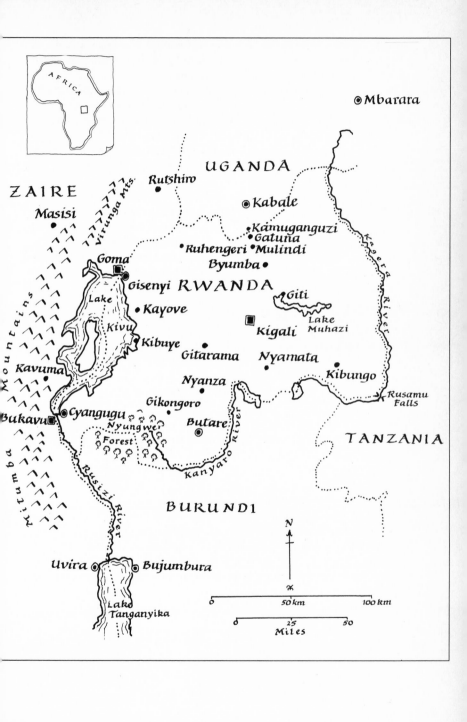

VISITING
RWANDA

PROLOGUE

Throughout April and May 1994 I was in South Africa, completely absorbed in that country's affairs, and I scarcely registered Rwanda's genocide while it was happening. At the time my knowledge of Rwanda could have been written on a postcard. I knew only that it had the highest population density in mainland Africa (some 7.15 million occupying a territory about the size of Wales), that it was very beautiful, mainly dependent on agriculture and terrifyingly prone to lethal conflicts between the 15 per cent Tutsi minority – for centuries the ruling élite – and the Hutu majority. I remembered too that in 1961, after the massacring of many Tutsi, the Hutu gained power as the Belgian rulers prepared to leave their grossly mistreated protectorate to its own sanguinary devices. Also, during a 1992 bicycle ride from Kenya to Zimbabwe, I met a few of the Tutsi who had settled in Uganda as refugees in 1959 and subsequent years. From them I learned that between '62 and '67 certain Tutsi factions had tried to fight their way back to Rwanda but were always defeated. These incursions provoked reprisals, usually government-organized, against Tutsi still living in Rwanda. During that period some 20,000 were killed and hundreds of thousands fled to neighbouring countries: Burundi, Uganda, Zaire and Tanzania.

In April 1995, a year after the genocide began, I suddenly had a personal reason to focus on Rwanda. My daughter Rachel, then two months pregnant, was moving to Kigali with her partner Andrew, who was to spend six months attached to a UNHCR team. (They first met in Mozambique when working as UN volunteers with a unit established to disarm the opposing armies in preparation for the elections of November 1994.) On their return from Kigali in October, they came to stay with me and I expected graphic accounts of life in post-genocide Rwanda; normally both enjoy describing their travels and analysing regional problems. This time, however, they had strangely little to say. Almost nothing, in fact; their faces closed if anyone asked about their impressions of Rwanda. This silence was in itself disturbingly eloquent and when they lent me two books I fully understood it.

Rwanda: Death, Despair and Defiance, published by African Rights, needs 1200 pages to report exactly what happened in each of Rwanda's 143 communes during the genocide. It is by far the most shattering book I have ever read, all the more so for being a straightforward record of facts and figures, dates and times, personal names and place names, unadorned by literary graces. Gérard Prunier's *The Rwanda Crisis* made me aware for the first time of the French government's unforgivable complicity in the genocide and of the shameful passivity-cum-duplicity of the UN before, during and after the tragedy.

On 4 August 1993 the Hutu government and the Tutsi Rwandan Patriotic Front (RPF) signed the Arusha Accords, designed to end the conflict that began in October 1990 when the Rwandan Patriotic Army (RPA) invaded from Uganda, determined to overthrow the extremist Hutu régime and make it possible for the millions of Tutsi refugees and their born-in-exile children to return to Rwanda. The Accords provided (in theory) for the integration of opposing armies and the presence of a UN peacekeeping force until the setting up of a transitional government, including members of the RPF, to run the country while elections were being organized. On 5 October 1993 the UN Security Council's Resolution 872 at last authorized the peacekeeping force (UNAMIR), but its troops were not deployed until December. Meanwhile the Hutu extremists were blocking the formation of the transitional government and training and arming thousands of militia, ostensibly for 'popular self-defence' and the 'neutralization of infiltrators'. Because of a shortage of firearms, army officers instructed civilians in methods of killing with machetes, spears, swords and bows and arrows.

On 21 October 1993 the first Hutu to be elected President of Burundi, where the Tutsi are also in a 15 per cent minority, was assassinated by Tutsi army officers. More than 50,000 – both Hutu and Tutsi – died in the subsequent violence but the so-called 'international community' made no significant comment. Rwanda's genocidal leaders exploited this situation to incite hatred and fear of Tutsi, and pointed out to their followers that a world indifferent to massacres in Burundi would remain equally indifferent to the extermination of Rwanda's Tutsi. They were soon to be proved right.

On 11 January 1994 a cable arrived at UN headquarters in New York from the head of UNAMIR in Kigali, Major-General Roméo Dallaire, reporting that Hutu militia were preparing to commit genocide against the Tutsi. (Dallaire's informant was employed by President Habyarimana's party to train these militia – the *interahamwe* – and to 'register all Tutsi in Kigali'.) The reply from the UN Department of Peacekeeping Operations denied Dallaire's request for permission to raid an *interahamwe* arms cache, on the grounds that such a move would violate UNAMIR's mandate. Dallaire was authorized only to pass on his information to the Belgian, French and US ambassadors in Kigali and, amazingly, to President Habyarimana. The matter went no further. Within three months the reliability of Dallaire's informant was confirmed.

Also in January 1994 France promised Habyarimana more than US$5.5 million in military aid for the coming year. During February the Hutu militia murdered forty people in Kigali, the UN troops making no effort to deter them though UNAMIR's mandate was 'to contribute to the capital's security'. When that mandate expired on 5 April no transitional government yet existed and the Security Council voted to extend the mandate for another four months. UNAMIR then consisted of about 2700 soldiers from twenty-three countries, the vast majority inadequately trained and ill-equipped – not at all the sort of troops the international community would send to an oil-rich battleground.

On the evening of 6 April 1994 President Habyarimana and President Ntaryamira of Burundi – and all others aboard – were killed when their plane was shot down as it approached Kigali airport, by a person or persons unknown. Within hours the slaughtering of Tutsi and their moderate Hutu allies had begun. 'Moderate', in this context, means Hutu opposed to the extremist régime and willing to implement the Arusha Accords. Not all Hutu so described had 'Moderation' as their middle name.

By 8 April blood was flowing in torrents; in just one attack on that date over 2000 were killed on the campus of the Adventist University at Mudende, near Gisenyi. Next day 300 French para-troopers arrived to take control of Kigali airport. A thousand Belgian troops and an Italian contingent followed, while 300 US marines moved into Burundi. In collaboration with UNAMIR, these crack troops efficiently evacuated more than 2000 expats. Very few chose to remain in Rwanda, where the massacres were being accompanied, day and night, by orgies of rape and looting. The foreign troops then withdrew and by 13 April some 20,000 Rwandans had been butchered – as the Security Council noted while debating the crisis without reaching any conclusion. Three days later, by which time many thousands more had been killed, it held another inconclusive debate. On 21 April Major-General Roméo Dallaire, the UNAMIR commander in Kigali, stated that he could end the genocide if given a force of 5000 to 8000 well-equipped soldiers. On the same date the Security Council's Resolution 912, prompted by the US government, directed the withdrawal of most UN troops, leaving only 270 with a mandate limited to helping to deliver humanitarian aid and acting as 'intermediary' – a fanciful notion since mediation was not on the agenda.

Three weeks later, after countless prolonged discussions, the Security Council was about to vote to send troops back to Rwanda when the US representative requested a postponement of the vote because she had 'no instructions' from Washington. Not until 17 May did Resolution 918 authorize the sending of 5500 troops to Rwanda with a mandate to protect civilians (of whom more than half a million had by then been killed) and the delivery of humanitarian aid. The US voted for this resolution but delayed deployment by insisting that the situation needed to be 'further assessed'. Six weeks later the Secretary-General admitted that only 550 troops were deployed in Rwanda, more than two months after the resolution authorizing ten times that number. It is surely not irrelevant that on 10 June US officials were instructed to avoid the word 'genocide', as its use might increase pressure on the US government to act.

On 1 June General Dallaire appealed to Washington for armoured personnel carriers, without which he was unable to save civilian lives. President Clinton's envoy to Rwanda promised Dallaire that his request would be 'taken to the highest authority'. On 22 June 10,700 bodies were removed from Lake Victoria for burial; those bodies, flung into the Kagera river some time previously, had become a major threat to the health of lakeside villagers. Next day the US delivered to Kampala the first of forty-seven armoured personnel carriers leased to the UN. On 28 June another four arrived but proved useless because they lacked radios or machine-guns.

The RPA took Kigali on 4 July, and on 15 July the US government withdrew recognition from the genocidal régime and ordered its Washington embassy to be closed. Members of the MRND and the FAR chief of staff then took refuge, with French assistance, in Zaire, and the RPF announced the formation of a new Rwandan government.

The UNHCR estimated that by the end of July some 1.4 million Hutu refugees had fled to Zaire, 353,000 to Burundi and 241,000 to Tanzania. Many fled because their leaders told them the RPA would kill them if they remained in their communes, others because they were forced to leave by local officials. In Zaire FAR soldiers and militia regularly looted food and medicines from some of the refugee camps and prevented the delivery of food to others. Soon cholera had broken out and eventually more than 60,000 refugees died of various diseases.

On 10 August the US Assistant Secretary of State, George Moose, demanded the arrest and prosecution of all those responsible for the increasing violence in the expanding refugee camps. Three days later the Zairean Prime Minister sought international help for the disarming of the ex-FAR troops and their separation from the other refugees. He was ignored.

On 15 August a plan to repatriate refugees from Zaire was abandoned because the Hutu troops threatened to kill any who might attempt to return home; four men brave enough to defy them were murdered in Goma camps. Soon after, the UN verbosely deplored the perilous insecurity – virtually a state of war – within the camps. On 8 September the Secretary-General's special envoy revealed that FAR troops were preparing to invade Rwanda from Zaire and had already sent raiding parties over the border and killed several Tutsi survivors and Hutu moderates. (The whole region was by then infested with 'special envoys', each more ineffectual than the last.)

At the end of September the UNHCR, Oxfam and several other aid agencies had to leave Kitale camp for security reasons. On 1 November Rwanda radio announced the killing of thirty-six people in north-western Rwanda by ex-FAR troops based in Zaire, and fifteen NGOs threatened to leave all camps in the Goma area unless the genocidal warriors and their civilian allies were brought under control.

Three weeks later the Secretary-General requested a peacekeeping mission (oddly named as there was no peace to keep) for the restoration of order in the camps, but not one member state was willing to provide troops or support of any sort for this operation.

On 25 January 1995 the UN decided to pass the buck to the notoriously corrupt and undisciplined Zairean army. Those thugs would, allegedly, be 'supported and aided' by the UNHCR, an agency lacking any resources with which to control the well-armed ex-FAR and militia, backed up by Hutu community leaders who had helped to organize the genocide. Aid workers then had no choice but to co-operate with the *génocidaires* in the day-to-day running of the camps.

In the middle of a long book about a difficult subject (South Africa in transition from apartheid to something else) one needs a break, 'a little holiday'. So said Rachel in January 1996 on the eve of her departure for Bukavu, the capital of Kivu Province in what was then eastern Zaire. She was departing to join Andrew; his new NGO job involved working with the local Zaireans, whose needs hardly impinged on an international community obsessed with the regional refugee problem. Rachel and Andrew and their first-born would be gone for an unspecified but certainly lengthy period. Therefore Nyanya (Swahili for 'Granny') could see the need for a break in Bukavu.

Grandmaternity, to my friends' amusement and my own astonishment, had brought about a personality change. Babies in general

I had always been able to do without. They are of course inevitable, but excessively tiresome while one awaits the stage when verbal communication is possible. However, Rose somehow seemed different. She was born on 10 November 1995 in her parents' London flat, where I saw her bloody face as she emerged from the womb and heard her first cry and then heard the Afro-Caribbean midwife say, 'Now what have we here – a daughter!' Instantly I was besotted. I don't recall being similarly addicted to the infant Rachel but maybe I was. That's a long time ago and one forgets ... Although Rose must have been as boring as any other baby, her every meaningless whimper and gurgle and wriggle riveted me. Within a month of her being transported to Bukavu I was conferring with my travel agent.

An urban destination unapproachable by road for security reasons and ignored by all commercial airlines is quite a novelty; from Nairobi one must take a twelve-seater MAF plane to Bukavu. Let MAF define itself:

Our new corporate purpose statement reflects a sharpening of perspective: 'The purpose of the Mission Aviation Fellowship is to multiply the effectiveness of the Church by using aviation and other strategic technologies to reach the world for Christ.' For half a century, the propellers of MAF planes have served at the very cutting edge of missions. Even now, our Electronic Communications Department operates a C-Standard Satellite terminal in Rwanda, enabling groups on the field to communicate directly with the US as well as with one another. In the absence of local communications, this system serves as a critical link to co-ordinate relief efforts on site and keep track of personnel in perilous areas.

Over the years, on various continents, MAF and the CIA have had occasion to collaborate on enterprises of dubious probity. Nevertheless, I was pleased to be able to book a seat (US$460 return) on their 9 April flight from Wilson Airport.

1

ON THE EDGE IN ZAIRE

From the air Bukavu was distantly visible at the base of a steep
mountain, its three narrow wooded peninsulas stretching far out
into Lake Kivu. As the plane descended towards the airstrip at 1
p.m. (two hours late), an immense expanse of blue appeared
amidst the bush – a city of close-packed hovels, sheltering 90,000
Rwandan refugees, its blueness created by UNHCR tarpaulin
roofs. Pre-grandmaternity, I would have been avid for information
about how this camp is being run. Today I merely observed it,
avid only for information about Rose's development since last I
saw her on 15 January.

I stepped off the plane into the arms – almost literally, he
seized my elbow – of a tall, fat, complacent-looking Zairean soldier. In French he asked if I was the grandmother. Proudly I said
'oui'. Briskly he led me past those numerous predatory bureaucrats who lie in wait for foreigners entering Zaire. Smiling, he
delivered me to Andrew. No immigration officer was interested in
my passport, no customs officer even glanced at my rucksack.
Importing grannies is costly, but the dollars are effective.

I had been forewarned, I knew that Zaire is not as other
African countries are – at least not those through which I have
travelled. Here no one pretends that there is a functioning government. And if soldiers and civil servants go unpaid for years they
must somehow acquire money, whenever and however and from
whomever they can. Dollar-rich foreigners are naturally their
main targets, but Zaire's real corruption happens at the top in

Kinshasa and for more than thirty years has been indulged by the US and French governments, among others.

We hastened to the Land-Rover, Rose peering at me rather suspiciously from beneath her wide-brimmed sunhat. One doesn't linger in Bukavu's 'airport', a huddle of flimsy shacks around two semi-derelict colonial office buildings. Numerous heavily armed soldiers stroll to and fro, eyeing all newly arrived passengers speculatively – and to deny their demands is unwise.

The main road bisects the refugee camp. Although small compared with Goma's 'metropolitan' settlements 120 miles to the north, it seems a vast intrusion on this rural scene. Reputedly it is less violent than Goma's camps, but one prefers, said Andrew, to drive through as quickly as possible. The vibes are disturbing. The pedestrian traffic on the verges was heavy as refugees carried WFP-donated foods to be sold illegally to Zaireans. Many women, using forehead straps, were bent double under the enormous sacks of grain on their backs. Scores of men, women and children, returning to the camp, bore headloads of firewood. No one was conversing or smiling – or looked capable of ever again smiling.

During that twenty-mile drive I fell madly in love with Kivu Province. Even my enchantingly cheerful granddaughter, who already seemed to be thawing towards Nyanya, could not entirely distract my attention from the lush hilly beauty – hills grassy or forested, overlooking the jade-green waters of Lake Kivu, matching other forested hills on the far (Rwandan) shore. Here, towards its southern end, the lake narrows and that shore is only a few miles away.

Sometimes banana groves line the road, and we stopped to spend 15,000 Zaires on three dozen bananas offered by three small boys, pitifully skinny yet bouncy and grinning. Watching this transaction, my heart sank. I'm bad at sums and in countries where three, four and five zeros complicate calculations I tend to lose my cool when shopping. Three months ago Z15,000 was one US dollar; now it's about forty US cents.

Not far from Bukavu a large military tent stands by the roadside, labelled UNHCR. Several soldiers lounge at the entrance, ready to register the exit from Zaire of refugees returning to

Rwanda. Because no refugees are returning to Rwanda this tent might be described as cosmetic, a symptom of the arcane political game being played by the various aid agencies, the Zairean, Rwandan and Tanzanian governments, the genocidal camp administrators, the sinister Hutu militia (known as the *interahamwe*), and representatives of that amorphous entity, the International Community. I was about to revert to my pre-grandmotherly state of mind when Rose smiled directly at me, for the first time ever. Thus beguiled, I forgot all about genocidal refugees, corrupt institutions, self-serving 'humanitarian' aid agencies and devious governments.

On the edge of Bukavu, Andrew pointed out the city's brewery. He knew this would make me feel secure and relaxed; a beerless holiday might overstretch Nyanya's equanimity. This being one of the few surviving local industries confirms the Lonely Planet *East Africa Guide*'s observation: 'In Zaire the beer rarely runs out. Aside from Australia and Germany, there are few other countries which place such a high priority on their beer supplies.'

Thus far the road had been surprisingly good; in Kivu Province only those twenty miles are tarred and few of the potholes exceed six inches in depth and a yard in diameter. But now, as we entered the city, its disintegrated streets reduced Andrew's speed to fifteen m.p.h. I noticed Rachel clutching Rose more tightly; the local drivers, not similarly inhibited, send their vehicles careering from side to side, swerving to avoid the worst chasms as though performing in a stunt film. Mercifully Bukavu is only a mini-city and we were soon out of the centre, in the almost traffic-free quartier de Muhumba. As for Avenue Walungu, it is a winding rural laneway where goats graze on the verges. And beyond the garden hedge of No. 19 a maize-field slopes steeply down to the lake.

A month ago, on Andrew's erratic satellite phone – an over-rated gadget, liable to induce frustration-ulcers, and, if often used, bankruptcy – I had heard about Budgie, the fourth member of the family. Prosaically, I had assumed him to be feathered. But – a joyful surprise! As I walked into the living-room, a minute ball of grey and white fur unrolled itself and stretched, then greeted me like an old friend, purring loudly. Of course I should have guessed; neither Rachel nor Andrew can live catless and Budgie was presented to them, at the age of six weeks, as a 'Welcome' present. Although born in January, he still looks too small to have left his mother. He is singularly ugly – the archetypal alley-kitten – but of ineffable charm and immensely composed. He and Rose are mutually devoted; they share the satisfaction of dominating all available adults, black or white, resident or visiting.

Towards sunset a three-minute walk took me down to the shore – to a secluded spot, overhung by tall pink and orange wild flowers – for my first swim in Lake Kivu. It's ten years since my last holiday but this one was worth the wait.

10 APRIL

No. 19 is a compact little bungalow: living-room, two bedrooms, a small kitchen and bathroom and – most important and most used – a patio, some fifteen feet square, of polished concrete, overlooking the colourful garden, the lake below and the opposite peninsula. That peninsula runs into Rwanda, as I realized last night when house lights went on across the water from us while the small dwellings to the north remained in darkness. All are unoccupied; fear of *interahamwe* incursions from the camps keeps them so.

Two servants go with this modest home, part of the deal made by Andrew's NGO with the Zairean owner who lives in Kinshasa. Paul is the elderly cook-cum-cleaner who lives two hours' walk away and arrives punctually at 8 a.m. six days a week. At 3 p.m. he leaves and Mpolo, the askari, takes over until next morning. Supposedly he stays awake all night; in his tiny mud-floored hut by the gate (its roof a UNHCR tarpaulin: these may be bought in the market for US$30) there is no encouragement to sleep, only a hard-backed, broken-legged chair. He also tends the garden and washes and polishes the Land-Rover – second-hand, imported via Dar es Salaam and Bujumbura, from where Andrew drove it at the beginning of January.

Two servants suggest affluence. But – there is no teapot so tea must be brewed in the kettle. And there are only two each of glasses, mugs, plates, knives, forks and spoons. It seemed my arrival would necessitate sharing until I pointed out that empty honey jars can be used as mugs. I revel in this zany lifestyle, the bizarre colonial leftover of two servants juxtaposed with the extreme frugality of a conscientious 1990s development worker.

And there is a hilarious incongruity about seeing my daughter thrust willy-nilly into a memsahib role. In some ways she is, I have to admit, slipping into this role with ominous ease, seeming very happy to recline on the patio watching Paul hanging out Rose's nappies – he of course having washed them. And then he must iron them because of the mango fly, which likes to lay its eggs on damp clothes. When these hatch out (if not killed by a hot iron) the worms invade bodies through the skin and make trouble – of what sort I'm not sure. However, Rachel's happy reclining is perfectly natural; to relish household chores is unnatural. Only those who take political correctness to the point of fanaticism (as I stupidly did thirty years ago when living in Pokhara), or who are obnoxiously mean, would decline to share their relative wealth by employing servants in a country as desperately poor as Zaire.

Vendors of fruits and vegetables, rabbits and chickens, souvenirs and scarves, bang hopefully on the gate shouting for 'madame'. Happily this title in Zaire does not have its South African connotation. Here there is a hint of amiable mockery in the voices of dignified elderly vendors as they thus address the 'mistress of the household' – barefooted, clad in threadbare shorts and T-shirt and looking younger than her twenty-seven years.

11 APRIL

The capital of Kivu Province must surely qualify for the Guinness Book of Records: a city of a quarter of a million people with no public transport, no postal service, no telephone service, no functioning bank, no newspapers in any language, no expat dentist, a doctor only at irregular intervals and hospitals without medicines. However, Bukavu's welcoming and cheerful citizens (who have nothing discernible to be cheerful about) more than compensate the visitor for those little inconveniences. As do the clear deep waters of Lake Kivu (a swimmer's paradise) and the perfection of the climate and the beauty of this whole region – in my experience never surpassed, and only rarely equalled, on any continent. Within forty-eight hours, Bukavu has become my favourite city in all the world.

Goma and Bukavu, at the opposite ends of Lake Kivu, were the Belgians' favourite retreats from the relentless heat and humidity of the Congo Basin – their Simla and Darjeeling, inherited post-independence by Zaire's Mobutu-pampered élite. Spacious holiday villas, and more modest homes for the permanently resident provincial officials, were built on the long wooded peninsulas rising steeply from the lake. These attractive dwellings are well spaced out, each surrounded by a glowing abundance of flowering trees and shrubs. Our Avenue Muhumba – on the middle peninsula, towards its tip – winds between plantains and tall trees swathed in purple bougainvillaea; plots of maize, beans and groundnuts separate the bungalows. None of these is large: probably lesser officials were the original inhabitants.

I have, by chance, arrived here at a most propitious time, towards the end of a rainy season. Now the vegetation is all new and vigorous and the dust is still being controlled by infrequent but heavy showers while high, gently drifting clouds constantly change Lake Kivu's colouring: from jade-green to black to blue to silver. On most of our walking routes the lake is visible and it never disappears for long – except in the city centre, the former commercial district. Well, not quite 'former'; some muted commercial activity continues despite galloping inflation and closed banks. The one thriving industry, already mentioned, produces a tolerable brew: Primus, sold in half-litre returnable bottles. So precious are these that there is no deposit system; without an empty you cannot buy a full ...

On the main avenues several 'European' stores (most now Indian-owned) seem large in contrast to the average African shop and still offer an amazing selection of non-perishable imported goods – at formidable prices. You can buy lavatory paper, shampoo, hand-cream, toilet soap, lipstick, sun-lotion, paper napkins, disposable nappies and edible items like biscuits and breakfast cereals made in Kenya and tinned Kraft cheese from the US. No one seems to know by which route American cheese travels to Kivu Province; it must be weirdly circuitous. And why import this repellent comestible when an excellent hard cheese is made on a nearby Catholic mission farm and sold in the butcher's shop? (Expensive but one of the staple foods at No. 19.) Perhaps the importer of Kraft (three times as expensive) is catering for those elderly American radio evangelists who drive their jeep round and round the city centre loudly relaying taped fundamentalist messages. In contrast to all else in the 'European' shops, authentic British booze is astoundingly cheap: US$15 for a bottle of Scotch (standard size) or Gilbey's gin. Rachel patronizes such shops only to buy Scotch for special occasions and Klim powdered milk for our tea. Rose, of course, has her personalized milk supply.

A Belgian returning after thirty years would certainly find Bukavu's centre dismal, proof that Africans can't govern themselves ... I, however, like its run-down grottiness, its wide hilly chasmic streets, its shattered pavements and peeling, once-imposing commercial façades. The provincial governor's residence and the old colonial administration offices – now the offices of moribund Zairean government departments – are clustered on the most densely wooded peninsula and guarded by unkempt soldiers, most of whom look mad or bad (sometimes both). These buildings are stuccoed, tin-roofed, pleasantly unpretentious – quite unlike their British equivalents, built to remind the natives that Britain's empire was unique in scale, power and wealth. Significantly, the city's dominant building is a Catholic church-cum-seminary and boarding school, a massive fortress-like complex on the highest ridge of our peninsula. Here, as elsewhere, the missionaries and the colonists worked closely together – were in effect part of the same team.

12 APRIL

This morning Rachel purchased Flopsy for US$5. (He has to be Flopsy because one ear permanently hangs down.) Far be it from me to question the purchase, we're all entitled to our eccentricities. But having impulsively acquired a rabbit (to save it from a neighbour's pot?), where to house it? Luckily there is a spare bedroom, the space Nyanya would be occupying if she didn't prefer sleeping out on the patio in her flea-bag. So Flopsy has been installed in the guest-room while alternative arrangements are being made.

Something unsettling happened this afternoon. Opposite the patio, a row of tiger-lilies flourishes in the rich soil below the hedge. Overnight one bloomed brilliantly – the first to flower – and at breakfast time Rachel rejoiced loudly, rushing down to admire it. Then we got back from the market at 4 p.m. to find that it had been uprooted and thrust through the hedge into the maize field. Only Mpolo could have done this, though of course he denied it. Seemingly an inane deed, yet unsettling because we felt it was not inane but mysteriously purposeful. Just occasionally, in Africa, one is made deeply uneasy by the operation of inexplicable forces no longer encountered (perhaps never encountered?) in our world. This was such an occasion.

When I first saw Mpolo, when he opened the gate on our arrival from the airstrip, he gave me the creeps. His eyes disconcerted me – as did his manner. No, 'manner' is the wrong word; in fact he welcomed me enthusiastically without being obsequious. I should have said his 'aura'. But these instant and apparently irrational reactions to another human being evade analysis, whether they be negative or positive. It's interesting – maybe even significant – that Paul, too, seems always ill at ease with Mpolo.

Sitting on the patio this evening, drinking our Primuses and watching the glow-worms on the lawn (they need to be protected from Budgie), we were all slightly subdued.

13 APRIL

The construction of a rabbit-run doesn't normally overtax human ingenuity. One needs only a few lengths of wood, a roll of chicken-wire, a few ounces of nails and a man with a hammer. But life in Bukavu is not normal: where to find chicken-wire? Yesterday and today Rachel, Rose and I roamed through the markets, enquiring. No one sold chicken-wire, no one knew where chicken-wire might be sold. It would have been easier to buy an AK-47 (US$25).

By now Rachel and Rose are well known and evidently well liked in both markets. 'Mama Rosa! Mama Rosa!' – the greeting comes from all directions as we appear. Nowadays these friendly vendors see no tourists and very few *muzungus* of any brand. Quite often their friendliness extends to giving well-meant but uncomprehending advice about how Rose should be carried. Her sometimes travelling on Rachel's front in a cloth baby-sling worries Africans who believe a baby's place is on the back. But even when she is on the back, in a purpose-built knapsack, they remain worried. This, to them, looks cruelly insecure, allowing her too much freedom of movement; when sleeping she slides down into what looks like an excruciatingly uncomfortable position. (Obviously it isn't: she often sleeps thus for hours.) Then kind advisers crowd around, eager to help this clueless young Mama (and equally clueless Nyanya) by adjusting Rose's head and limbs. Understandably, Rachel finds this trying; any mother lucky enough to have a sleeping infant wants to keep it that way. But for the sake of inter-racial harmony she contains her irritation.

In recent years, technology has begun to invade some of Africa's traditional markets – calculators, digital weighing machines, even mobile phones. Of such innovations Bukavu's markets are innocent. Here even the accursed plastic bag, global befouler of landscapes, has not yet arrived. You bring your own basket or container, or accept goods wrapped in the pages of used copy-books – allowing shoppers to appraise the academic standards (low) of Bukavu's youth.

Rachel and Andrew favour the smaller (but still large) hilltop market some fifteen minutes' brisk walk from No. 19. After rain its narrow paths, between close-packed ramshackle stalls, become canals of liquid mud. And always the aromas of decaying vegetation and rotting fish envelop the area. Here we buy fresh fruits and vegetables, rice and beans and Budgie's tiny sardine-like fish. It is a joy to see fruits and vegetables of irregular shapes and sizes, knowing that what the food industry would consider their 'blemishes' are evidence of their flavour and wholesomeness.

The larger market, near the centre, sells every sort of foodstuff (indigenous) and hardware, cloth and meat. Two or three men, grunting and sweating, may be seen pushing a handcart up the street laden with whole skinned bullocks – or maybe, here, they are young bulls? The butcher's hefty young assistants then dismember the carcasses with machetes, a procedure that too vividly recalls the other uses of machetes in this region not long ago ... Flies swarm, enthusiastic and undeterred. Cravenly, but perhaps sensibly given our European lack of immunities, we buy from a more 'Western-style' butcher in the centre. His slaughtering and dismembering methods are akin to the market butcher's but he doesn't permit flies to alight on the meat – at least not within view of his customers.

Eggs are most often available from pavement stalls along the main streets, stalls that also sell cigarettes, fizzy drinks, combs, bread and second-hand shoes. No one can explain why eggs should be so scarce and expensive: fifteen pence apiece for what we would consider pullets' or bantams' eggs – half a dozen are needed to make a decent one-person omelette. Fresh milk is unobtainable because of the lack of transport and refrigeration; the nearest herd grazes twenty-five miles away. But sometimes, at unguessable intervals, yoghurt comes from the mission farm and Rachel avidly stockpiles it. Fish is not as plentiful or as cheap as one would expect. Lake Kivu is volcanic and occasional releases of poisonous gas from the lake floor are said to be responsible for limiting the fish population. End of market report.

There's more to rabbits than meets the Irish eye. At home they are jolly, furry, hoppity, cuddly creatures, most often seen at dawn nibbling the dewy grass. A Bukavu rabbit is a much larger creature with – I discovered this evening – a kick like an ostrich if not held firmly in a certain position.

14 APRIL

Nyanya is having a holiday with a difference. Somehow I have become responsible for Flopsy-care, which gives me an unusual insight into the workings of a rabbit's bladder and bowels. Flopsy's prodigious output of urine baffles us. 'How and why?' we ask ourselves; he drinks none of the water diligently changed in his dish morning and evening. We can only deduce that his fodder (Flopsy-sized mounds of greenery freshly cut twice a day on nearby verges) has a 50 per cent water content, at least. Unfortunately, by the time this water emerges it has been so processed that it indelibly stains the concrete floor and anything else within reach – like my rucksack. When Flopsy took up residence I placed the empty rucksack, invitingly open, in a corner of the guest-room, thinking Flopsy might fancy it as a burrow-substitute. Instead, he fancied it as a latrine and peed copiously within, bleaching the back forever.

Rabbit urine is pungent. Thrice daily I get down on my hands and knees and mop it up, then scour the floor with whatever substance Paul uses – which is causing the skin on my hands to flake off. As for a rabbit's bowel movements, these of course are extremely civilized: neat, dry marbles – but unbelievably numerous marbles and strewn all over the floor. I hand-pick them one by one, risking a dislocated back as I insinuate myself under the low bedstead (it's too heavy to move) in pursuit of the almost inaccessible. Then I fling the fistfuls into the garden where they annoy Mpolo by besmirching the concrete rain-channel he so assiduously sweeps every afternoon. When on duty, the adorable Paul observes my endeavours with a twinkle in his eye; he has adjusted well to working in a nut-house where *la belle mère* sleeps on the patio floor while a rabbit occupies the guest-room. Mpolo is less adaptable; he looked quite alarmed, the evening Flopsy arrived, on seeing me apparently weeding the garden by torchlight, a task Mpolo is paid to do by daylight.

For all this hard labour, my reward is Flopsy's increasing acceptance of his skivvy – almost amounting to affection, or so I tell myself. He no longer hops under the bed when I open the door but wriggles his nose quite frenziedly in what could be interpreted as a greeting – even a welcome. He also takes food from my hand and, if I hold one of his favourite herbs out of reach, he is trusting enough to climb on my lap, place his forefeet on my chest and stretch up for the treat. Rabbits can elongate in the most extraordinary way, as though made of elastic.

Sometimes during these sessions I see out of the corner of my eye a very small grey paw being inserted under the door. Budgie has taken to spending hours outside the guest-room, his posture that of a cat by a mouse-hole; instinct tells him that what he smells within is a feline's natural prey. However, when formally introduced to Flopsy (at least eight times his size) poor Budgie was momentarily paralysed with terror – then fled. Flopsy, on the other hand, seemed amiably interested; he hopped through the open door and stared rather wistfully in the direction of the vanished potential friend. Rachel intuits he's lonely – needs a wife ... Andrew looks ahead to the demographic consequences and discourages this idea. 'Unless,' he said, 'Nyanya plans to settle in Bukavu.'

15 APRIL

This morning Paul staged a protest. The household's only floor-cloth, with which he washes the floors every day, became over the weekend so powerfully redolent of Flopsy pee – despite my scrupulous rinsing and re-rinsing, then hanging out in the strong sun – that Paul dreads the whole house being polluted. I promised to buy another floor-cloth today.

Then Paul reported a rumour that chicken-wire might be available in a commercial area very far away, serving what old South Africans would describe as the 'township'. (During the Belgian era that is what it was, in fact if not in law.)

Galvanized, Rachel (Rose-encumbered) and I set out to walk to this distant possibility. In the centre a Zairean friend noticed us, offered us a lift and – what was most urgently needed – his assistance as guide, translator and mentor. On the way to the semi-derelict industrial zone we passed the prison – outwardly, one of the best-maintained buildings in Bukavu. Then Louis's gleaming new Land Cruiser slowly lurched up a steep flood-grooved track lined with small jerry-built shops stocking very little of anything. Louis was determined to solve our problem; he seemed to regard the procurement of chicken-wire as a worthwhile challenge and patiently investigated shop after shop, following up on clues given by numerous friends and acquaintances.

At last, from the darkest corner of a cramped scrap-iron store, a roll of chicken-wire was dragged out with difficulty. (Flopsy should be forever grateful to Louis: no way could we, unaided, have found it.) Then arose a serious question: how many metres did we need? Half a dozen friendly men converged on the scene to give advice. They spoke only Mashi and/or Swahili. Louis translated into French for Rachel's benefit, Rachel translated into English for my benefit. There was no sense of anyone's trying to exploit the *muzungus*' ignorance; the advice offered was practical. Were Flopsy to be caged and fattened – his destiny the pot – we needed only six metres. If, however, he was destined to be a member of the family, living happily ever after in the garden, we needed thirty-six metres. So we bought thirty-six, at US$1 per metre. Then we had to find the wood and the nails: two more sagas. A man with a hammer is proving absurdly elusive; that will be tomorrow's saga. In Bukavu, housing a $5 rabbit costs more than $50. Some might argue that Flopsy is not a cost-effective addition to the household. But I disagree.

This is my first 'family' experience of the expat life, as distinct from being the guest of expats. Yet it hardly counts as that; Rachel and Andrew have no white social circle and, given their happy state of unwedded bliss, don't need one. That is yet another of Bukavu's charms: it is free of the obtrusive expat colony to be found nowadays in most Third World cities. Its foreign aid workers number fewer than a hundred and are mostly UNHCR, who work in their own enormous compound and are disinclined to emerge from it. The missionaries, of various denominations and nationalities, are equally self-sufficient though in general more friendly.

I'm told the missionary presence in Zaire (particularly eastern Zaire) has always been exceptionally strong – and surprisingly eclectic, whereas in Rwanda and Burundi the Catholic Church led the field by many lengths. Here you get all sorts in hot pursuit of 'native' souls: Mormons, Seventh Day Adventists, Jehovah's Witnesses – the lot. The Belgians were happy to see any sort of Christian setting up shop – or rather, setting up schools, hospitals, clinics, orphanages, homes for the handicapped. Thus the colonial authorities were let off the hook and could concentrate on exploiting the Congo's amazingly lucrative natural resources. To this day, many Zaireans remain dependent on these foreign-funded social services. Some missions have been established for several generations and in their areas of operation regard themselves as the real ruling power, perhaps in coalition with a local Big Man who scorns the Kinshasa (mal)administration.

16 APRIL

Rachel rightly identifies No. 19's electrical equipment as the greatest threat to life (our lives) in Bukavu. The kitchen is the area of maximum hazard, where an out-of-control cooker delivers mighty shocks to the unwary. To avoid these – when you need to pick up a kettle or lift a saucepan-lid to check on the stew – it is essential to unplug the cooker. But that action is itself life-threatening. The flex is frayed and unravelling, the plug's pins are wobbly and from that menacing plug-socket droops a tangle of multi-coloured bits of wiring. To compound the kitchen's hazards, the plumbing is defective. Water sprays wildly from the sink tap so one is standing on wet concrete while interacting with the homicidal cooker. I marvel that we're not all underground by now, leaving Rose to fend for herself. Last evening the living-room, hall and patio lights repeatedly came on and went off without human intervention. Andrew decided an electrician was needed and volunteered also to find a man with a hammer; the two manhunts could be combined.

After breakfast I shouldered my granddaughter and walked into the centre in search of cheese – a traumatic expedition. Perhaps Rose is teething, or had colic, or was hungry at the wrong time. For whatever reason, she registered misery very loudly on the way home. It would have been futile to pause and attempt to console her: obviously she needed Mummy. But often I was stopped by reproving women – occasionally by reproving men – who pointed out that the baby was distressed, raging with hunger, demanding attention. How could I ignore those strident, agonized cries? What sort of callous brute was I? Quickly demoralization set in; rarely do you see or hear an African baby-on-back howling and apparently being ignored. Africans take baby-care seriously and I was a blatant failure, should never be left in charge of any child ... Given the language barrier, self-defence was impossible. I couldn't begin to explain that Rose was not being ignored, that each howl pierced my grandmaternal heart and stimulated me to walk at Olympic speed towards maternal comforts. Even worse than the spoken reproaches were the silent hostile stares as I went on my harassed way – stares accusing me of a crime against humanity. We were only halfway up Avenue Walungu when Rachel came hastening towards us. Reunited with her milk supply, Rose fell silent.

Unless out of Bukavu, going about his business in the bush, Andrew returns from his office at lunchtime for forty-five minutes. The magnet is not food but his daughter, usually awake at midday and energetically rolling around on the patio. Rolling is her latest achievement and now she can't be left alone for an instant; there is a four-foot drop from the patio's unguarded edge into the concrete rain-channel. I feel sorry for Paul, who has a considerable reputation as a chef (Belgian-trained when young) but whose culinary talents are wasted on No. 19. He is never required to cook a meal; the ingredients are unavailable and so are utensils, apart from one very large saucepan. However, Rachel and Andrew look pretty fit on their diet of bread, cheese, fruits and vegetables.

Today, Andrew did not return at 12.40; the manhunt was taking longer than expected. An hour later the Land-Rover appeared, loaded with three electricians and a carpenter. Andrew, unusually for him, was looking a trifle fraught. He led the trio with their box of tricks into the house, leaving Rachel and me as spectators of the carpenter's creativity. He unrolled the wire and thirty-six metres suddenly seemed an awful lot; as a privileged *muzungu* rabbit, Flopsy is going to have more personal space than the average Zairean human.

Africans are amused by harmless *muzungu* foibles, like building a fortress-equivalent for a rabbit. Also, they enjoy novel diversions. Soon Paul, and several of the neighbours' askari, and sundry passers-by, were assembling around the carpenter, considering with him the wire and lengths of wood which, we could see, were seriously challenging his creativity. Neither Rachel nor I had any advice to offer; our skills lie in other directions. Much calculating ensued, the design was eloquently debated, many suggestions were made, lengths of wood were measured without benefit of a measuring-tape. Although Mashi was the language in use, facial expressions and graphic gestures made clear the general drift. Eager volunteers stepped forward to help the carpenter cut two of the lengths. Then, after much experimentation, it was realized they had been cut too short and must be nailed together again ...

It was time for me to give Flopsy's floor its second scrubbing of the day. Indoors, I paused to observe the electricians' progress. The fuse-box in the garage had been disembowelled, various plug sockets had been removed from the walls, the cooker's intestines were exposed, two light switches hung loose, two more lay on the floor and the trio were in contention about what to do next – what was the core problem ...? Of course experts often disagree. But I had the impression these three were 'electricians' only in their own estimation.

That was many hours ago. Now Flopsy's fortress is half-built (to be completed tomorrow) and the trio have left things looking normal, though the light switches remain idiosyncratic – in fact rather more so than before. When they demanded an $85 fee Andrew gave them $10 because they do seem to have brought the cooker under control.

It's been a long hard day, by Bukavu standards. And now, as I write in my flea-bag on the patio, yet another landmine has exploded on the opposite peninsula. One can only hope it was set off by a wandering animal rather than a reckless human.

17 APRIL

Until recently, essential faxed information, like the date of my arrival, could be received by Andrew – courtesy of UNHCR – and Rachel was able to fax me a list of 'Urgent Requirements!', though the inclusion of a baby's toothbrush made me question that adjective. Now the UN has withdrawn this 'personal faxes facility' for NGO employees, leaving us at the mercy of Andrew's capricious satellite phone. Such a degree of cut-off-ness from Outside is, for me, holiday-enhancing. Here escapism is effortlessly achieved; one isn't deliberately running away, the rest of the world has somehow floated off, become remote to the point of unreality, leaving the visitor free to respond ecstatically to Bukavu's beauty. Perhaps I should feel guilty about being so happy in one of Africa's unhappiest regions. But how could I be other than happy, practising my grandmaternal skills in this dotty household on the shore of this loveliest of lakes?

However, though Bukavu is Paradise to me, it must, at present, seem otherwise to the indigenes. On my very first morning here, when we set off to walk to the big market, Rachel stopped as we approached the centre and said, 'Let's turn back, there's trouble in the air.' I, drunk on the beauty all around, had noticed nothing. But Rachel was right. Soon after we turned back a student demo erupted along our route, the market stalls closed hastily, a young man was shot dead by the army. I asked Rachel how she had detected 'trouble in the air'. Succinctly she replied, 'People's body-language.'

In my holiday mood I felt no compulsion to try to understand what goes on here. Does anyone understand? Probably not. Is anyone in control of events? Apparently not. Zaire is in a state of suspended anarchy. Rumour Rules OK. One senses, among ordinary Zaireans, a preference for not knowing 'the facts'. Like who shot a father-of-six last evening as he stood fishing for his children's supper on the bank of the Rusizi where it marks the border with Rwanda? And who lays the landmines occasionally heard going off after dark on the little paths crossing the border? And who planted the ground-shaking bomb that woke me the other night in the small hours? That mighty explosion has never been explained – or rather, it is explained in half a dozen ways, none ever confirmed. Two nights ago several gunshots and much angry shouting were heard nearby and next morning our neighbours had disappeared. They were reputed to be sinister Rwandans, Hutu officials who, having helped to organize the genocide, fled to Zaire after the RPA victory. Were they shot dead or merely forced to move?

This morning Andrew and Pascal, one of his Zairean colleagues, took off on a three-day journey to inspect rural projects. Normally Rachel is stoical about physical danger but this evening I sensed some anxiety, cheerfully suppressed yet detectable by the maternal antennae. A few weeks ago Pascal's mother-in-law was killed by a landmine while driving home from Uvira. The Zairean army, which roams all over, setting up roadblocks where it fancies, is universally feared. It isn't, of course, a real army, as we understand the term, but an unpaid uniformed rabble who feel (and are) free to terrorize the population. Significantly, the troops stationed in Kivu Province come from far away, from other tribes: they are, in effect, an alien force.

Last evening in the bar of Chez Chris (our nearest source of Primus, a hotel five minutes' walk from No. 19) I met a young Italian NGO worker who had just had a typical encounter with the army and was still looking slightly shaken. Two soldiers stopped him in the city centre and asked to see his passport. Foolishly, he had left it at home. The soldiers demanded an on-the-spot $100 fine. Antonio explained that he never carries cash and proposed going home to fetch his passport – vain hope! The soldiers got into his Pajero, pushed their rifles against his back, and ordered him to drive to his office and pay the 'fine'. He did so. He had no alternative. Bukavu lacks any Higher Authority to whom one can appeal feeling confident that justice will be done. SNIP (the secret police) don't quite fit into that category though they do wield a great deal of power.

18 APRIL

One of our favourite walks is to an alternative swimming spot, directly across from No. 19 on the opposite peninsula. A rough track, high above the lake, winds around the bay formed by the two peninsulas and for much of the way is shaded by towering trees, some now aflame with crimson blossom. The feeling remains rural, despite this being one of Bukavu's rather affluent areas – an expanding suburb where several new homes are being built. Although ambitiously designed, these may not last very long; the bricks look dodgy and the builders' workmanship even dodgier. Here too are a couple of those abandoned half-built houses so often seen in Africa where entrepreneurs seem peculiarly vulnerable to the boom-and-bust syndrome.

From the track we scramble down a precipitous slope on which a few cattle graze, handsome lyre-horned beasts, their chestnut coats glossy – the property of a local Big Man. The teenage boys who herd them sprawl in the shade of a solitary bluegum and observe our progress wonderingly. While Rachel swims, Rose looks slightly anxious, not quite sure whether that bodiless head means Mummy is still around. While I swim, Rose has a compensatory feed. Across the quarter-mile stretch of water, Paul can be seen hanging out nappies.

Lake Kivu is the world's third deepest lake, after Lake Baikal and the nearby Lake Tanganyika; it is 1400 metres deep in the centre. The water temperature is almost perfect, just a few degrees too warm for my taste. However, that allows one to stay in more or less indefinitely. Opinions vary as to whether or not the bilharzia snail resides around the Bukavu shores. We choose to believe that it doesn't.

When we bathe *en famille* I stay near the shore to entertain Rose with splashy aquabatics. Serious exercise happens during my solitary sunrise and sunset swims, starting from below No. 19. Sometimes I cross our bay to the opposite peninsula, sometimes I swim down the centre towards the Rwandan shore, never approaching too close lest there be snipers lurking in the forest. (Snipers do lurk there, I'm not being fanciful.)

By now the local fishermen have adjusted to meeting a *muzungu* mama in the lake and they greet me with jolly shouts as they row past. Their pirogues come in different sizes, from six-foot canoes easily managed by one or two small boys, to thirty-foot craft manned by six men or more. These often work in threes, joined by ropes – but several yards apart – to form a trawler. When fishing is over, the raised net hangs in front from a pole frame; seen from afar by a swimmer, this contrivance looks like some giant insect. As they row home up the bay – standing, wielding their broad paddles with graceful power – the sunset glows golden on their naked black torsos. Always then they sing, a deep-throated traditional fisherman's chant – a wondrous sound, floating across the darkening water, matching the rhythm of their movements. If they had outboard motors and ghetto-blasters, would they really be richer?

19 APRIL

Nyanya won't be swimming to the opposite peninsula ever again. This morning, as I approached my turn-around spot – where Rachel and I dive in and the cattle come down to drink – an appalling stench wafted towards me. At first I assumed a calf or goat must have drowned and was beginning to decompose; in my home river one occasionally comes upon dead livestock caught in the reeds by the bank. But this was a dead human, enshrouded and carefully tied in two semi-transparent nylon sacks and dumped at the weedy edge of the lake. For one horrified moment I trod water while taking this much in. Then, while quickly turning away, I glimpsed a second sack containing a child's body. In future my swimming will be confined to the centre of the bay.

Andrew returned this evening after an uneventful journey – or if there were any 'events' he didn't mention them. I told him and Rachel about my unpleasant encounter but swore them to secrecy. They, I suspect, thought this rather absurd – Nyanya being melodramatic. However, in places as lawless as Bukavu it's prudent to keep your mouth shut. Corpses in Lake Kivu are none of my business.

20 APRIL

Rose-care, predictably, generates the most squalid feature of daily life in No. 19. I'm not referring to her bowel movements – admittedly less tidy that Flopsy's but swiftly cleared away, with skill and discretion, by an alert parent. (While awake she leads a naked, nappy-free life on the patio.) It's her ingesting, not her excreting, that revolts Nyanya. For some reason (reading too many modern baby-care books?) Rachel and Andrew feel their daughter should, *aet.* five months, be 'onto solids'. Nyanya says nothing ('mustn't interfere!') but suffers in silence.

Solids, in this context, are mashed banana and/or mashed avocado. Neither is, from a practical point of view, solid. Both have the potential to render everything within reach sticky, smelly and stained. Rose, whose mother's milk is delivered on demand throughout the twenty-four hours, naturally has no interest in solids as nourishment. But solids as a game – one that totally focuses parental attention on Rose – she simply adores.

A ceremony precedes Rose's 'meal'-times. The cushions are removed from the relevant chair, leaving only bare wood; a large basin and a cloth are placed nearby to deal with the aftermath; Rachel and Andrew strip to their underpants (Nyanya likewise, if she is participating in this repulsive ritual) – and then away we go. The too easily imagined details need not be recorded. Parents and infant seem thoroughly to enjoy themselves from start to finish. Rose – cunning beyond her months – swallows just enough to keep the game going and make her parents feel their effort is worthwhile. But were they neurotic types, who really believed their five-month-old needs solids, they would now be in a psychiatric ward.

Just once I broke my vow of silence, casually mentioning that Rachel, a child of proven strength and stamina, spurned solids until she was two and a half. However, my suspicion is that those 'meal'-times are in fact a game for all three, an entertaining if messy bonding process. And of course the Bukavu environment favours the playing of such games. In a climate not conducive to stripping naked, and with carpeted instead of concrete floors, solids might be less fun.

21 APRIL

Family routines develop quickly; early on weekend mornings I go walkabout with Rose for a couple of hours to give her parents a break from parenting. It is then my fervent hope that the sky will remain overcast (as quite often happens here at this season) to spare me the fag of holding a large umbrella at precisely the right angle over my precious burden. The fact that Bukavu's altitude keeps the temperature down is deceptive; we are almost on the equator and the sun's rays are dangerous. Moreover, Rose is a carbon copy of Andrew: red-gold hair, dark blue eyes, very fair skin. (You'd never guess Rachel had also contributed genes.) In consequence, if even five toes briefly escape from the umbrella's shade they turn bright red, her parents are traumatized and Nyanya is blamed for having allowed her to become seriously sunburnt. Happily this morning was overcast at 6.30 a.m. But of course I took the umbrella.

Quite a few Important Persons live in quartier de Muhumba. Turning right from No. 19's gate, one walks along the up-market end of Avenue Walungu where dense flowering hedges half-hide spacious bungalows and an EU flag flies above the high walls of an invisible mansion and soldiers regularly prowl in groups of three or four. (Much to Paul's discomfiture: he dreads meeting them.) Whether these patrols are guarding the homes of the affluent or planning to rob them is a moot point. Farther on, the French consul's shrub-studded lawn slopes down to the shore where his large speedboat is moored. This is one of the few sources of pollution (oil and noise) on Lake Kivu; the others are the UNHCR launches that take supplies to the refugee camp on a nearby island.

This morning I turned left out of Avenue Walungu to continue up a much wider avenue shaded by magnificent trees, the large gardens flooded with colour – and here it was that Rose turned bolshie. She was objecting to being on my back instead of hanging in front, the position to which she is more accustomed. Or so I intuited; I'm re-learning that with babies you have to do a lot of intuiting. She was on my back because as she gains weight (which she is doing rapidly, despite minimal solids) the frontal position becomes increasingly arduous for the carrier. After half an hour one's neck muscles are aching, after an hour they are throbbing. However, I now paused to make the loudly demanded change. But I chose the wrong spot, near the gateway to an imposing mansion set well back from the road. As I laid my burden on the wayside grass a scowling soldier appeared, bristling with suspicion. Aggressively he questioned me in pidgin French and demanded to see my passport. Slowly he thumbed through it, then complained that it was 'dirty'. True enough; it is battered and rain- and sweat-stained and full of smudgy African visas and arcane bits of paper pasted in at intervals by South African bureaucrats who were try-ing, unsuccessfully, to keep track of my movements in and out of their country. As the soldier began to criticize my Zairean visa Rose intervened at maximum decibel level; she had had enough of lying, ignored, by the wayside. I grabbed my passport, turned my back on the enemy, picked up my granddaughter, shoved her into the sling and harnessed myself the right way round from her point of view. The soldier shouted something abusive as I hastened away. Later, Andrew told me that the mansion is the residence of the military commander-in-chief of Kivu Province, a very Big Man indeed. But this inadequately explains the hassle; it is hard to imagine any activity more blatantly innocent than a Nyanya adjusting a baby-sling.

Soon Rose was asleep and an hour later (my neck muscles throbbing) we were on another peninsula, on a deserted stretch of road out of sight of any dwelling – an unusual circumstance in Bukavu. This was not our lucky morning. Here a ragged elderly man – unmistakably a Rwandan refugee – suddenly emerged from the roadside bushes and demanded dollars. Truthfully I said I had none, was carrying no currency. He didn't believe this. He was a nasty character; one could easily imagine him participating with relish in a genocide. I was scared – badly scared. He pulled at the sleeping Rose's feet and repeated his demand. Rose woke and yelled. Then he made to undo the sling's zip and I was about to use the umbrella as a weapon when a group of pedestrians came into view on the far side of the wide road. Through two fingers I whistled piercingly (one of my few skills) and without hesitation three young men rushed to the rescue. The refugee fled but was furiously pursued and beaten up – how badly I couldn't see.

Meanwhile the womenfolk of the group had joined me, all carrying prayer-books and wearing brilliantly patterned flowing gowns and piled-up turbans. They abused all refugees in torrential French (I can understand more than I can speak), then concentrated on Rose, who had picked up the vibes and was (I intuited) howling for Mummy.

When my rescuers returned, panting and sweating and indignant, one of them said in English – 'You are stupid! Here is safe no more, we have too many criminals from the camps.'

Having made grateful noises and shaken hands all round I turned towards No. 19, another hour's walk away. Luckily the walking rhythm works wonders; within ten minutes Rose was asleep again.

In the West we play strangely little attention to the impact of a million or more refugees on their host country (apart from statutory exclamations of horror about the damage done – inevitably – to the environment.) Busy with our humanitarian efforts on behalf of the Rwandan refugees, we seem to regard Zaire and Tanzania as the obvious and appropriate locations for city-sized camps. But just supposing some magic carpet had deposited those refugees in Europe – would our affluent countries have accepted them? I very much doubt it. Most of us prefer to be 'humanitarian' by remote control, donating money – the easy way out. Impoverished Africans, however, are expected to be 'humanitarian' by tolerating disruptive concentrations of refugees from other countries whose presence grievously exacerbates local problems. True, dollars beyond reckoning cascade into host countries; therefore some African governments are said to be very partial to refugees – the more the merrier. But aid money indiscriminately sloshing around has a deleterious effect on the economies of poor countries, or so I'm told by those who understand such matters. Little trickles down to the indigenes who most need it; instead, it circulates among the already wealthy who have houses to let to expats, or who run import businesses, or who in other ways can ride on the 'humanitarian' gravy-train.

Can it be true that things tend to happen in threes? Rose and I were on the home peninsula when a tall, heavily pock-marked young man came towards us, stared hard as we passed, then turned back to walk close beside me demanding money in French. Again there was no one in sight, though a few houses stood far from the track, on the slope above. I walked on steadily, feigning to ignore this latest demand. The man followed, jostling me quite roughly and now using English: 'You have many dollars, give me – quickly!' As we approached an Italian NGO residence I decided to bang on the gate; with luck an askari would immediately appear. Then a side-gate opened, two Zairean men walked out and abruptly my molester turned away. Rose, still asleep, didn't register this third 'incident'. It really is odd – three unpleasant encounters packed into a few hours on a Sunday morning when otherwise I have found Bukavu trouble-free.

22 APRIL

Even on the shores of Lake Kivu, escapism can't be allowed to take one over completely. Before leaving home, an old friend now working with an Irish NGO in Bangladesh had assigned me a task. Niamh is considering applying for a job in one of Zaire's refugee camps and wants my impressions of that particular humanitarian scene. Until yesterday I had no hope of collecting any impression; visitors are forbidden to enter most camps and discouraged from entering the rest. Then last evening a Land Cruiser arrived with a note from an aid worker who had heard that I was 'around in Bukavu' and invited me to visit her NGO's residence-cum-office.

Eagerly I set out after breakfast, bearing Rose on my back because Rachel was in agony (severe toothache) and needed a Rose-free interlude while her painkillers were taking effect. With the nearest reliable dentist 700 miles away in Nairobi, I can't think of a less suitable location for a dental problem. In times past it made sense to give a bush-dentist a chance to sort things out – but not now, not in the Age of AIDS.

The NGO's headquarters, three-storeyed and outwardly ugly, stands on the edge of a wooded cliff. Its long, high-ceilinged sitting-room is comfortably furnished and well equipped with the latest electronic music-making gear – a far cry from frugal, tranquil No. 19! Enormous picture-windows overlook miles of shimmering water with a superb range of rugged blue mountains lying along the horizon to the north-west. (Mountains so tantalizing that at the back of Nyanya's mind a plan is germinating ... More of that anon.) A grey parrot, hopping around the floor pecking at biscuit crumbs, conveniently distracted Rose while I talked with Bridie and three of her colleagues – young people of different nationalities, all on their first posting in Africa. None is informed about or interested in the political background to the Rwandan refugee crisis. However, I will after all be able to collect a few impressions for Niamh. Bridie has suggested my visiting a small camp (population 29,000 or so) twenty miles north of Bukavu. Tomorrow she is taking medical supplies there and on Thursday another vehicle will return me to base ...

2

LETTER TO NIAMH

Dear Niamh,

You asked for my opinion and here it is: I don't think you'd enjoy working in a Rwandan refugee camp. The one I have just visited is, by regional standards, minute – population 29,000. Many came from the French Operation Turquoise camp, closed on 21 August '94. Others came from Cyangugu prefecture, just across the Kivu Province border near Bukavu. Their arrival wasn't emergency-creating; as they were expected, the UNHCR's infrastructure was already in place.

From Bukavu a rough track (one of Zaire's main motor roads) climbs a series of precipitous hills, densely forested: bamboo, pines, bluegums, indigenous trees aglow at this season with red and yellow blossoms. At first one is looking down banana-blanketed slopes into the narrow valley of the Rusizi river; the forested slopes on the far bank are in Rwanda. Then comes a wide grassy plateau – broken but not rugged country, surrounded on three sides by the Mitumba mountains, rising to 8000 feet and more.

Twenty miles from Bukavu we turned onto an even rougher track – very narrow, gently undulating – and passed a couple of small villages where our shiny luxury vehicle was observed without friendliness. This fertile region is not overpopulated, yet the local welcome for the refugees was, shall we say, mixed ... There is a large impoverished village close to the camp and 'incidents' (sometimes fatal) are not uncommon.

From a high ridge-top, one first sees the edge of the distant camp: huge hospital-tents on an opposite ridge, beyond a wide green valley, and the glinting tin roof of the food-store shed – the only permanent building. The synthetic UN blue of the roof tarpaulins seems a harsh intrusion on an otherwise unspoiled landscape.

Soon we were on the scene of a minor crisis: near the camp entrance the track had collapsed into a deep culvert. Our vehicle could find a way round easily enough but the giant World Food Programme trucks, due to arrive next day, could not. The camp leaders were panicking at the prospect of food rations running out. A UNHCR expat road engineer and his local team had been requested to come immediately and stones were being carried to the chasm by corvée labour from the camp. I asked why these young men couldn't also carry food-sacks from the trucks to the store and was told that that would involve 'an unacceptable security risk'. There are a lot of very hungry Zaireans out there but no one regularly drives 1200 miles from Mombasa, transporting a carefully balanced diet, to sustain them.

The strictly guarded gate of rusty tin was opened by a beaming askari. He welcomed me warmly; elderly expat visitors are treated as possible sources of extra funding. The staff's neat compound holds a hamlet of tents, each measuring eight feet by eight and minimally furnished, standing a few yards apart on the level ridge-top. Marigolds and miniature cacti grow between the white-painted stones marking the edges of little paths. The loo and showers are in portacabins, far down a steep slope overlooking the main camp on its wide valley floor. The dining-room-cum-kitchen is not a room but a lean-to. Many square yards of canvas awning, attached to the top of the high compound wall, are supported by bluegum poles. Beneath, on the earthen floor, benches serve as chairs on either side of a long trestle-table. A generator provides light and keeps the fridge going – most of the time. An excellent Hutu cook, once employed in a Kigali luxury hotel, transforms basic foods into delicious meals. Now the expat staff is down to three – contented folk who, relishing the simple life, rarely visit Bukavu.

Jeejee appointed himself my guide. A volunteer worker in his forties, idealistic and compassionate, he has spent almost a year teaching in the camp school and is adored by his pupils. Scores converged on him, cheering and laughing, as we walked for miles through various 'zones'. I won't even try to describe the surrounding landscape: never have I been anywhere lovelier. In November I hope to return to trek through the Mitumba mountains – and others.

One associates refugee camps with overcrowding and squalor but here the zones are well spread out, some on the valley floor, others on steep hillsides or high ridge-tops approached by lung-testing footpaths. Most mud-brick huts (nine metres by six) stand in small plots where maize and/or vegetables may be grown. A minimum of ten people must occupy each hut, even if a family numbers fewer. A 'bloc' is a group of nine huts under a *responsable*. A zone comprises twenty blocs under a controller. The camp 'chief' is the equivalent of the burgomaster of a Rwandan commune, who in this small camp is in fact an ex-burgomaster. We passed clinics, schools, churches, shops, shebeens, a 'hair-stylist' – all in mud huts – and dressmakers and tailors working by the wayside. On the highest hill American evangelicals have built a red-brick church: large, circular, brash. This permanent structure infuriates those who argue that the whole camp should look 'temporary'.

The orderliness of this 'town' both impressed and chilled me. I've read about these places being modelled on Rwanda's communes – many refugees living with the same neighbours as before and taking orders from the same (genocidal) local authorities. This camp certainly contradicts the standard image of a great flood of panic-stricken wretches fleeing into a strange land where they suffer as uprooted people. It felt like a disciplined segment of Rwandan society successfully transplanted, at vast cost to the international community. Yet it didn't seem to me a relaxed or contented segment. The small children clinging to Jeejee, and to me as his friend, were cheerful enough though filthy and malnourished; everyone else looked morose. And on all my walks with Jeejee (he discouraged me from walking alone) I saw numerous frightening faces – with killers' eyes. I've seen similar faces elsewhere: in Croatia, in South Africa, in Northern Ireland. Not surprisingly, the camp contains a horrific number of men with such faces. Yet Jeejee remarked that it is reputed to be the calmest, safest (for expats) and most tension-free of all Zaire's camps; otherwise I wouldn't have been invited to visit it.

After the culvert had been repaired, I watched a food-distribution. Again, all very orderly: people queuing with their ID cards, every name being entered in a ledger – so-and-so received such-and-such on 25 April. This immensely long queue was submissive, subdued – too silent. The four men in charge were hard-faced, powerful figures who habitually fiddle the books. It's unlikely that the camp supports 29,000, as the expats tacitly admit. Most Hutu refugee 'community leaders' inflate numbers, then sell the surplus rations and buy guns. Since the collapse of the USSR, cheap guns have been showered on Africa. The significance of that grisly economic fact is not sufficiently recognized.

I toured the rows of enormous hospital tents with Muriel, a nurse attached to this camp since its establishment and proud of its medical facilities – as well she might be. Last week I visited Bukavu's main hospital and was shattered by its lack of facilities: at present it is a hospital in name only. Medically, the refugees are privileged people, cared for by their own Hutu refugee doctors, surgeons, radiographers, physiotherapists. Zaireans, hearing about this super-hospital, naturally hope it will treat them too, at least in cases of serious illness. But unless they can pull powerful strings they are denied access, their children allowed to die at the hospital gate. This perhaps is inevitable; the UNHCR and its satellite aid agencies cannot be expected to cater for all local medical emergencies. But, equally inevitably, the local people ask, 'Why does the UN think Rwandan refugees are so much more deserving of help than we are?'

One morning I sat watching the sunrise in a little thatched 'summer-house' on the edge of the expats' compound – their verandah-substitute. Here an askari joined me; Jean is one of the few refugees who speak fluent English and we had talked before. He comes from Kibuye, a town on the Rwandan shore of Lake Kivu where some of the worst genocidal atrocities took place. In June 1993 he graduated from a Kinshasa college as a hydraulics engineer but now has no hope of getting a suitable job, unless the UN needs someone with his qualifications. I asked why he wouldn't go home to a country desperately short of every sort of graduate. His reply revealed that he believes the camp leaders' reports about all returnees being killed by vengeful RPA soldiers. In every camp, this intimidating 'warning' campaign is relentlessly maintained.

At 7 a.m. Jean tuned his trannie to a Kinyarwanda channel purporting to provide a news bulletin. As he translated, I realized this was virulent propaganda, a direct descendant of the infamous Radio Mille Collines broadcasts during the pre-genocide period. It shocked me to find RMC brainwashing still in operation and effective.

The camp's 'English Literature' students expressed a wish to meet me. These seventeen middle-class refugees (eleven men, six women, all professionals over thirty) have evidently accepted that even if the ex-FAR troops one day 're-take' Rwanda, the English language – though hated by most Francophones – will be useful in the twenty-first century. (English is the first European language of Tutsi returnees from Uganda.) On four evenings a week they meet to practise their spoken English in a tent furnished only with twenty camp-chairs – and lit that evening by a kerosene lamp, the generator being off sick. None looked like a refugee; all were well dressed – the women elegant in a Gallic way – and obviously from affluent backgrounds.

Following Jeejee's introduction everyone clapped loudly, crowded around to shake my hand and welcomed me with genuine friendliness. However, when I tried to switch the conversation from my travels to Rwanda's tribulations the atmosphere became somewhat strained, though *la politesse* prevailed to the end.

My referring to the killer militia as the *'interahamwe'* (in Kinyarwanda, 'those who work together') caused great offence. It is, everyone told me, 'a derogatory and abusive term'. They protested even more strongly against the word 'genocide'. What happened in Rwanda in '94 was a war, they asserted, with killings on both sides. 'Genocide' should never be used unless proven to the satisfaction of an international tribunal. If proof exists, they asked, why have the leaders not been punished? I could see how, two years after the 'war', the ineptitude of the UN's Arusha Tribunal has emboldened the guilty, making them feel the 'culture of impunity' will always protect them.

It was disconcerting, almost unreal, to be associating with people whom one knew to have been responsible, as commune leaders, for helping to implement the genocide. They appeared normal, affable, intelligently interested in me as I had been presented to them: an Irish travel writer. 'Normality' was the most sinister aspect of the sort of people I met that evening. Doctors, school principals, lawyers, university lecturers – the authority figures who gave their imprimatur to the attempted extermination of all Tutsi. Tutsi who were often their patients, their pupils, their clients, their academic colleagues, sometimes even their relatives by marriage.

An emotive word, genocide – too often wrongly used nowadays. In '94 confusion persisted for some time, while the massacres were taking place, about whether or not they could be defined as genocide. Naturally Rwanda's 'interim' government put a lot of thought into fudging the issue, but by now few deny that genocide happened. Plus the slaughtering of some 30,000 'moderate Hutu' – certain politicians, and their supporters, who wished to see the Arusha Accords being made the basis for 'a new Rwanda' which would have disempowered the *génocidaires*.

I left the camp asking myself, 'Why does the UNHCR, in collaboration with various NGOs, continue to collude with the *génocidaires*, docilely playing their game? At a cost of US$2 million *per diem* ...' This is a political rather than a humanitarian crisis. Two million refugees became victims of the *génocidaires*, having been intimidated into leaving their homes by leaders who were looking ahead. As one (Jean-Bosco Barayagwiza) boasted publicly, 'Even if the RPF has won a military victory, it will not have the power. It has only the bullets, we have the population.' Barayagwiza now lives in luxury in Goma, running one of the camps.

As early as August '94 the UNHCR knew they were nurturing evil people. An official spokesman, Ray Williamson, admitted this. In November '94 a UN report stated, 'Former soldiers and militiamen have total control of the camps', and General Dallaire of UNAMIR II was willing to try to separate the militias from their victims; he had no doubt these would then return home. However, he was opposed by the UNHCR commissioners, and by several major NGOs, and denied the necessary mandate. His proposed operation might have involved the deaths of some UN troops, and that institution fears the effects of body-bags being seen coming home (to wherever) on CNN. William Shawcross, writing about the genocide, has angrily observed, 'So often today, humanitarianism is a figleaf for political inaction.' The UN is efficient only at disguising its own moral flaccidity by 'doing good' in a way that soothes uninformed, TV-prodded Western consciences.

It's unlikely you'd feel happy and fulfilled working amongst these refugees. But don't get me wrong. I'm not, post-genocide, anti-Hutu, pro-Tutsi. That would be ridiculous, banal. Past Tutsi behaviour was outrageous, brutal, consistently demeaning of the Hutu. Although nothing justifies genocide, that past (both distant and recent) does explain why the organizers succeeded so dreadfully. Also, Rwanda's peasants were and are peculiarly vulnerable to having their inherited antagonisms manipulated. The structure of their society – in pre-colonial times, during the Belgian protectorate, since independence – has been tightly authoritarian in a way atypical of Africa. That counted for much, after 6 April 1994. When told to kill, the peasants killed. When Authority sanctioned the slaughter of their neighbours, tens of thousands of them slaughtered their neighbours, accepting that their own survival demanded the extermination of Tutsi – not sparing the children, this time, as they did in 1959. Repeatedly they were reminded that thousands of those children had recently returned to Rwanda wearing RPA uniforms.

Everywhere aid workers are supposed to be politically neutral, helping all those in need with no questions asked. But maybe it's time to revise that code? Have we not seen enough of where its abuse leads? In this respect, too, my camp visit was disquieting. The three expats are admirable: innovative, resilient, dedicated – not escapists, like some of the younger generation of aid workers, or cynical passengers on the NGO gravy-train. Yet they are actively supporting a morally indefensible operation. Perhaps in such situations most aid workers become ghettoized, their lives for the moment centred on the physical welfare of their charges, their horizons restricted to 'humanitarian' considerations. Obviously those three have a good relationship with the camp leaders; they seem to have no difficulty accepting the 'war' explanation – maybe they need to believe in it, for their own peace of mind? Or maybe they are genuinely ignorant of the background to this 'humanitarian' crisis. It is extremely complicated. I certainly wouldn't understand any of it had Rachel and Andrew not been living and working in Rwanda in 1995. If solely dependent on media interpretations, I'd probably have pushed the tragedy aside as one more distant horror beyond my comprehension.

On 9 May I go home to Ireland, sustained by the prospect of returning to Kivu Province in November. My friends will certainly assume that this wish to revisit Bukavu is entirely Rose-inspired, another symptom of my personality change. A reasonable assumption, but false. Kivu Province pulls me as a traveller – forget grandmaternal urges. Rwanda, too, sounds like good trekking country; I may also spend some time there. But I hope to see you before then.

Your old friend,
Dervla

3

A DISAPPEARANCE
AND A PARTY

26 APRIL
Last evening I arrived back from the camp to find Rachel still in a
bad way. Andrew has tracked down an elderly Norwegian mission
doctor who works here on and off and happens to be in the city
this week; he diagnosed a tooth abscess, prescribed the appropriate antibiotic and advised drastic action post-infection. Today we
heard of a reputable Zairean dentist, attached to a mission hospital near Lake Tanganyika. Soon Andrew is due some local leave
and after my departure they will drive south to consult him. I am
now striving to control my AIDS paranoia and be a good non-
interfering mother-out-law. Such situations can bring one's racism
rapidly to the surface.

27 APRIL
At weekends, if we feel like a long lakeside session with frequent
swims, we take a picnic to the Safari Club. The name at first made
me baulk but nowadays this is a quiet, *muzungu*-free zone. On Sun-
days a few Zaireans come to picnic and/or swim but for some reason other expats avoid the cove. It is on the far side of our peninsula, a glorious half-hour walk along a track riven by two-foot-deep
erosion channels and criss-crossed by massive, contorted pine tree
roots. The garden walls are draped with purple bougainvillaea,
banana groves line some sections and Lake Kivu stretches away,
multi-coloured and magical, to the distant blueness of a hilly shore.

A side-track descends to a rambling colonial hotel, its restaurant
popular with UNHCR folk; this means few others can afford to eat

there, so inflationary is UN spending-power. Here we stock up on Primus, paying a normal price because not drinking on the premises. The bar floor is scattered with what appear to be fragments of a discarded carpet. These are in fact the owner's geriatric poodles: stiff, smelly, overfed. A long steep path, partly stepped, winds through the garden – ablaze with hibiscus, porcelain roses and anthuriums, bristling with candelabra cacti. Beyond a stand of pine trees is our secluded destination, a half-acre of short green grass. The opposite western peninsula, its slopes too steep to be built on, is densely forested; this bay is wider but not as deep as our fjord.

The hotel's neglected-looking motor launch is moored at a little jetty; when Bukavu drew fun-seekers they rented it to tour the peninsulas or visit the islands. Beside the jetty, in a small shack, live the groundsman and his family: a friendly wife and five happy, energetic children, aged fifteen months to eight years. When we appear the eldest, a girl, shyly brings a straw mat, striped red and white – obviously a cherished possession – for Rose to roll on. This is an act of kindness and a gesture of welcome, not a tip-seeking ploy. On the scrubby hillside above the grass forage the family's small herd of goats and kids, rounded up towards sunset by a tiny boy and tethered near the shack. Here the lake is shallow for some ten yards out from the shore and the older children spend much of their time at the edge of the water scrubbing pots or washing clothes which quickly dry when spread on the grass.

This afternoon, at the Safari Club, we began to plan The Party. (So formidable are the logistics involved that all our voices give it caps.) Andrew will be thirty on 2 May, an appropriate occasion for him to return the helpful hospitality he has been receiving since January. But the festivities are scheduled for 4 May, a Saturday, leaving Sunday for recoveries. That's one week from today.

Paul is elated at the prospect of having some serious cooking to do. 'But what's he going to cook in?' I asked. 'Your saucepan is usually busy boiling Rose's bath-water.' (In this area *muzungu* babies must have all their bath and washing water boiled – not merely heated – lest they pick up bilharzia or some other ghastly water-borne disease.)

'I can borrow from colleagues,' said Andrew, which made sense. Africans customarily deal with such emergencies by lending and borrowing. He will also borrow plates, dishes, glasses, cutlery – in varying amounts from different households, all to be collected at different times.

Thirty guests have been invited but Pascal has reminded Andrew that when thirty Africans are invited forty are likely to arrive.

Rachel asked the crucial question. 'How much food do forty people need?'

There was a brooding silence. We all gazed over the lake with furrowed brows. None of us is accustomed to throwing parties for forty people. Our imaginations were boggling in unison. 'And what sort of food?' continued Rachel, showing symptoms of rising panic.

'Roast chicken,' said Andrew.

'Grilled steaks,' said I.

'Kedgeree,' said Andrew.

'Potato salad,' said I.

'Tomato and avocado salad,' said Andrew.

'Cheese and salami on sticks,' said I.

'Won't that be enough?' asked Rachel, paling beneath her tan.

'And oceans of Primus,' I concluded.

'Also oceans of fizzy things,' said Andrew. 'Half of them are teetotal, good fundamentalist Christians.' Suddenly he looked alarmed. Eyeing me, he hesitated – then pleaded, 'Do please keep off the Primus till the party starts!' Poor fellow, he had had a nightmare vision of *la belle mère* in too jovial a mood by 8 p.m. when his fundamentalist friends began to arrive. A not irrational fear; normally I retire at 9 p.m. and do not wait until 8 for my first Primus.

'Back to basics,' said Rachel grimly. 'When do we cook all this stuff?' That was another crucial question; No. 19's fridge is small and feeble. It makes a lot of noise but does very little preserving.

'I suppose on the day,' said Andrew, 'starting very early.'

'You must be mad!' said I. 'On the day for forty people? With a two-ring cooker and a snail's-pace oven?'

'Where are people going to sit?' wondered Rachel. 'We've only got chairs for five.'

'I think we should go home,' said Andrew. 'The midges are beginning to bite.'

By unspoken mutual consent we postponed further planning for The Party to another day.

28 APRIL

This morning Rachel and Andrew decided to give Nyanya a Sunday treat by taking her to Km. 18. They knew it only by repute: a very beautiful swimming spot eighteen kilometres from the city, down a side-track off the airport road.

First there was a slight parental argument about Rose's car-seat, to which she is allergic: it prevents her from seeing the world go by. Andrew, however, refused ever again to expose his unconfined daughter to Bukavu's traffic. Nyanya approvingly watched Daddy winning that round.

On the airport road swarmed hundreds of pedestrians (many from the camps) carrying goods to the Sunday market. A privileged minority rode on ancient noisome pick-ups, insanely overloaded, their shouting and singing passengers squeezed between bulging sacks, ten-gallon jerry-cans of banana beer and five-foot stalks of bananas. As these death-dealing vehicles swayed and swerved through the crowds, shrieking women and children scampered out of the way. But for the roads' speed-lowering properties, Zaire's traffic mortality rate would be even higher than Kenya's.

Here our lack of speed allowed a young man to hang on to the back of the Land-Rover, vigorously trying to wrench open the door – his expression angry and full of hate. This, apparently, is a common occurrence. Any *muzungu* foolish enough to leave a vehicle back door unlocked loses whatever lies within reach. In Zaire daylight robbery is easy, the robbers confident of incurring neither blame nor punishment however many witnesses there may be.

For two miles from the turn-off a narrow track zig-zags down to the shore. High, richly scented hedges, laden with tiny pink or blue flowers, brushed the windows. A meeting with another vehicle would have entailed one driver's backing up, for a long way. Here I felt a spasm of acute frustration. What superb trekking territory, what a waste to be traversing it in a Land-Rover!

We began to have doubts about Km. 18 before we arrived, when two water-skiers appeared far below. Already the grating whine of their speedboats' engines could be heard. Then a grassy expanse came into view, shaded by scattered pine, mango and avocado trees. From a small jetty several pirogue-owners were taking people for trips up and down the shore. Scores of Zairean yuppie types were visible, and at least a dozen expats, and ghetto-blasters disseminated the psychotic wailings of American pop-singers.

At the foot of the mountain we had just descended, on a long wide ledge above the shore, a pole barrier stopped us and two shabby men sternly demanded a one-dollar entrance fee from each adult; in return, they guard all vehicles parked beyond the pole. About thirty small refugee boys, better dressed than many of their Zairean peers, were standing on an earthen bank beside the barrier, staring at us. They weren't selling anything or begging (we guessed they didn't dare beg in front of the two men), but one of them leaned forward to shout, 'We are unfamilied!' He presumably meant that they had lost all their relatives, through violence, disease or otherwise, and belong to the category known officially as 'Unaccompanied Children'. I found their little faces disturbing: neither sad nor happy, neither expectant nor resigned but curiously enigmatic – withdrawn. We cannot even begin to imagine what they must have seen and suffered.

I also felt disturbed, in a different way, as we left the Land-Rover and walked around the fire-blackened ruin of quite a large restaurant, its walls lavishly bullet-marked. Here was a story; but no one could (or would) remember it.

Down on the shore a few solitary men lay under trees in drunken stupors with empty whiskey bottles beside them. (It was 11.30 a.m.) The yuppie types, wearing psychedelic swimming-trunks, were horsing about on the grass with beach balls, shouting at each other above the blaring of their ghetto-blasters. Other young men were leering at giggling young women prancing about in bikinis – with no intention of swimming. And brash UN expats were insidiously throwing their weight about, being patronizingly friendly to the locals. The slim white speedboats were, we noticed with interest, inscribed 'World Food Programme' in large blue letters. What do speedboats do to facilitate the provision of food to the island camp?

We sought the quietest spot and shared a bottle of Primus while Rose was having a feed. None of us wanted to swim here and we soon agreed that we would prefer to spend the afternoon at the Safari Club – which we did. But why were the vibes so very bad at Km. 18? It wasn't the vulgarity of the scene that unsettled us; that could be amusing for a few hours. There was something else, something peculiarly oppressive – almost malign – in the atmosphere. All three of us reacted to it immediately.

29 APRIL
Because the patio faces east I open my eyes every morning to the splendour of another Kivu dawn. These sunrise cloudscapes are infinitely varied in their tints and shapes. Standing on the edge of the patio, I watch the lake change colour as it briefly reflects the pale clear green of the sky over Rwanda or catches the pinkness of high-floating cloud shreds. Or there may be one massive immobile cloud, a golden sculpture poised above the wooded heights beyond the water. Or, after a rainstorm, the jaggedness of long low purple clouds hurrying north, or banks of silver mist drifting away to the south, towards the city.

Recently we have enjoyed several dramatic storms, usually during the afternoon or early evening – only once at night, forcing me to retreat into the living-room. These break with little warning, the blue sky suddenly becoming black while mighty thunderclaps cause the earth to tremble and one's ears to tingle. (And cause Rose to blink and look perplexed.) Then comes an abrupt drop in temperature and the roar of the rain as a tropical deluge obscures the opposite peninsula and quickly floods the patio – driven under the roof by a gale that makes the lemon and papaya trees bend and toss as though in pain. Blue sheet lightning flares in the semi-darkness, white lightning flashes starkly over the water. An hour later it's all over – the sky clearing, the air calm, the whole world glistening and growth almost perceptible as the sun takes over again.

Yesterday the border-crossing into Cyangugu was closed to expats for an indefinite period: reason unspecified. Could the reason be a new government diktat, dated 14 April, compelling all foreigners to enter Zaire through Kinshasa? Kinshasa is a thousand miles west of Bukavu as the plane flies, and a month's boat and truck journey by surface transport, so this regulation will present me with a major problem in November. We at first took it to be an attempt by Kivu officials to extend their opportunities for dollar-collecting but we were being over-cynical; it really is of Kinshasa provenance. Some of Andrew's friends believe it was inspired by a determination to vet potentially critical observers of the unsavoury scene in and around eastern Zaire's refugee camps.

30 APRIL

A grim day. I was setting off for my sunrise swim when Mpolo appeared, all agitated, and beckoned me towards Flopsy's fortress. Following him along the lawn – he gesticulating wildly and talking volubly in Mashi – I expected the worst. And indeed Flopsy was gone. Mpolo pointed to a hole in the wire at ground level, then towards large tufts of rabbit fur leading towards a gap in the hedge. He expected me to believe that Flopsy had dismantled the wire and run away. That is a physical impossibility. Rabbits are strong, but not strong enough to rip apart tough chicken-wire. It is also a psychological impossibility. Flopsy was very content hopping about his roomy fortress in the spreading shade of an avocado tree. He was well fed, much talked to, the recipient of lavish affection from Rachel, Andrew, Paul, Nyanya and the neighbour's fascinated children. (And a wife was about to be provided, though he couldn't have known that.) Besides, the earth is soft here and a rabbit seeking to escape would dig his way out. I didn't try to conceal my anger as Mpolo trailed me back to the house, still pretending to lament Flopsy's loss.

Over breakfast (I had abandoned my swim: I didn't have the heart for it) we tried to analyze the implications. Had Mpolo simply stolen Flopsy to sell him for $5? That could make sense; no askari dare admit to a thief having gained access while he was on duty – Flopsy himself must be made to seem responsible … Yet we knew it was not so, we recognized this as a sequel to the flower-destruction episode. Then Andrew, as Head of the Household, issued a diktat: Nyanya must give up sleeping on the patio. Momentarily I was disposed to argue, then I saw the point. With Mpolo, we do have an unquantifiable problem.

Usually Mpolo slopes off before he should, not waiting for Paul to take over. This morning, however, we saw him greeting Paul at the gate, leading him to the fortress, telling his story. We followed. Paul's face was a study in scepticism. Yet he didn't dispute the implausible escape story but turned to us, commiserating in French. Again I sensed his fear of Mpolo. Clearly the wire had been cut, then folded back – bent with human fingers – to make a hole. When Mpolo volunteered to search for Flopsy in the maize-field beyond the hedge Andrew told him to get lost. This evening we held a sombre indaba on the patio while a golden half-moon rose and the frog chorus croaked and wood-smoke wafted towards us from Mpolo's fire – his hut only thirty yards away.

I am now worried about Budgie and would be worried about Rose were she ever within reach of Mpolo – which she isn't. Nor do I much like the idea of his being around when I've gone home and Andrew is off on one of his two- or three-day journeys into the interior. All the windows are barred but the door leading off the patio is frail, as is the garage door, which gives access to the hall and bedrooms. I feel (have felt for some time) that Mpolo should be sacked. Unpunctuality could be the reason given; he often arrives an hour or more late. Rachel agreed with me, until Andrew wisely pointed out that Mpolo would depart nursing a mega-grievance; NGO wages paid in dollars are not easily come by these days. And might he not then be more of a threat? Especially as he is very matey (remarkably so for a Bukavu citizen) with the soldiers who frequent Avenue Walungu; this has been uneasily noted by Paul. Moreover, his contract with Andrew's NGO (signed, sealed, witnessed) makes it extremely difficult to sack him. Our indaba ended inconclusively.

1 MAY
Planning of The Party can no longer be postponed. Given forty (or thereabouts) guests, and no experience of mass-catering, we must surely err: but it better be on the side of lavishness. During breakfast we made a list:

10kg potatoes	1kg onions
5kg rice	10 bulbs of garlic

5kg tomatoes	2 litres of mayonnaise
2kg fish	60 bread rolls
2kg cheese	10 avocados
1kg salami	2kg groundnuts
20 steaks	1kg raisins
10 chickens	3 boxes paper napkins
20 eggs	80 bottles of Primus
160 bottles of fizzy soft drinks	One 50kg block of ice to keep
One sack of charcoal	the drinks cold in the bath
to grill the steaks	

'Let's try to get this sorted out,' said Andrew. 'The chickens can come alive on Friday afternoon for Paul to kill on Saturday morning.' (Rachel shuddered but said nothing.) 'The fish we should also get on Friday afternoon and cook it that evening. The eggs we'll get whenever we can find them.'

'When do we begin cooking?' asked Rachel.

'That,' replied Andrew, 'is up to you.'

'Perhaps tomorrow we can scrub the potatoes,' I suggested, feeling Nyanya should seem vaguely constructive.

'And hard-boil the eggs for the kedgeree,' added Rachel.

'If we have found them by then,' said Andrew.

Given the local (in)security situation, no one wants to possess physically more dollars than are immediately needed, and now Andrew had to acquire some cash – actually quite a lot – to cope with that list. We all, including Paul, set off in the Land-Rover and our first stop was in the centre where Andrew collects his salary from an Indian merchant whose London account has received it in dollars. To such stratagems are even the most respectable NGOs driven by Bukavu's lack of a bank. Next stop: the open-air money-exchange area near the big market, where dozens of men sit around on chairs holding suitcases stuffed with millions of Zaire notes. Today the rate of exchange is 45,000 to the dollar. As these notes are in 1000 or 500 denominations it takes time to change $100 – counting 450 (or 900) very sticky, tattered notes likely to fall apart in your hand if not treated gently. Throughout Zaire, how many man- and woman-hours must be devoted every day to note-counting? Though I have noticed, in both markets here, how often vendors trust their customers and don't check the bulky bundles.

Two and a half hours later we were back in No. 19, laden with provisions. Then Paul organized the far-flung borrowings; for the next three evenings, after work, Andrew will be discovering bits of Bukavu hitherto unknown in quest of saucepans, plates, bowls, glasses, cutlery.

'This evening,' said Rachel, 'we must come to terms with that barbecue thing. We need to find out how it works before Saturday.'

The 'thing' in question had long been puzzling me. A concrete and tin contraption, it stands to one side of the patio, the fire-space at waist level, the high tin roof without a smoke exit. Nor is there any draught or any grill, merely a bare floor on which to light the fire. Paul has never used it and doesn't want to.

At dusk, when Rose was out of the way and while Andrew was collecting crockery, Rachel and I brought the full force of our intellects to bear on the contraption. As there was no paper available we collected wisps of dry grass, put thin twigs on top, ignited the wisps and gently blew on them. When tiny flames began to spread we added small pieces of charcoal and the flames went out. 'I think,' said Rachel, 'one of us should keep blowing.' She was right. By the time Andrew appeared a few small pieces of charcoal were tentatively glowing. He stood and stared – then demanded, 'But will anything ever cook on that?'

Rather peevishly I retorted, 'You've got to wait!' – and added slightly larger pieces of charcoal.

An hour later cooking seemed possible. Rachel balanced the shelf from the oven over the crimson embers and placed on it our experimental steak, carefully seasoned. When the experiment proved delicious (just a corner or two slightly charred) we all relaxed. Said Rachel, 'It'll be just a matter of timing, getting the charcoal going long before people arrive.'

On that reassuring note we retired.

2 MAY

We've had no time today to celebrate Andrew's birthday; under Party pressure he is beginning to look older than his thirty years. The crockery he collected last evening obviously hasn't been used for a very long time and wasn't thoroughly washed before being stored away. It needed scouring. I seized on this opportunity to do my bit (I'm diffident about getting involved on the food side) and when Paul departed I took over the kitchen and spent hours soaked to the skin (that tap!) while Budgie, perched on the window-ledge above the sink, had fun trying to catch bubbles. (Washing-up liquid was an expensive emergency purchase.) The last of the plates was being dried when Andrew entered from the garage bearing a tower of saucepans. They, too, needed scouring.

Weeks ago Rachel and Andrew were talking of going to a nightclub this evening; there are no babysitters and they have never had time off together. (Improbably, there is a nightclub on Avenue Walungu, in one of the small bungalows.) They didn't then foresee how drastically pre-Party tasks would diminish their energy. By 10.15 they wanted only to sleep.

3 MAY

The smallness of the kitchen and the cooker's limitations mean that we must do things in shifts. Before sunrise this morning No. 19 was all action: Rachel boiling potatoes (scrubbed yesterday), Nyanya peeling them as they cooled, Andrew chopping onions in the living-room while Rose explored her baby-gym's possibilities on the floor beside him. Later, Paul cooked the rice and made the dressing for the tomato and avocado salad.

Today's first crisis concerned steaks; the butcher's fridge has broken down so they have prematurely become our responsibility. Hastily Rachel reorganized her fridge, exiling those items least likely to go off. Now we're hoping for the best and I'm preparing for the worst.

The second crisis concerned eggs, lack of … I opined that you can make an excellent kedgeree without eggs but this concept offended Rachel's perfectionism. Andrew was despatched to a nearby village where Paul reckoned it might be possible to find a few eggs, though probably not twenty. I then put in a request for a large bottle of the cheapest vinegar. 'What for?' inquired Rachel. 'Don't be so nosy,' I replied. 'It's just one of Nyanya's little whims.'

For five hours this afternoon Rachel and I sat on the patio creating bowl after bowl of potato salad, essentially a simple dish but

in ten kilos there are a daunting number of potatoes. And the gar-
lic-peeling was truly gruelling; Bukavu's garlic has minute cloves
with abnormally adhesive skins. Occasionally the rolling Rose
thrust a foot into a bowl of potato and onion, or garlic and may-
onnaise, and when next she sucked her toes (a favourite pastime)
she looked slightly puzzled. In mid-afternoon the chickens arrived
noisily (actually elderly hens, their laying days over) and were
locked in the garage. At 5.30 Andrew arrived, fish-laden and
looking triumphant: he had found eight eggs.

After a quick round of Primuses I gutted the fish and Andrew
fried them while Rachel washed the raisins for the kedgeree.
Somehow none of us had any appetite for supper. We retired even
earlier than usual.

5 MAY

Last night I slept in the guest-room for the first time while The
Party continued until 3 a.m. I never have been a party person and
by 10 p.m. was more than ready for bed after an eighteen-hour
day.

At 4 yesterday morning Rachel woke me looking so grief-
stricken I feared a cot-death. But it was only the steaks.

'Come and see!' she said. 'What are we going to do?'

Piled on their dish on top of the fridge, the steaks looked faint-
ly green, smelled rather strongly and felt very slimy. This was
Nyanya's finest hour.

'Not to worry,' I said cheerfully. 'It's nothing scalding water
and vinegar won't sort out. My generation grew up in households
with larders instead of fridges. In fact they'll taste better for having gone slightly ripe.'

'Well get on with it then,' said Rachel testily, 'and be quick
whatever you're going to do. Andrew would die if he saw them
now.'

'I can't be quick,' I said. 'First the water has to boil and you
know how long that takes.' The cooker, though no longer homicidal, had not been speeded up by the electricians' attentions.

Paul, arriving early as promised, nodded approvingly when he
saw me in action; obviously he understands about halting meat-rot.

Happily Andrew slept on until 6. An hour later he was to be

observed emptying the bookshelves in the living-room, stacking their contents in the bedroom.

Bewildered, I asked – 'What's all this about?'

'Music,' replied Andrew. He was not in a conversational mood.

'You can't have a party for Africans without music,' said Rachel.

It transpired that Pascal and two of his friends had been able, after prolonged efforts, to borrow a music centre, complete with enormous speakers. Soon the three would arrive to install the equipment.

While I was deboning fish Rachel peeled eggs and outside the kitchen window Paul began his slaughtering of the innocent. We pretended not to hear.

Paul and I did the plucking and gutting with Budgie in rapt attendance, anticipating a change of diet; normally he lives on fish and cheese.

Meanwhile life was getting complicated in the living-room, where Andrew and his friends were engaged in deadly combat with a surreal tangle of flexes and wires and plugs that didn't fit and connections that wouldn't connect. As Paul was about to put the first batch of 'chickens' in the oven everything fused.

'Really we should have had this party in a hotel,' said Rachel to no one in particular.

Andrew had to go into the city centre at some stage anyway, to fetch the bread and salami, and Pascal knew exactly where to find a new fuse. It was decided to fetch the ice also on this trip because who could guess how long it might take to render the music centre operational?

My next task was to move the crates of drinks from garage to bathroom.

In due course the ice arrived – a rectangular block, a miniature iceberg weighing seventy kilos. Andrew and Pascal staggered in with it, laid it gently in the bath and left Nyanya to pack the 240 bottles around it. I didn't quite see the logic of this – surely only those bottles in contact with the ice would remain cool?

There followed an indaba in the kitchen. The chickens, as crowded in the oven as European chickens in a battery unit, were cooking unevenly – one side almost burnt but blood trickling when a leg was pulled. Various opinions were given, much repositioning took place, more dripping was added.

Then Paul had occasion to go to the bathroom, from where he returned with bad news. Our cooling technique was defective. First the block of ice must be shattered, then the bottles are buried under and between the chunks. But great care has to be taken not to chip off small pieces ...

Stoically I removed the 240 bottles and Andrew brought a hammer from the Land-Rover. It is extraordinarily difficult to achieve chunks rather than small pieces. I left him to make his travail alone.

Half an hour later I was back in the bathroom, burying 240 bottles. By the time I had finished there were only 239. I hadn't promised Andrew not to have *one* Primus before 8 p.m.

By then Paul had converted the guest-room into a larder. Conveniently, there is only a bare wooden bedstead (no mattress or bedding), on which were laid all the dishes and platters and bowls and tureens, an array that made me question our calculations for the first time. Here surely was enough to feed at least one hundred very hungry guests. And in addition there were steaks ...

In the living-room, the scene was set. Rachel had worked hard, both mentally and physically, to make the most of what little furniture there is – and of course chairs had been borrowed. Also the music centre was operational, its miles of flexes and wires so ingeniously disposed that no one could trip over them.

At sunset, our thoughts turned to braaing. Rachel had already collected an ample supply of dry grass and twigs, and a sack of charcoal stood by the contraption. Rather to our surprise, there were no complications. But the timing of the grilling became a small bone of contention.

'We want people to eat when they feel like it,' said Rachel. 'It's no good making a big thing of the braai so they think they have to eat then. Everything else is cold.'

'The chickens will be warm,' I pointed out pedantically.

'They're not going to ask for steak,' argued Andrew. 'They can only eat it when it's there to be eaten. We should decide now on a grilling time.'

'But we don't know when they'll arrive,' protested Rachel.

'So what?' said Andrew. 'Latecomers can have chicken.'

'It's my opinion,' said Nyanya, 'that we all need one good stiff drink before anyone arrives.'

There was no disagreement about this and Andrew opened his birthday bottle of Scotch.

The first guests arrived at 7.50, the last at 9.30. Men and women tended towards segregation; several of the latter were baby-laden. A few spoke only Mashi, or another of this region's innumerable languages, and none spoke English – which left Nyanya undistracted while looking after their drinks. Everyone ate lots of nuts and salami-and-cheese nibbles. Pascal's wife arrived with a gigantic oblong chocolate birthday cake and insisted on its being passed around quite soon. Thinking of the array on the bed, my heart sank. I had a horrid feeling no one expected a real meal – they had probably eaten already ...

At 9.00 Rachel decided that all the food should be displayed and she and Paul began to grill. (Paul, rising to the occasion, had overcome his distrust of the contraption.) To my relief the steaks were rapidly devoured and the half-chickens also went down well – each had been bisected by Andrew, somewhat jaggedly with a blunt carving knife. But when I retired not much impression had been made on the kedgeree and salads.

As I unrolled my flea-bag in the guest-room I felt a pang; the floor still smells of Flopsy.

At midnight I woke to pee and heard The Party going well: much singing and dancing and loud laughter. I hoped the dancing would stimulate their appetites.

At dawn I put on the tea kettle and anxiously investigated. Yes, some appetites had been stimulated, but not enough to justify the effort put into those salads and that kedgeree. Never mind, Paul would be the beneficiary.

A pathetic call came from the bedroom – 'Is Nyanya brewing tea?'

Rachel and Andrew looked frail, after two and a half hours' sleep. (Rose doesn't yet know about making allowances for late nights and hangovers.) They confessed to a slight misjudgment, in their eagerness to impress Andrew's fundamentalist friends with their virtue. Sometimes they appeared to be drinking Pepsi-cola –

furtively fortified in the bedroom. An empty whisky bottle explained their red eyes and sensitivity to loud noises. Neither is accustomed to drinking spirits.

'Mixed with that horrendous stuff,' said Rachel, 'it doesn't taste like whiskey, you don't realize how much you're taking in ...'

'But now we realize!' groaned Andrew. He looked the worse case so I gave him my last Alka Seltzer. Gratefully he accepted the fizzing glass with a palsied hand.

We spent the day washing up, me in a gloomy mood because tomorrow I fly away from Bukavu. Rachel and Andrew also seemed slightly gloomy, quite apart from being hung-over. This touched me; apparently Nyanya has not outstayed her welcome.

6 MAY, NAIROBI AIRPORT

Driving past the brewery this morning, en route to Kavumu, we noticed its long-neglected façade being painted. A direct result, Andrew deduced, of Nyanya's holiday in Bukavu.

MAF arrived from Nairobi an hour late, having first gone to Goma, and then the 'Kinshasa only' diktat delayed my departure for another two hours. I had already said goodbye to the family – a dismal business, to be got through as quickly as possible – and Pascal had seen to all my dollar-dispensing negotiations, and we were sitting in the 'departure lounge', a row of rough wooden benches, shaded by a sheet of loose rusty tin. There was tension in the air, Kavumu airport's normal tension. Anarchy breeds stress and strain; none of us *muzungus* – the rest were missionaries – could relax until airborne. Although we had completed our formalities, more dollars might be demanded at any moment for some invented reason. The octogenarian Norwegian nurse sitting in front of me (retired, but unable to settle in Europe after a lifetime in Zaire) complained that things were never like this before the refugees came, trailing clouds of UNHCR dollars.

As the twelve arriving passengers – eight Zaireans, four expats – came towards us across the bare dusty ground, one *muzungu* was conspicuous. Middle-aged, very tall and stout, he wore baggy jeans, a sage-green bush-shirt and a red baseball cap. He carried a laptop computer and was draped with cameras, binoculars, a tape-recorder, a mobile phone. The tension became abnormal when he was told he must go back to Nairobi on our flight, proceed to Kinshasa and from there return to Bukavu. Was this, mysteriously, a contretemps not amenable to bribery? Or had he refused to bribe on principle? But he didn't look exceptionally high-principled.

Soon we gathered that he is a German development consultant with influential contacts in Bukavu. Then why, we wondered, had those contacts not met him? As he strode angrily to and fro, always followed by four soldiers, one could feel the Zaireans' hostility increasing. So did mine. Any sympathy I might have felt for a *muzungu* diktat-victim was short-circuited by his arrogance.

As Herr X's luggage (four ginormous zebra-skin suitcases) was being re-loaded, we debated which passenger would be forced off to make room for him. And why four suitcases? Was he planning to settle in Bukavu? That, somehow, seemed unlikely. Perhaps he was on an extended entrepreneurial tour of Central Africa? These days, with Zaire on the edge of collapse, there are many of his sort roving around.

By now a peculiarly African miasma had risen above the scene. We watched Herr X's luggage being again unloaded, only to be reloaded ten minutes later. On MAF flights the pilot and co-pilot double as baggage-handlers and a tall, gangling blond American was po-facedly doing as bidden by a small, fat, uniformed Zairean. Meanwhile Herr X, sweating and snarling and crimson with rage, continued to stride from the police office to the customs office to the immigration office and back to the police – where the lengthiest arguments took place. All these offices are cubby-hole shacks unlikely to awe a German developer.

I longed to rejoin the family, so near though invisible, but Pascal advised me not to move lest dollar-extraction start all over again, prompted by a *muzungu*'s leaving this 'departure lounge' which it costs so much to enter.

Forty-five minutes had passed since the plane's arrival. I marvelled at the cheerful patience of three small missionary children, excited about their trip to Nairobi but born and bred in Bukavu and conditioned not to expect anything to happen on time.

Suddenly Herr X's military escorts faded away, slinging their rifles over their shoulders, and he stood alone on the empty space between us and the plane, guarding his luggage – unloaded yet again and lying on the dusty field looking absurd. From his subsequent behaviour we inferred that he knew he had won. When a large UNHCR plane landed far away from the airport shacks he adjusted his telescopic lens and photographed it. A frisson of horror went through the waiting passengers, black and white; in Bukavu, *muzungus* have been jailed for much less provocative uses of their cameras. Four blue-capped officials emerged from this plane and stepped into a waiting vehicle – and the plane at once took off again. UNHCR staff – privileged everywhere by protocol agreements – avoid all the hassle to which lesser mortals are exposed. However, $100 bills often find their way to the top Kavumu bureaucrats, who had also driven out to meet this plane from a tiny red-brick office at the far end of the runway.

Half an hour later she arrived, one of Herr X's influential contacts: an unmistakable Kinshasa type, young and svelte and brisk, reeking of money and power. In her presence, the police, the customs officers, the immigration officers, the loutish strolling soldiers, counted for nothing. She commanded two soldiers to carry her guest's luggage to a shiny Land Cruiser driven – I was bemused to notice – by a traffic policeman. Zaire is rich in these Alice-in-Wonderland touches.

Ten minutes later we were off, and never shall I forget our flight over Rwanda. Something deep within me distrusts aeroplanes; every time I fasten my seat-belt I look Death in the face. Statistics, the sort that tell you flying is much safer than motoring, don't help. It just doesn't feel that way. And over Rwanda we encountered extreme turbulence. As the little plane dropped horribly my seat-belt hurt my hips and I wanted to vomit but couldn't. As it turned on its side, and moments later on its other side – giving new views of Rwanda – I felt sad about never again seeing Rose. The missionary children, inured to MAF flights since babyhood and with Daddy as co-pilot, were ecstatic. Their eyes glowed, they told me that this was their most exciting flight ever, they chortled with glee as yet again we fell like a stone towards the green forested hills very close below. Then we plunged into clouds all torn and black and lightning leaped around us like devils dancing. The children squealed joyously (they were running loose in the aisle) but soon their delightful experience was over. We were out of the storm, over sparkling Lake Victoria.

4

SEEN FROM AFAR

Soon after my return home in May 1996 I had a premonition that by November Kivu Province would be unsuitable territory for a granny-trek. Even during my visit there were, as I have recorded, 'noises off'. Then, five days after I left Bukavu, a convoy bringing food to the Goma camps was ambushed near the Gisenyi border-crossing and thirteen Zaireans were killed. Next day a thousand Zairean Tutsi (from communities settled in Kivu for generations) sought sanctuary at Mokoto monastery in the Masisi region and were attacked by Hutu militia. Many – the number as usual disputed – were killed.

On 19 May *Le Monde* reported that in northern Kivu local tribes (the Hunde, Nyanga and Nande) had formed their own militia in response to the influx of *interahamwe* and ex-FAR, which they saw as a 'foreign invasion'. They were observed fighting with these troops in the Rutshiro region along the border with Rwanda – the area I had been planning to trek through, entering from Uganda.

At the end of June Ron Redmond of the UNHCR admitted that 'Rwandan extremists have been involved in the ethnic cleansing of Tutsi in the Masisi region'. When he went on to complain that 'The UNHCR has this year received less than half the funds needed for the refugees', I thought – 'Jolly good thing too!' Then he announced 'a search for some new options. We are considering relocating 1.7 million refugees further into the interior of Zaire where they might be able to grow food and be at least partially self-sufficient.' But why, I wondered, did Mr Redmond expect the tribes of the interior to be more welcoming than the Hunde, Nyan-ga and Nande when 1.7 million Hutu began to cultivate their land?

During September, Rachel, Andrew and Rose were home on leave. On 26 September we noted but refused to seem concerned by a statement from the US State Department: 'The United States deplores the recent exchange of fire between Zairean and Rwan-dan armed forces along their common border near Bukavu and calls upon both parties to defuse the situation. The United States also condemns the persecution of the Banyamulenge who live in the area around Bukavu.'

Andrew returned to Bukavu a week ahead of Rachel and Rose; they had to wait in London for some infant booster inoculation that could only be given on a certain date. That was a providential delay. Only days before they were to have departed from Heathrow, Laurent Kabila's army, then on its way to overthrow the Mobutu régime, invaded Kivu Province at Uvira, some forty-eight miles from Bukavu on the northern shore of Lake Tanganyi-ka. Rachel stiffened her upper lip and admitted that she had been wondering, since 26 September, if she, Andrew and Rose – the RAR unit – would ever again be able to relax happily on the patio facing Rwanda.

I stayed on with Rachel and Rose in their London flat. Daily we bought all the newspapers and avidly read their confused reports about what was happening – might be happening – could happen ... Nightly we listened to the World Service, which on the whole made more sense. Regularly we received UN press briefings on the situation. Every few days Andrew – gallantly risking bank-ruptcy – used his satellite phone briefly, to reassure Rachel. Mean-while Rose scampered ebulliently around the flat, not giving a damn whether Daddy was dead or alive. From the age of ten months and three weeks she had been walking briskly.

On 22 October all fifty-eight expat aid workers were flown out of Uvira, having endured quite an ordeal. Twice Kabila's troops had prevented their departure by the simple expedient of forcing hundreds of locals to sit on the airstrip. Now the UNHCR was tending towards panic. Within the previous few days about 220,000 refugees had fled from the camps around Uvira, leaving them empty. Some were hiding in banana groves on the nearby hills; most were on their way to Bukavu, where 10,000 had already arrived and were squatting on the outskirts. Simultaneously, 194,000 refugees had begun to trek south from the Goma camps. (All UNHCR figures to be taken with a few grains of salt.) These mass movements were prompted by hunger as well as fear; for weeks it had been virtually impossible to get food supplies into Kivu Province.

On 25 October Chris McGreal reported in *The Guardian*:

Tutsi fighters were bearing down on the panic-stricken city of Bukavu last night as government troops continued to flee from a powerful week-long offensive. The rapid advance of the Banyamulenge raised the spectre of conflict consuming the whole of Eastern Zaire as Kinshasa threw in more troops and accused Rwanda of invading ... Tutsi fighters have taken at least three towns in recent days and are reported to be within ten miles of Bukavu. Zaire's army said it was bringing in heavy weapons to defend the city. Planeloads of troops have already arrived.

Rachel chewed her nails and said nothing. Neither of us slept well. And in Bukavu Andrew didn't sleep at all because – as we learned much later – he spent that night, and the next, under tables and beds with Pascal's family while shells fell all around them. One of his office askaris was killed on the second night. Then he was airlifted out to Nairobi with all the other expats. (All except the resident missionaries, who are differently motivated and rarely leave 'their people'.)

Suddenly Bukavu – a place most people had never heard of before – was in the news. For a few days it got first mention on Radio 4 news bulletins, front-page headlines and half-page photographs, while sketch-plans of the area showed the refugees' routes as they stampeded every which way. The swift advance of Kabila's troops was not really so astonishing given the support they received from the Kivu folk and the degeneracy of the Zairean army, who mostly ran away, looting and raping as they went, before Kabila arrived. The most serious fighting took place, soon after the capture of Bukavu, around Goma. We deduced that that fight was Kabila's force versus Hutu militia, but by then all journalists had been banished from the province so there was nobody around to confirm our deduction.

Quite apart from Andrew-anxiety, that was a stressful time. Human nature being as it is, we became more emotionally involved than if all this suffering had been happening in some unfamiliar region. Rachel's flat is blissfully TV-free but the newspaper photographs were harrowing enough to inspire nightmares.

On 28 October Zaire suspended all commercial flights to Kivu Province. Next day Bukavu was heavily shelled, an RPA commando openly crossed the border from Cyangugu and remnants of the Zairean army looted NGO offices, beat up their local staffs and 'requisitioned' their vehicles – in which they then deserted the battlefield. That evening the Jesuit Archbishop of Bukavu, Christophe Munzi Hirwa, was murdered in an ambush not far from No. 19. A few days previously he had written to the UN Mission in Bukavu absurdly accusing Rwanda of using the Banyamulenge 'to seize power in Zaire'.

International reactions to events in eastern Zaire came to verge on the hysterical. One headline proclaimed 'Catastrophe Could Reshape a Continent', and some commentators even wrote frenziedly about 'global destabilization'. Soon representatives of the UN, EU and OAU, accompanied or followed by senior politicians, military men and NGO directors, were rushing around in circles – from New York to Arusha to Geneva to Kinshasa to Brussels to Nairobi to Stuttgart to Kigali and back again. There was much controversy about sending in a UN military intervention force, and we ground our teeth when the leader of this as yet theoretical force emphasized that its objective would be 'strictly humanitarian, it would be politically and militarily neutral'. This dithering and squabbling about the force's 'mandate' would have been comic were it not a repeat performance of the UN's 1994 inaction, which had such tragic results.

When we thought Andrew was safe in Nairobi, the *Irish Times* disillusioned us; it quoted him reporting on how things were looking in the interior of Zaire, which he had been flying over, very low, in some tiny plane.

During those trying times Rose was the cheering factor. I became fascinated by the one-sided verbal communication already possible; toddlers seem to acquire a considerable vocabulary long before they can use it. When I handed Rose an empty beer can and said, 'Please put it in the bin', she trotted off to the kitchen, down four steps, and put it in the bin. When Rachel said, 'Please bring a nappy', she trotted into her room and returned with a nappy. Is this why many toddlers go through a stroppy phase? To be able to understand so much but express nothing in words must be extremely frustrating.

When Kabila publicized his plan to 'overthrow the régime in Kinshasa and all it stand for', most commentators scoffed – then we were puzzled when he declared a three-week unilateral cease-fire on 3 November.

During the following week the Rwandan government chose ten NGOs, out of the 200 or so then competing in Rwanda, and authorized them to provide food and medical care in the Kabila-held areas of Kivu near the Rwandan border. Thus were the refugees encouraged to overcome two fears: of Kabila's mainly Tutsi troops and of returning home. At a meeting in Kigali on 9 November between Rwandan government officials and the chosen NGOs, the Rwandans made it plain that they had only one thing on their minds: the return home of the dispersed and disorganized refugees. They feared the arrival of a 'neutral' UN force, which would enable the ex-FAR and *interahamwe* to continue to re-arm within Zaire. When EU political and humanitarian representatives invited themselves to attend this meeting they were refused admission, despite their indignantly pointing out that the EU provides most of the region's relief and development money. A Rwandan explained bluntly that repeated EU demands for a UN military intervention disqualified the Europeans from participating in the new Rwandan plan.

Because Mobutu fully supported the Hutu militia, Kinshasa rejected Kigali's home-grown solution to one of Rwanda's major problems. Therefore no UN agency accompanied those ten courageous NGOs across the border into sovereign Zairean territory. To the UN, diplomatic niceties usually seem more important than human lives. However, on 13 November Dr Boutros-Ghali created a precedent by sanctioning the movement of UN agencies into Zaire in defiance of the government. It seemed some furniture was being shifted behind the scenes of the international community.

Happily, Andrew was back in Nairobi (evacuated again) by 10 November, in time to ring a rather forlorn Rachel on Rose's first birthday. Most of the displaced aid workers from Kivu were stuck in Nairobi for weeks, living in expensive hotels and occasionally attending futile meetings called by the UNHCR. No NGO would risk their staff's being absent should some unexpected media-attracting development arise – as one did, in mid-November, by which time I was at home in Ireland.

The government's plan had worked and suddenly most refugees were moving in the right direction. Journalists who for weeks had been dwelling on the pitiable plight of the starving flee-ing hordes now marvelled at the stamina of those 700,000 (or so) returnees as they sturdily trekked home carrying their possessions. In *The Irish Times* Mark Brennock reported from Gisenyi:

Aid workers had waited in dread for this day, fearing that they would be faced with diseased emaciated people. Word of the scale of the movement had spread on their radio network during the morning. Several hundred raced to the scene and what they saw was extraordinarily uplifting. Peo-ple looked well and said they were happy to be coming home. It was like a miracle, a peaceful return of healthy refugees ...

On 19 November 'confidential' documents were found in a broken-down bus near one of ex-FAR's abandoned Goma bases. These revealed that a British company, trading as Mil-Tec Corpo-ration, had supplied the genocidal government with £3.3 million worth of mortar bombs, grenades, rifles and bullets between April and July 1994. The shipment went to Goma via Albania and Israel, with Zairean end-user certificates, and began on 17 April – ten days after the start of the slaughter. According to British offi-cials, these shipments broke no British law (though some broke the UN 17 May embargo) because they did not travel through British territory. A recent letter from Mil-Tec to the exiled former Minister of Defence requested the payment of debts totalling US$1,962,375 and included invoices and bills for air freight. It concluded, 'We have supplied your ministry for more than five years ... You will realise that we have gone out of our way to assist your ministry in times of need.' It soothes me to think of Mil-Tec losing $1,962,375.

On 27 November the UN's press briefing contained an uncommonly meaty exchange when Sylvana Foa, who then spoke daily to the world press on behalf of the Secretary-General, was challenged by a few journalists. One asked if it were true that on 11 January 1994 'central elements had been left out of the briefing to the Security Council? Specifically was the Council alerted to the possibility of a plan for systematic killing in Rwanda?'

Ms Foa did not reply 'Yes' or 'No'. Instead she recalled

a story now familiar to everyone. On 11 January 1994 General Roméo Dallaire, UNAMIR head in Kigali, sent a cable to Maurice Baril saying basically that an informant in Kigali – someone he felt comfortable with, but with whom others did not feel so comfortable – had told him that plans to commit genocide against Tutsis were being formulated and arms caches were being hidden everywhere by the *interahamwe*. The Secretary-General then asked General Dallaire and his Special Representative, Jacques Booh-Booh, to go and immediately brief the ambassadors of the US, Belgium and France on the informant's story. He had also instructed him to go immediately to the President of Rwanda and inform him that what the informant reported would, of course, be in major violation of the Arusha Accords and that the international community hoped he would take some action. They had also gone to the Prime Minister of Rwanda with the same message. The next day, at a regular briefing to the Security Council, the concerns of UNAMIR over the possibility of increased violence had been presented. Evidently, the word 'genocide' had not been used in the briefing. But let's get real here. The cable could not be passed around because it named names and General Dallaire was very concerned about the informant's life. This was just one person telling us something and some people were comfortable with that person and some were not. The discussion about the cable was whether to go public with it or work to try and stop whatever was happening before it happened. If the UN had gone public at that time, if it really believed that cable – and some did and some did not – would it then spark the *interahamwe* into immediate action to do their dirty work? These dilemmas the UN routinely faces. Yes, we had an informant. Yes, this informant used the word 'genocide'. Yes, this informant told us about arms caches. But were we positive this informant was right? No. Did we try to do it through diplomacy? Did we ask the three major players in the area – the Americans, the French and the Belgians – to help us with this? Yes.

Another journalist said she understood General Dallaire had

asked the Secretary-General's permission to check out the arms caches but permission was denied on the grounds that the UN did not have a mandate to that effect. At that point could the Security Council not have reviewed the mandate if the Secretary-General had requested it to do so?

Ms Foa replied:

The Department of Peacekeeping Operations had cabled the Special Representative authorizing UNAMIR to respond positively to requests from the authorities, on a case-by-case basis, for assistance in recovery of the illegal arms. But we have to have a request. This was not a Chapter VII operation. This was a Chapter VI operation. As correspondents know, the UN's hands are tied in such matters.

When it was suggested that 800,000 lives might have been saved by more immediate action Ms Foa recalled

the mood of the time. The UNAMIR force, organized two months earlier, had been authorized up to two battalions but only one had been sent. By the end of December 1993 the Council was already looking at a possible reduction of the operation. We did not know what was going to happen. No one – no one – did enough to stop this. But it sure is a lot easier to Monday-morning quarterback what we should have done almost three years ago with the knowledge we have today than with the very scant knowledge we had then.

Asked who had opposed publishing the cable, Ms Foa said:

There was no one person in opposition or in favour. The information simply was not firm. We have to tread warily. We went as far as we thought we could. We went to three governments with extensive intelligence capacities ... We told them we were going to the President and Prime Minister of Rwanda with this information.

What Ms Foa's smooth talking revealed was the UN's unwillingness to find out what was really going on in pre-genocide Rwanda. The 'scant knowledge' need not have been scant; General Dallaire's cable was not the only warning of the imminent catastrophe. It was unnecessary to seek help from 'three governments with extensive intelligence capacities'. By January 1994 there existed a mass of public circumstantial evidence – in print and on tape – that genocide was being planned. Between 1991 and 1993 nine periodicals were regularly published that specialized in incitement to extreme anti-Tutsi violence. Had the UN made it their business to have these translated even they might have felt obliged to heed that cable from the man to whom they had given responsibility for seeing Rwanda safely through the interim period before elections, as agreed at Arusha. They could also have considered the statements by the International Committee of Lawyers, and numerous human rights organizations, after the publication of the Ten Hutu Commandments – which created an international uproar – in *Kangura* in December 1990. This twice-monthly journal, described by Gérard Prunier as 'the spearhead of the ideology of Hutu fundamentalism', was defended in Paris in April 1991 by President Habyarimana – in the name of 'freedom of the press'. The founder of *Kangura*, Hassan Ngeze, was the chief organizer of the Tutsi massacres in Bugesera in March 1992.

The UN could also have acquired scores of Radio Mille Collines cassettes. This 'private' radio station, in Gérard Prunier's words 'a main orchestrator of the genocide', was set up in April 1993 and reached every corner of Rwanda. Nine of its fifty founding shareholders belonged to the Habyarimana 'inner circle', the *Akazu* – then the source of all power in the country. Its staff was high-powered, no mere mob of fringe fanatics. Ferdinand Nahimna, whose brainchild it was, became its director. A distinguished historian from Ruhengeri, he had studied in Canada and France and his 1986 thesis – *Le Rwanda, émergence d'un État* – was published by Harmattan, Paris, in 1993. In his acknowledgments he thanked 'my friend Jean-Claude Habyarimana' – the President's son. RMC was allowed to use Radio Rwanda's network of transmitters free of charge, and its studios, opposite the presidential palace, were connected to the palace generators during power-cuts. Moreover, RMC's chief technician was sent to Germany to buy the very latest electronic equipment – a stark measure of the distance between Rwanda's slaughterings and 'primitive tribal warfare'.

Given these public and prolonged preparations for genocide by the *Akazu* and its henchmen, why did the UN Department of Peacekeeping Operations cable M. Booh-Booh on 11 January 'authorizing UNAMIR to respond positively to requests from authorities, on a case-by-case basis, for assistance in the recovery of the illegal arms'? This grotesque reaction to General Dallaire's cable highlights the incompetence of those senior officials who sit at their desks in New York making momentous decisions in total ignorance of the nature of the problems for which they are responsible. Contentedly they go through their ritual dance of the bureaucrats: the Department of Peacekeeping Operations cables authorization to the Secretary-General's Special Representative in Rwanda, who conveys it to the Commanding Officer of the UN troops – and don't forget, the request must come from the 'authorities' and it must be 'on a case-by-case basis' ... All this mumbo-jumbo while those same 'authorities' were arming the peasantry in preparation for genocide – to be committed under the noses of UNAMIR, with the foreknowledge of their helpless General. And no less lunatic was the notion that the French (one of the 'three governments with extensive intelligence capacities') would help the UN to sort out things Rwandan. It was plain to be seen – plain then, not just with hindsight – that President Mitterrand's government gave unqualified support to the Habyarimana régime.

Resolute UN action in January 1994 would have saved hundreds of thousands of lives. Mass killing was being planned on the basis of its not being defined as 'genocide'. The outside world was to be confused with talk of 'civil war' while the Tutsi and 'moderate' Hutu were being systematically slaughtered. The organizers were confident of getting away with this precisely because the UN had turned its back on Rwandan realities.

On 14 December 1996 Dr Boutros-Ghali was replaced by Mr Kofi Annan from Ghana, the US government's choice – he who had ignored the significance of the Dallaire cable when Under-Secretary-General for Peacekeeping Operations. Simultaneously it was announced that the proposed 10,000-strong multinational force would not after all be deployed in eastern Zaire. *The Guardian* reported that 'The scheme was crippled by procrastination and uncertainty about what it could hope to achieve in the face of increasing opposition from the Rwandan government and the Banyamulenge'.

At the beginning of December Andrew briefly revisited Bukavu and reported that all seemed calm, though many residents (not including the loyal Paul) had fled to the hills to escape the fighting. In a way, he said, the tension was less than during my visit – partly because the refugees had gone home, partly because Kabila's army had freed Kivu from those lawless and predatory Zairean soldiers.

In January 1997 Andrew's NGO promoted him. In his new job he would have to spend three months annually in Angola (at intervals) while Rachel and Rose remained in London. I sympathized with Rachel, who has always longed to travel in Angola, but such are the constrictions of motherhood. Well I remember them, having spent Rachel's first five years confined to Europe.

By January Nyanya's sights were again fixed on Kivu Province. No, not *fixed* – in the circumstances that would have been unrealistic – but my plan was: fly to Nairobi on 15 January, bus to Kabale near the Uganda-Rwanda border, then onwards by foot to Kigali and points west. How far west? Time would tell. Sitting in darkest Ireland (dark in January at 4 p.m.) it was impossible to gauge what the situation might be in Cyangugu. But with luck I could cross into Bukavu – and perhaps trek on into those unforgettable mountains? At least I could check on Budgie's welfare. Only to Rachel and Andrew was it possible to admit how much it mattered to me. In the middle of major humanitarian/military/political crises rational people do not fret about cats. But for a month Budgie had shared my sleeping-bag and I had endured his fleas, so our relationship became seriously meaningful, the bonds enduring ...

5

INTO THE GREAT
UNPLANNED

Each evening at 7 (or soon after) an Akamba 'luxury' coach
departs from Nairobi for Kampala. The journey takes sixteen and
a half hours owing to frequent and prolonged stops – to eat, to
cross borders, to negotiate Uganda's contraband-seeking military
roadblocks. At 11.30 this morning we reached Kampala's bus station and I emerged stiffly into a steady drenching downpour; it
had been raining and foggy over the last fifty miles. An hour later
I left for Mbarara in another sort of vehicle, a grievously battered
rural bus.

In front of me sat two young women with five babies and toddlers between them, all going to Kabale. Four of the juveniles
were model travellers: sleeping, or suckling, or quietly content.
The fifth was a two-year-old who could not be deterred from
banging on the window with a tin spoon. Her expression of jolly
defiance replicated Rose's and induced grandmaternal nostalgia.
But for Laurent Kabila, my granddaughter would now be ahead
of me in Bukavu instead of behind me in London.

That five-hour journey ended on Mbarara's High Street, where
the Pride Lodge provides an adequate £3 room leading off a small
concrete yard. The receptionist is a charming youth who carefully
wrote out my tiny receipt despite lacking forearms and having
only three-fingered hands where his elbows should be. When the
town's electricity supply failed at 7.40 he brought a candle within
moments. Over the bed hangs a 1991 calendar depicting a simper-
ing Indian film-star and advertising Roadmaster Cycles: 'Any

Road, Any Load', a text very germane to this part of Africa. As the bedding is damp I must use my sleeping-bag.

In a café-bar across the street I quickly downed two Nile beers to give me Dutch courage before I set out to look for my Tutsi friend, Marie. Since our first meeting in '92, when I was cycling through Uganda, we had corresponded – until January '94. Then, in her last letter, Marie mentioned that she was about to visit her mother and seven-year-old son in Kigali. Three letterless years suggested the worst but I continued to hope; possibly she remained too traumatized to write.

Two tables away I noticed an elderly man studying me with that furtive intentness one employs when trying to work out whether or not a person is known. At last he approached, diffidently, and asked, 'You were Marie's Irish friend?' Were ... So I had been silly to hope. Marie had rented Mr Kanabalula's flat; he recognized me from a photograph of the two of us that once hung on her living-room wall. She had remained longer than planned in Kigali because her mother fell ill. In April '94 she and her son and two brothers were murdered. Her mother survived but has since died. I have just repacked the three paperbacks I brought for Marie, as requested in her last letter.

KABALE, 18 JANUARY

By 6.45 I had secured a front seat in a minibus about to depart for Kabale – according to its driver. Two hours later it was full and we took off, or seemed to. But that was an illusion. Beyond Mbarara several individuals and groups appeared by the wayside, desperate to get aboard, and a vehicle licensed to carry fourteen passengers ended up carrying twenty-two. Delay-wise, the extra passengers themselves are no problem. But it does take time to load their chairs, poultry, matoke, planks, sacks, cartons, baskets, bundles, blankets and rolled-up mats. Then it turned out that not all passengers were going to Kabale. At intervals we stopped and much hectic unloading took more time – much more, if the disembarking person's sack was under other passengers' possessions. And always, before anyone's belongings could be retrieved, it was necessary to remove the two chairs roped to the open back door. Happily, I readjusted to the rhythm of African life. But the Kampala businessman beside me registered extreme impatience. 'Time is money!' he fumed, repeatedly unzipping and rezipping his brief-case in a near-paroxysm of frustration.

For the first twenty miles or so we were driving through fertile level farmland, interspersed with wide papyrus marshes and wooded hills. At this season the hedges are aglow with blossoms: scarlet, blue, yellow. Despite the fertility, the local folk look wretchedly poor: skinny, many with infected sores on their legs, all clad in dirty rags. Scores of mothers and children – not fathers – were walking to their fields in single file. Some of the children, carrying child-sized hoes, seemed no more than six or seven years old. A few herds of Ankoli cattle paced along ridge-tops towards valley pastures, their lyre-horns a mobile frieze etched against the pale blue morning sky.

Leaving the cultivated land behind, we climbed slowly into hunky green mountains, boulder-strewn and steep, unpredictably shaped and so irregularly spaced that every bend presented a surprise. The superbly engineered road rises – and rises – and rises. Then it levels out to curve around the rims of deep valleys, some lightly wooded, some with orange-red erosion gashes furrowing their sides. Next come longer and still steeper climbs, the air now perceptibly colder. Suddenly one is aware of leaving East Africa, entering a region more remote and quite distinctive, a temperate well-watered zone that remained inaccessible for so long no Arab slave-traders ever penetrated here. Which is one reason why Rwanda and Burundi are Africa's most densely populated countries.

In April '92 Marie had urged me to do a detour from Mbarara to visit her family in Kigali. (At that date an impossible detour, I discovered; there was sporadic fighting along the border.) I remember her exact words: 'The climb to the heights, it is of the greatest magnificence!' – as indeed it is. Today a curious incredulity is mingling with my sorrow. Genocide lies far beyond the grasp of one's imagination; it is illogically hard to believe that anyone known personally was among the victims.

In this south-western corner of Uganda one is already within the Rwandan 'sphere of influence'; the Kigeza district was part of Rwanda until the British and Germans did a boundary adjustment deal in 1910. By now Kigeza might be described as a Banyarwanda home-from-home-land. Some of the Hutu peasants who escaped the Belgian forced-labour barbarities of the 1930s settled around here, as did many of the Tutsi who fled after 1959.

From the pass above Kabale I glimpsed the Virunga chain of volcanoes far away to the west, their rugged austerity seeming extra-dramatic in contrast to Kigeza's lushness. I longed to disembark here and walk the last few miles. But the disinterring of my rucksack would have caused such a time-consuming upheaval that the Kampala businessman might have succumbed to hypertension.

From the pass the road plunges into a narrow valley, then rises again, gently, to enter Uganda's highest town (about 6000 feet), where a cool breeze tempers even the noon heat. During the afternoon blue-black clouds suddenly filled the sky and soon delivered an hour's torrential rain to lay the dust and fill water-barrels. In this congenial little town the local traffic consists mainly of bicycles; scores are registered cycle-taxis with cushioned carriers and number-plates. Kabale is the 'base-camp' for backpackers and overlanders en route to the mountain-gorilla reservation near Kisoro, most of whom stay in the Visitour Hotel (£2 per night).

MULINDI, RWANDA, 19 JANUARY

I was unwise to leave Kabale in darkness; within a mile three speeding lampless cyclists had missed me by inches. But soon came a subdued dawn, the pale light filtering through low grey clouds. As the invisible sun rose, those clouds sank to ground level and became a shifting mist, a silver veil that sometimes briefly revealed the nearby hills, the clumps of tall wayside trees or stands of bluegum saplings, the wide valley pastures where imported Ayrshires were being milked. Baboons, near but unseen, were barking loudly, and the calls of stately crested cranes (Oh Ann! Oh Ann!) sounded harshly plaintive as they waded through marshy hollows.

This area is densely populated and the locals look quite prosperous. By 7 the mist was dispersing and there was much traffic – all of it two-wheeled, cyclists with gleaming milk-churns strapped to their carriers pedalling fast towards Kabale. Twice young men who were about to load their carriers pointed to the mug hanging from my rucksack and offered me delicious frothy warm milk. In the several villages en route I was greeted with waves and smiles and shouted questions and made to feel welcome as an amusing oddity – one more daft *muzungu*. Topographically I was already in Rwanda, the road winding between steep rounded hills, cleverly terraced and overlooking long, wide, flat valleys.

It took me five hours to cover the fourteen miles to the border. At 11, in the straggling, down-at-heel village of Kamuganguzi, I walked past a queue of twenty-seven oil-tankers and trucks, their drivers evidently taking Sunday off in Uganda where prices are much lower than in Rwanda. The ramshackle frontier barrier-gate stood open and a predatory Ugandan policeman, masquerading as a customs officer, beckoned me into his small round tin-roofed hut and ordered me to unpack my rucksack. Pouncing on 200 mini-cigars he accused me of 'smuggling and illegal import' and demanded a US$25 bribe. Then he was distracted – fascinated – by those books I had hoped to give Marie. He checked my passport, to confirm the name, then exclaimed that he had never before met a writer of books. We negotiated. He settled for *In Ethiopia with a Mule*, autographed and personally inscribed. As I remember noticing on a previous visit, many Ugandans are gratifyingly addicted to books.

In the customs building across the track a genuine customs officer was uninterested in my rucksack. The immigration officer, while stamping my passport, warned, 'Be careful over there, be very careful – they don't like *muzungus*.'

The quarter-mile of no man's land is a wide rough track, mangled by truck traffic: no one's responsibility. Piles of burnt-out vehicles lie on either side, too heat-deformed to be identifiable, relics of the desultory 1990–94 civil war – Tutsi RPA versus Hutu FAR.

Three lanky teenage soldiers, lounging in a tattered tent by Rwanda's pole-barrier, stared in disbelief as mama walked around it. Then I saw the first evidence of this country's relatively responsible use, since Independence, of foreign aid money. The Gatuna customs and immigration buildings are large and well built and in comparison to their Ugandan equivalents give an impression of orderliness and efficiency.

At noon on the Sabbath the immigration office was queue-free. At one desk sat a very beautiful young Tutsi woman. When I addressed her in English her male colleague, sitting behind a bigger desk – not obviously Tutsi or Hutu – snarled, 'She doesn't speak that language.' Then he asked, 'Why do you travel by feet? What are you looking for? What is your career? Who is paying you?'

Blandly I defined myself as a tourist who likes walking and pays her own way.

A long pause. Then: 'You cannot walk to Kigali. It is impossible, it is far. There is nowhere to sleep, no hotels. At this season there is heavy rain. And there is dangerous traffic on this road. I can organize transport to Kigali. Sit and wait.'

I thanked him for his kindness while remaining adamant; my holiday must be a walking tour, I enjoy nothing else. He became agitated, looked to his colleague for support. Briefly she met my eye before saying something dismissive in Kinyarwanda. My would-be protector shrugged, stamped my passport, then released me to combat heavy rain and dangerous traffic as best I could.

The road is quite narrow but well maintained. I walked on – feeling vaguely unsettled by my introduction to Rwanda – in the shade of ancient trees rooted in high embankments. There was no traffic, pedestrian or otherwise, over the next two miles. At the first roadside hamlet – two small stores, a dozen tin-roofed mud-dwellings – the few visible inhabitants had closed, unsmiling faces. The stranger did not feel welcome. Suspicion hung in the air like fine dust. I didn't linger. Trekking on, I accepted being in another world. Even to a visitor unaware of Rwanda's recent trauma its 'otherness' would, I am convinced, be immediately apparent.

Then I reminded myself that this area's trauma long predates the genocide. By '91 the RPA were in control of the north of Byumba prefecture and had closed the Gatuna border-post, forcing all imports from Mombasa to use the far more expensive roundabout route through Tanzania – a serious blow to Rwanda's economy.

At that stage most of the RPA were Tutsi born and bred in Uganda, the offspring of refugees. The RPA/RPF loathed the Habyarimana régime but ostensibly were not anti-Hutu, per se. Having fought in Museveni's army, many had absorbed his Get-Rid-Of-Tribalism ideology and seen for themselves the effectiveness of the system he imposed in Uganda in 1986. Instead of political parties competing nationally for power there was village democracy, each community electing its own leaders and taking responsibility for its own welfare. (A system now being undermined by the World Bank/IMF demand for Western-style 'democratic elections' and privatization.) The RPA/RPF claimed to think of themselves as Banyarwanda rather than Tutsi, this being the generic term for all Kinyarwanda speakers – Tutsi, Hutu and Twa – whether their homeland be Rwanda, Uganda or Zaire. However, although the RPA presented themselves as an enlightened army of liberation, dedicated to freeing Rwanda from a hideous tyranny, the Hutu peasants saw them (and were vigorously encouraged to see them) as vengeful Tutsi returning to re-establish their traditional dominance in Rwanda. By the middle of 1992, 300,000 terrified Byumba peasants had become Displaced Persons elsewhere in Rwanda. Undoubtedly the RPA invasion made it much easier for the organizers of the genocide to present all Tutsi as The Enemy. But – had the RPA not been present to fight the FAR and the *interahamwe*, there would have been no Tutsi or moderate Hutu survivors.

As I trekked on, beginning to feel tired and thirsty, I decided that here and now honesty is probably the best policy. Plainly Rwanda is not at present a tourist-magnet and the immigration officer knew I was lying. To admit to being a travel writer, even if few understand what that means, might diminish suspicion.

I had just reached this conclusion when a young man hailed me from a large, tree-shaded compound on a steep slope high above the road – the first habitation since the hamlet. 'Let us help you!' he called. 'Have food, have water!' My progress up that skiddy incline was observed by twenty or so elders – men and women – standing around in little groups wearing Sunday clothes. They ignored my greetings.

Pierre met me halfway, beamingly shook hands, then led me to one of five low, rectangular tiled dwellings, solidly built of mud bricks. His petite bride sat within, expensively dressed, obviously an urban lass – a Bujumbura-born Tutsi returnee, it transpired. Monique showed a friendly interest in the visitor but hesitated to

speak English. Pierre's English was limited: 'I learn as visiting relatives in Mbarara.' While his much older sister prepared a meal he
went to fetch his mother, my contemporary but semi-crippled by
rheumatism. She hobbled in on two sticks, murmured a welcome
in French, embraced me with one arm, then rejoined the elders –
now settling down to what looked like an indaba, the men and
women sitting in rows on wooden benches, facing each other.

For lunch: a plate piled with hunks of stale white bread, thinly
spread with margarine, a communal omelette, a communal dish of
bone-infested fish stew – more gravy than fish. I was mainly interested in the tea, already milked when poured from a huge kettle.
My companions added several heaped spoons of sugar to their
enamel mugs; the visitor was given a chipped cup. As we ate
Pierre told me he works for an evangelical American NGO in
Kigali, where Monique is about to start teaching at a primary
school. I got the impression that he had, as we say in Ireland,
'married above himself'. His bride seemed not quite at ease,
perched on the edge of a sagging brown velveteen sofa, being deferential to her new in-laws who in turn were being deferential to
her. She whispered a reproof when Pierre began to spit his fish-
bones onto the earthen floor; he ignored her.

'In before days we have nice things,' said Pierre apologetically,
looking around the bare little room. 'In war days we went gone
from shooting and grenades. Coming back, the houses is empty.'
He asked then where I would spend the night.

I explained – at a tea estate-cum-factory a few miles farther on,
ruined during the war and now being restored under the supervi-
sion of an old friend of mine, John Walton, whom I first met in
Peru in 1978.

'Is far,' said Pierre. 'Too many kilometres. Stay here and I talk
and talk, is good for my English. Is room and bed for you. Tomorrow you foot on to your tea friends, we have *matatu* to our little
new home. In Kigali, you become visiting us again. I go say my
sister, make bed.'

Monique and I then achieved a limping conversation in embry-
onic English and French. Pierre was visible outside, being interro-
gated – it seemed – by the elders. His mother looked agitated. One
man, tall and grey-haired, stood up to speak loudly and angrily to

Pierre. Monique leaned sideways to peer nervously through the doorway. Moments later Pierre returned, discomfited, and withdrew his invitation.

Two months ago, this hospitable family sheltered a Kabale-bound Frenchwoman, travelling alone, whose NGO Pajero had broken down nearby at sunset. Throughout the night stones were thrown into the compound, the roof tiles were badly damaged and every window in the hut was broken. I had noticed that they remain broken: glass is very expensive.

'Our Tutsi father has died,' said Pierre. 'Dead in October 1990, they say he like very much RPA. Now hate for him go on. For all our family. Father Tutsi, all are Tutsi. Hutu mother is Tutsi if she marry him. They like reason for attack and make us fear. I have apologies, I like to give you shelter. But mother have right, she have all to protect in this houses.' Inconsequentially he added, 'Mixed families have big confusions, from six children you can see three Tutsi, three Hutu.' Pierre himself has Hutu features but Tutsi stature.

I made understanding noises and left soon after, Pierre insisting on filling my two-litre water-bottle with costly bottled water brought from Kigali. The elders again ignored me as I descended to the road.

So – giving refuge to a *muzungu* in distress could provoke the vandalizing of a compound and the terrorizing of its inhabitants. Or was that attack because the Frenchwoman's vehicle identified her as an aid worker? I have heard that in Rwanda foreign aid workers are popular only among the communities they are aiding – and not always there.

The smooth tarred road (a motorist's delight but unkind to trekking feet) continued to wind around the bases of intensively cultivated slopes. Beyond the wide flat valley on my left rose forested hills. This is a very beautiful country. And today provided perfect trekking weather: no wind, no rain, no sun until 3.15 when the high pale grey cloud cover dispersed. Then came the beginning of the tea plantation – Rwanda's first, established in 1946. It covers 8000 level hectares and employs 2000 locals who work six days a week from dawn to noon and are paid piecemeal. Looking at the low, neatly pruned bushes in their symmetrical rows, with drainage channels running through them at intervals in straight brown lines, one would never suspect the extent of the recent war-damage. Soon a large wayside notice directed me to the factory and the last few miles were uphill on a dirt track through woodland – the ubiquitous bluegums, mighty pines and many indigenous unknowns. Round and round went the track, affording splendid views of other valleys and hills. The variety of birds was astounding; I counted fourteen species, some like jewels being thrown through the branches. From one distant commune across a valley – the little huts invisible amidst banana groves – came the sound of drums and hymn-singing and hand-clapping.

The tea factory's domination of this area for the past half-century means that Mulindi is not a typical commune. The large settlement below the summit occupies a saddle between two hills and is a dreary collection of tin-roofed, one-storey buildings serviced by a few mini-shops, hawkers' stalls and shebeens. The Sunday idlers hanging around the track junction viewed me with an astonishment undiluted by friendliness. I paused to ask which way to the factory but no one understood – or tried to understand – my rudimentary French. I turned right and the track became steeper, climbing between rough stretches of grass behind which stood rows of shoddy shacks. Here a few goats were tethered and hens pecked and children swarmed. Then two young men came towards me and smiled a welcome. Both are Kenyans, employed by the tea company as engineers. When I introduced myself as John Walton's friend they asked eagerly when he would be returning from the UK and escorted me to the hilltop. In a battered sentry-box, by the factory compound's closed gate, sat a soldier whose duty it is to keep out the locals.

My escort explained that I am now on historic territory, the headquarters of the RPA for three years and nine months while they struggled to gain power in Rwanda. Much fighting took place on this site and bullets and shell-cases may still be picked up as souvenirs. The completely destroyed and looted factory has been made as good as new with EU money – in fact, better than new. Given modern equipment, it takes only twenty-four hours for each day's crop of freshly picked leaves to be dried, finely ground and packed into sacks ready for export – to be added to those blends that go into tea bags. However, many of the former workers' dwellings and their health centre and school and community hall remain derelict: bullet-pocked, shell-blasted, windowless, blood-stained, aggressively graffiti'd. The bunker of the RPA leader Paul Kagame was pointed out to me, and later, as I walked alone across a disused soccer field on a flat ledge, I found my own special souvenir in the long grass: a military helmet, camouflage green, destined to adorn my study.

Surprisingly, the enormous shed-like factory, with its adjacent colossal stack of firewood (grown nearby by the company), does not give this hilltop an industrial aura. All around are fine bungalows, large and small, set amidst colourful gardens and connected by hedged laneways. Even now, post-war, the general effect is agreeably villagey – as long as one doesn't dwell on the socio-economic implications of tea estates ...

I am writing this on the verandah of the guest-bungalow, perched on a narrow ledge on the periphery of the 'village', bright with flowering shrubs and semi-encircled by towering indigenous trees – old and dignified and busy with bird-life. Otherwise the silence is unbroken. Far below lies a tranquil valley, already in shadow as the sun pours a gentle golden light onto the opposite hills. These seem to be strewn with mirrors; my binoculars have just revealed the glinting new tin roofs of huts being hurriedly built with aid money for some of the returned refugees.

It feels odd, on my first evening in Rwanda, to be staying in this bungalow where so much has happened – so many historic confrontations, speculations, gambles taken, decisions made, statements issued – all going to the shaping of the new Rwanda. And now it has reverted to its original role and the normality of this hilltop – the genocide regarded as a mere hiccup, briefly halting tea-production – seems unreal. And perhaps is unreal? Yet this is how things should be: people industriously picking up the pieces and getting on with life.

This has been a taxing day, both physically and emotionally. Not that I expected Rwanda to be emotionally non-taxing. But I am in an unsettled mood this evening – really rather an absurd mood. The contrast between Rwanda's natural beauty and its present atmosphere has thrown me. Atmosphere: meaning 'mental or moral environment, pervading tone or mood'. I think back to 1968 when I trekked through eastern Turkey by way of taking healthy exercise while pregnant. One day I walked through a region that made me feel as I do this evening. It deeply disturbed me though I didn't then know why. Back home, a little research revealed that I had been traversing an area marked by one of the worst atrocities of the Armenian genocide. There, half a century before my journey, the Turks had flung thousands of men, women and children into deep ravines and left them to die – some quickly of their injuries, others slowly of starvation. That experience taught me that an awareness of psychic stains on the atmosphere is not dependent on foreknowledge, is not imaginary or in any sense subjective.

KIGALI, 20 JANUARY

A late start this morning: until 9 no one was available to whom I could say 'Good-bye and thank you'. Last night there was a post-poned New Year's staff party, to which the Rwandan director kindly invited me – but by then my bed beckoned.

While descending to the main road I was overlooking miles of tea flecked with bright colours as scores of pickers moved amidst the waist-high bushes, delicately picking the end buds and their two tiny adjacent leaves. Demanding work, on which depends Rwanda's reputation for exporting only the highest quality of tea. Men, women and children (older children) are employed here, the women most numerous.

Down in the valley, I walked for hours along the edge of the plantation, meeting many pickers carrying their morning's harvest to the nearest collection point. It is obvious that this immensely valuable foreign-exchange-earning crop does nothing to alleviate local poverty – rather the reverse. The wages paid are worth much less than the food that could be grown on Mulindi's rich soil. Moreover, the right to use a given plot of land – which right may be passed on to the next generation – greatly enhances a peasant's status. The government's past cash payments, in exchange for expropriated land, cannot compensate for this loss of status.

Eventually the road swung away from the tea valleys and climbed quite steeply towards the pass near Byumba town, winding through a landscape of heart-stopping loveliness – abundantly

green, some slopes wooded, others cultivated, all apparently unin-
habited. But only apparently; the peasants' small huts are usually
concealed by banana groves. Given the pivotal significance of this
road, for Rwanda, Burundi and Kivu Province, there was surprisingly little traffic: no private cars, only two NGO vehicles, a few
massive trucks coming from the port of Mombasa over a thousand miles away.

Soon after 3, life took an unexpected turning, as I guessed it
often would on this rather dotty journey.

Flashback to my London-Nairobi flight. Beside me on the
plane sat a Baptist missionary of American parentage, born in
1926 in a remote corner of what was then the Belgian Congo. He
has lived there ever since, apart from three years at an American
theological college where he 'felt like a gorilla in a zoo'. Mentally
I labelled Matt 'not the worst sort of missionary'. He speaks three
of Zaire's innumerable languages, in addition to Swahili, French
and 'just enough Kinyarwanda to get along'. Moreover, he is so
sympathetic towards ordinary Zaireans that he cannot forgive the
US government for its backing of Mobutu throughout the Cold
War. He told me that when Kabila's forces had taken Goma they
requisitioned his huge mission compound as a barrack. For two
months he remained nearby, then saw his precious buildings being
set on fire when Kabila's troops moved on. 'I quit then – I hated
quitting but my kids and grandkids are all in the States and wanted me out. Now that things are quieter I'm going back to see what
can be salvaged and check out our guys there.'

Matt was flying on to Kampala to pick up his vehicle to drive
to Goma, staying in Kigali overnight. As we parted on the plane
he said, 'May see you on the road!' And so he did, this afternoon,
as I approached the military roadblock outside Byumba town.

Matt braked with a squeal, backed rapidly, leaned out to grin at
me and asked, 'Have you heard the news? My guys in Goma reckon there's an invasion of Kivu due soonish. The Zairean army aims
to retake the whole province before February. OK, so we can laugh
at that. But maybe Mobutu's foreign buddies will do the job. You'd
better get shifting if you're so keen to see Bukavu again. Don't
waste time walking, come to Gisenyi with me tomorrow. Maybe
the Goma-Bukavu ferry is running again, maybe not. No matter –

I've good friends can fix you a ride on the Gisenyi-Cyangugu brewery barge. Then you're thirty minutes' walk from Bukavu. Or less, the rate you seem to go if you only left Kabale yesterday morning.' He opened the Land-Rover's passenger door. 'Hop in, throw your gear in the back.'

I didn't hesitate. Of the 285 passengers on that flight from London, almost certainly only two were heading for Kivu. When Fate seems to be intervening so directly it's best to pay attention. Anyway, two soldiers had stopped their jeep half an hour before to warn me I'd not be allowed to continue on foot beyond the Byumba roadblock.

From the pass – one of Rwanda's highest points – the road descends around the precipitous flanks of uncultivable mountains. Alas! Matt is a horribly fast driver; we covered the forty-five miles to the outskirts of Kigali in thirty-five minutes, during which time I learned a little more about my companion. In 1896 his missionary grandfather settled in Kenya, then became a pioneer bringer of the gospel to the Belgian Congo, directly supported by both US President Cleveland and the unspeakably vicious King Leopold II. (At that point in Matt's account I thought, *inter alia*, how odd it is that Mobutu so closely resembles that monarch in personality and behaviour.) Subsequently Granddad was awarded all sorts of honours, royal and presidential, for his successful Christianizing endeavours. I intuited that Matt has been saddened by his own progeny's declining to continue those endeavours. He believes reconciliation in Rwanda is 'no way ever going to happen', not for the reasons commonly offered but because too few Rwandans have been reborn.

Tonight Matt is staying in a missionary hostel and I am staying in the Gloria Hotel, paying US$20 for a cramped windowless room, unfurnished apart from the bed, with a waterless bathroom – and nobody brings buckets. As Rachel warned me, Rwandan prices are, by African standards, very high.

In a nearby bar (where this is being written) I felt a pang on again seeing bottles of Primus, brewed in Bukavu and recalling all those happy days on the patio of No. 19 and the shore of Lake Kivu. If I do get back there, I'm going to miss the RAR unit (especially the junior R) most dreadfully.

Here I have a table to myself, beside a long picture window overlooking a jumble of rusty tin roofs. Mount Kigali is visible across the crowded valley, changing colour – from grey to blue to umber – as the sun declines. This big bar is as yet uncrowded and quiet, the scattered pairs or groups conversing in low voices, the few lone drinkers looking gloomy. I find myself wondering, 'Who is what?' – a morbid but inevitable reaction to the shadow of genocide still darkening this country. Of course it's not now p.c. to acknowledge the physical differences between pure-bred Hutu and Tutsi; we are supposed to deny the evidence of our eyes and go along with the reconciliatory RPF assertion that the Banyarwanda are 'one people'. Which is true, culturally; all Rwandans speak the same language and share the same traditions and customs. Yet it's plain to the detached observer that at some time in the distant past the Tutsi's ancestors migrated from some region (Ethiopia? Somalia?) where people are much taller than the Hutu and have straighter noses, thinner lips and longer fingers. At the end of the nineteenth century, when the various colonial powers hijacked physical anthropology (then a new discipline) for their own ends, the Germans – Rwanda's first colonizers – classified the Tutsi as 'Hamitic' (more like 'us', therefore 'superior') and the Hutu as primitive Bantu. So they were not surprised to find the Tutsi ruling over the rest in most regions, though not yet in the north-west where the Germans helped them to get a grip – if not a very tight grip.

After World War I the Belgians took over Rwanda and Burundi (then run as a single entity) under a League of Nations Mandate. In pre-colonial times it was possible for a Hutu who had accumulated a certain number of cattle to climb the socio-political ladder and gain Tutsi status. This flexibility – though the transition was rare enough – prevented the evolution of a Hindu-type caste system. It also prevented the development of a Hutu élite capable of disputing Tutsi domination. Then, between 1926 and 1933, the Belgians put a stop to upward mobility. Every Rwandan, from infancy to senility, had to carry a pass identifying him or her as Tutsi or Hutu. The colonists also established indirect rule, as so many of their kind were wont to do. But first it was necessary to smash the tradition whereby the Mwami (king) appointed three chiefs to administer his territories: a Tutsi with responsibility for gathering taxes and recruiting warriors, a Tutsi in charge of cattle and grazing rights, a Hutu in charge of matters agricultural. By concentrating authority in one hand-picked regional chief, the Belgians eliminated these ancient and healthy checks and balances. And all Hutu chiefs were dismissed.

Through their over-indulged puppets, the Belgians ruled with sickening cruelty, and few Tutsi protested on behalf of their enslaved fellow-Banyarwanda. Meanwhile, the colonists' missionary allies – mainly Catholic with the White Fathers in the lead – exacerbated the situation by going along with the official educational policy: only Tutsi were deserving of schooling. Before World War II, Hutu were excluded from all Church schools, the only schools in rural areas. However, clerical attitudes changed dramatically after World War II. The missionaries then recruited came from the less privileged layers of their own society – and from the French-speaking provinces of Wallonia, which made them more sympathetic towards the wretched Hutu peasants. By the mid-fifties an increasing number of Hutu were graduating from the Groupe Scolaire at Astrida (now Butare). But still all civil-service and private-sector jobs were reserved for Tutsi; only the Church offered the Hutu a livelihood. It also allowed them an opportunity to agitate against discrimination. They took over several Church publications, with clerical approval, and began a political campaign (with clerical guidance) that was to end, very bloodily, with the 'revolution' of 1959–62, the departure of the Belgians and the inauguration of the Hutu Gregoire Kayibanda as first President of the Republic of Rwanda. That 'revolution' was closer in spirit to a genocide. Uncounted thousands of Tutsi died, thousands more saw their homes burned down and/or their cattle herds stolen. By 1961 about 120,000 had gone into exile, leaving the Hutu and the Church in charge of the newly independent Republic.

My 'physical anthropological' survey of the bar's customers was inconclusive. I remember Rachel's noting the fact that generations of mixed marriages have blurred visible differences. And naturally, given the percentages involved, Hutu genes predominate. However, one of the young bartenders was unmistakably

Tutsi: tall and slender with an oval face and large luminous eyes. Had I seen him in London I would have assumed him to be an Amhara. While I was buying my third Primus we got into conversation. He is the son of '59ers, as they are known: a returnee from Kinshasa, where he learned English while working in the US Embassy.

'It was fine and dandy', said he, 'to be able to come home last month. The Zaireans turned against us after Kabila got going. They fired all Tutsi from their government service.' (What government service? I wondered.) For this young man 'coming home' was, in fact, his first experience of Rwanda.

6

GUERRILLAS
IN THE MIST

The impeccable Kigali–Gisenyi road was built with World Bank money by Chinese convicts – 'Probably dissidents', said Matt. From the capital's outskirts it snakes steeply upwards for miles through dense bluegum plantations, then crosses a high narrow plateau overlooking scores of hilltops on both sides. Here the guidebook cliché 'Land of a Thousand Hills' seems literally true. But unfortunately I've come at the wrong season for panoramic views. During the months ahead, according to Matt, these will be permanently obscured by haze. And the Virunga volcanoes on the northern shore of Lake Kivu are likely to remain in cloud purdah. As we were descending from the plateau, Matt slowed to point out the graves of nine Chinese 'killed in action' and buried on a hillside, each awarded a tombstone and a row of cacti.

Every square foot of the surrounding countryside is cultivated, yet few pedestrians use this road. Matt, on the lookout for bargains to present to his 'Goma guys', slowed again as we passed a few roadside trading centres. Towards one colourful weekly market, lines of very small Twa women were head-carrying high stacks of shapely, intricately painted pots. The pygmy Twa were Rwanda's earliest inhabitants; now they make up about 1 per cent of the population.

We overtook several swaying lorries packed with soldiers; their guns, poking upwards and through the side slats, made these vehicles look from a distance like magnified hedgehogs. 'Are they going to Gisenyi?' wondered Matt, a trifle nervously. But most seemed to be heading for Ruhengeri's important military base – extra important now because this north-western corner was a Habyarimana stronghold and under the present government is notoriously disaffected.

Today the splendour of Rwanda's landscapes tormented me; there can be few forms of emotional torture than motoring worse from Kigali to Gisenyi. Many tracks lead off the main road, winding up to hilltop communes. Longingly I gazed at them, planning a cross-country return to Kigali from hilltop to hilltop ... Then I exulted, as the oceanic width of my beloved Lake Kivu appeared far below – only to vanish as the road dropped to the shore through mightily flourishing banana groves.

At noon, from the Palm Beach hotel, Matt made a few phone calls and learned that both the Goma-Bukavu ferry and the Gisenyi-Cyangugu brewery barge are 'in abeyance'. Last week, it is rumoured, a rocket was fired at the barge from the Bukavu shore. By whom and why? 'Nobody knows,' said Matt. 'Or if they do they're not telling. Maybe it's not even true. But my friends have left suddenly – the brewery manager and his wife. A bad sign ...' Matt was almost tearfully apologetic about having led me astray. To soothe him I pointed out that in Gisenyi I am at least nearer to Bukavu than when he picked me up at Byumba. We may meet again on his return from his quick recce to Goma. I plan to spend a few days here, trying to winnow fact from rumour, before settling on a trekking route.

The seed of Gisenyi was sown in 1894 when Lieutenant von Goetzen set up an army post on the lake shore. The Belgians developed the place as their main Rwandan holiday resort and built opulent lakeside villas, many now rented at vast expense by foreign NGOs and UN agencies. A mile-long avenue of very tall palms runs along the low grassy shore to the super-luxury Meridien hotel, at present a dispirited place, dependent on aid workers (a dwindling breed since the Goma camps closed) in lieu of holiday-makers. Halfway down the avenue is the Palm Beach hotel, which I at once recognized from Andrew's photographs; he and Rachel (and Rose *in utero*) stayed here eighteen months ago. From my room it's a two-minute walk to the water, and I have had three blissful swims today, though not as blissful as below No. 19. Here the water is shallow near the shore, there is less privacy and the 'holiday resort' after-taste lingers. Also, Gisenyi cannot compete with Bukavu's unique beauty.

After all my efforts to obtain US one-dollar bills in London, I find the bigger denominations more valuable in Rwanda. The rate for $50 bills and over is RF310; for under $50 it's only RF295. But my immediate dollar-problem concerns a rabbit; it's odd how those creatures impinge on one's life in the Kivu region. Matt bought a comely young doe en route, from a wayside livestock trader, for breeding purposes – Kabila's troops having eaten all his mission's colony. She sat on my lap over the next fifty miles and peed copiously into my money-belt, and the hotel receptionist refused to accept wet dollars. He was, however, reasonable (I didn't explain the source of the wetness), and agreed to wait until this evening for payment. I then sat by the lakeside (windless and at that hour deserted) with dollars spread out on the sand all around me, drying in the sun. In Rwanda one needs such 'light relief' problems.

The Palm Beach is now dependent on my dollars; yesterday the three expats who were lodging here left for Kigali, obeying orders from their NGO director. He had been made twitchy by rumours of an imminent mercenary invasion of Kivu Province which might spill over the nearby border into Gisenyi. In the bar just now, a Primus-primed RPA major, speaking excellent Ugandan English, assured me – 'We're ready for them, we're ready to go over.' Meaning ...? I'm not even trying to understand what goes on, apart from sussing out whether or not it's safe for me to trek from here to Cyangugu via Kibuye, on the dirt road that runs through the mountains high above the lake. Luckily there are quite a few English-speakers around, all Tutsi returnees from Uganda. One Mbarara-born MSF worker mentioned those refugees back from Goma who have refused to return to their communes on the UNHCR trucks and are roaming the Kibuye area, hungry and desperate. They are said to be ruthless robbers (their only survival mechanism) though they rarely kill. My informant described them as 'genocidal peasants', but as I'm not a Tutsi they sound an insufficient deterrent to trekking.

Hereabouts the bird-life is fabulous but the major warned me against using either a camera or binoculars 'at this moment in time' – even within the hotel grounds, where all day soldiers have been patrolling with rifles at the ready. Gisenyi is included in 'the blessed region' (so described by the *Akazu* criminals) where support for Hutu extremism is strongest. In July '94 a local trader told a French journalist, 'We never had many Tutsi here and we killed them all at the beginning without much of a fuss.'

THE SAME, 22 JANUARY

While crossing the hotel's inner courtyard, on the way back to my room after a long dawn swim, I saw something I should not have seen. Outside the kitchen door lay nine fat grey dead rats, all caught during the night. Obviously they had been thriving in the hotel's larder. The cook was quite put out when he saw me photographing them.

After a breakfast of bread and bananas in my room (the restaurant is too expensive), I walked the mile or so to the Zairean border. Hundreds of refugees are still crossing daily and now that the flow is down to this mere trickle their processing is brisk and efficient. As they step across the border they are carefully counted and each individual's age-group, sex and place of origin is noted by Rwandan UNHCR clerks. Then soldiers escort them a quarter of a mile down the road to a securely locked compound where trucks wait to take them back to their hilltops. They have remained in united commune groups, which greatly simplifies life for their minders.

Standing near the barrier-pole, I observed this morning's returnees loading their possessions onto crudely made but sturdy wooden hand-carts – to be pulled, for a small fee, to the compound gate. These are some of the people who, according to the international media, 'fled into the interior of Zaire as the Tutsi rebels [Kabila's troops] advanced, and endured severe hardships'. Many wore weary expressions but none seemed to have recently endured any form of physical deprivation. Quite the contrary: they looked much healthier and better dressed than the average peasant I met on the way from Gatuna to Byumba. One often wonders who is playing what variation on this refugee theme – and why?

Suddenly a trio of UNHCR officials (Rwandan, American, French) pounced on me, asserting that without written permission

from the burgomaster it is forbidden to photograph or communicate with any refugee. (At their own request, I had already taken
several photographs of children and mothers with babies.) Why
this curtailment of the returnees' freedom of speech? Is there a
good reason for it, related to media misreporting? But no: accred-
ited journalists with press cards are not similarly restricted. So is
this yet another manifestation of the UNHCR's tendency towards
authoritarianism? (I simply don't believe it has anything to do
with the burgomaster, and my new friend, the RPA major, agrees
with me.) Or do they have something to hide from foreign snoop-
ers, possibly representing a subversive group dedicated to rocking
the UN boat?

On the way back I paused by the UNHCR compound gate to
observe the activities within and was enchanted by a solitary girl
toddler (aged fifteen months or so) playing a game identical to one
of Rose's current favourite activities. On the flat surface of a low
volcanic rock (her equivalent to Rose's stool) she carefully placed
a leaf, then swept it off, replaced it with another, swept that off –
replaced it – and so on and on, with exactly Rose's expression of
self-satisfied concentration. Then the signal was given for a truck
to be loaded and the toddler yelled indignantly as an older (sev-
enish) sister dragged her away. She looked none the worse for
having been born in a refugee camp; life may be considerably
tougher back on the family's hilltop.

At lunchtime my communicative major reappeared and
remarked to the barman (I was meant to overhear) that he likes
this Irish *muzungu* – 'She reminds me of my mother, she is a
strong woman, she could frighten men.' Perhaps because of this
resemblance, and a few Primuses, he later confided that Goma is
now, in practice, controlled by the RPA. He may have been exag-
gerating but not many doubt that massive support is being given
to Kabila's force by Rwanda and Uganda.

This afternoon I had a swimming companion, a young Rwandan employed by a British NGO who worked for two years in
Mugunga camp. As we sat on the grass afterwards he gave me his
eyewitness's (and ear-witness's) impression of events in and
around the camp in mid-November. The refugees' sudden return
was not, in his view, caused simply by the overnight retreat of the

interahamwe and ex-FAR militia. It was a direct result of Kabila's troops, supported by the RPA, threatening to annihilate them if they didn't return AT ONCE! This version of events is not implausible. If left to themselves, would all those hundreds of thousands have immediately and simultaneously realized that now they were free to go home? And would they have got organized so rapidly? Heavy pressure from those who dreaded the re-establishment of the camps elsewhere, by the UNHCR, could explain the abruptness of that mass-return which astonished the whole world. Since August '94 the genocidal militia have been abusing their 'refugee' status to rearm heavily, with Mobutu's help, while recruiting from among the refugees for the stated purpose of returning to Rwanda to 'finish the work'.

At sunset, as I sat alone on the hotel terrace enjoying a spectacular flaming sky above the Zairean mountains, a woman drove up in her white UN vehicle. Shirley introduced herself as an HRFOR (Human Rights Field Operation in Rwanda) monitor based in another prefecture but visiting a friend here. Earlier, I had passed HRFOR's imposing lakeside mansion, set in an acre of garden. This is the first operation run by the UN High Commission for Human Rights – established, coincidentally, during the genocide. In Rwanda this agency is by now notorious for its squandering of scarce (very scarce, we are often told) resources. Also, it has neglected to take seriously its post-genocide obligations and has frequently and blatantly favoured opponents of the government, which in many cases means those implicated in the genocide. No wonder the high walls of Gisenyi's HRFOR compound are defended by a triple barrier of South African razor-wire.

Shirley, a cheerful brash young American, arrived in Rwanda three months ago, fresh from college, having never before been out of her home state. She admitted that to justify her existence she is reduced to sending regular reports to Geneva giving minute details of incidents of RPA soldiers being nasty to street children. I wasn't surprised. And one can't blame poor Shirley, who doesn't know whether she's coming or going. But who selected her for such a delicate and arduous job? This country urgently needs the help of experienced lawyers (who don't have to belong to a UN agency) to investigate, most meticulously, accusations of 'complicity' in the genocide and to co-operate with the government as it tries to establish a respect-worthy judicial system. Instead, the competent and dedicated members of HRFOR's team (a minority, but valuable) find themselves repeatedly frustrated by a leadership whose ineptitude is, even by UN standards, off the scale.

Today's rumour-mill output: The Zairean army's invasion of Kivu Province has been postponed to allow negotiations between Kabila and whoever is now in charge in Kinshasa. This is not credible. Said my major, 'Their silly invasion, 'twas never more than a bluff!'

THE SAME, 23 JANUARY

An exhilarating two-hour storm – the lightning frenzied – cheated me of my morning swim. At 7 the sky remained black all over, though the sun had risen, and the thunder was Wagnerian.

Poverty breeds, among other things, ingenuity. In Gisenyi it has bred the home-made wooden scooter, resembling a saddle-less, pedal-less, brake-less bicycle; even the wheels, some eighteen inches in circumference, are wooden. On a broad shelf between the wide handlebars and the back strut, enormous loads are carried: two (even three) huge sacks of maize, or sweet potatoes, or bananas, or jerry-cans of banana beer. Gisenyi, at lake-level, gets most of its food from hilltop communes, and every morning an awesome spectacle may be witnessed on the precipitous final mile of the descent. Down a smooth tarred road hurtle dozens of these machines, each steered by a boy or young man – sometimes two boys, the passenger embracing the one who steers. This is an insanely dangerous feat and the fatality rate, I'm told, is 'fairly high'. These machines achieve thirty m.p.h. – or more – and at the foot of the hill must be steered around a sharp bend before they reach level ground and have space to lose momentum. The loads are insecure and the machines wobble sickeningly. Many riders' expressions are fixed rigidly and some eyes are quite fearful, though the *muzungu* spectator can prompt an unconvincingly insouciant grin. This of course has long since become a macho thing; the bigger your load and the faster your speed the more kudos you acquire among your peers. Fifteen of those death-defying 'dray-scooters' passed me on my way up the hill after the storm.

I planned to leave the main road on the summit and return to the town centre via a hilltop commune. Near the summit two soldiers, standing at a path-junction, stopped me. The English-speaking captain, a pleasant young man, asked, 'Where to?' He disapproved of my plan; I must not walk alone off the main road, his comrade would escort me.

His comrade was a moronic-looking teenager whose frayed uniform was a few sizes too large and whose rifle had a very worn butt. Silently he followed me on a squelchy footpath through a mile or so of thirty-foot-high banana plants. We emerged near a hamlet of rectangular mud huts – many rusty roofs askew, most of the walls disintegrating, the windows unglazed, the inhabitants surly. Here a bullock had just been slaughtered beside a butcher's stall. A young man was carrying the head away – upside down on his own head with blood dripping onto the back of his shirt and the long curving horns framing his face, giving it a diabolical look. A small boy trotted after him, carrying a foreleg in one hand and the tail in another. I wanted to explore the hilltop and compare the choice of downward routes but my escort, suddenly vociferous, would not permit this. I know not why; he spoke only Kinyarwanda.

We took the main, ladder-steep path to the town – not yet visible, hidden by two lower intervening hills. From the edge of the hamlet I was baffled to see a line of about thirty men ascending with hoes over their shoulders, uniformly clad in apparently brand-new pale pink shorts and bush-shirts (without pockets). Only when I noticed their four guards, wearing scruffy civvies but carrying rifles, did I realize that these must be prisoners from Gisenyi's enormous jail. Most looked cheerful and reasonably well-fed – of course by their families. Then suddenly one powerfully built young man leaped off the path and vanished amidst the banana plants crowding the steep slope. His fellow-prisoners stopped, stood still, stared after him. Glimpses of pink could be seen for moments through the drab green of the foliage. Evidently the guards' rifles were not loaded because two flung their weapons towards the escapee. Then I came as near to death as ever I have. From close behind me my escort fired, shouting angrily. I felt his bullet passing my left cheek and stumbled sideways as the soldier led the guards in pursuit – all the guards, leaving the rest of the work-gang to their own devices. They were grinning from ear to ear, leaning on their hoes, peering into the bananas. The shot had brought a score of youths to the scene and now the atmosphere was all excited violence. Rather shaken, I hastened on my way, then realized that my left ear was aching and my head buzzing. I sat under a tree to recover.

The path was thronged with men, women and children hurrying down to the central market. Some male heads were loaded with skilfully woven circular baskets holding six or eight stalwart, brilliantly handsome cocks. On other heads were balanced boxes and pails, bundles and basins, sacks of fruits and vegetables, rolls of matting and the omnipresent jerry-cans of banana beer, corked with leaves. All those banana plants, covering vast areas of Rwanda, supply more drink than food. Every young woman had a baby on her back; there was no exception during my fifteen-minute rest, apart from those carrying toddlers and followed by an older child (usually female) carrying the baby. From the age of four every child was loaded – sometimes overloaded, seeming distressed.

Cursing myself for not having brought a stick, I cautiously continued down this slightly rain-skiddy path. At times it became a stairway, the steps rocks and tree-roots, and the gradient allowed me to look into the head-loads of those in front. All the locals nimbly overtook me, their bare feet confident even on smooth slippy stretches of packed red earth. No one greeted me but when occasionally I almost fell those nearby laughed mockingly.

This path joins the main street, which has an air of having given up on everything. Its most pleasing feature is a scarcity of motor traffic. Yet the numerous large, two-storied business premises and offices – closed or only half-occupied – recall what a bustling place Gisenyi once was. Now all the bustle is around the open-air market-cum-taxi terminus, where tethered goats bleat loudly when not devouring discarded cabbage leaves and defective tomatoes.

I am avidly curious about the enormous Islamic college, complete with minaret, being constructed halfway up the long main street, dwarfing all other buildings. 'It's Arab money,' said my major. 'We don't know any more.' Arab money also funded two fine new red-brick primary schools on the edge of the town; each has a discreet little star and crescent on the roof over the main entrance. The post-genocidal era doubtless favours Islamic expansionism. None of the killers, whatever their Christian denomination, felt bonded by a shared faith to their fellow-church-goers. Only the Muslims (1.2 per cent of the population) saw each other as Muslims first. Without any known exception, the Hutu Muslims hid and protected the Tutsi Muslims – which fact deeply impressed their Christian compatriots when it became public knowledge.

Still feeling slightly bullet-shocked, I sought a therapeutic litre of banana beer in a grotty little restaurant where people were eating mounds of matoke and beans, accompanied by bones with a little meat attached. Gisenyi is not *muzungu*-friendly, but my choosing banana beer, when commercial alternatives are available, does something to lower the barriers. Not that those are one-sided. How much does my perception of Gisenyi as a bastion of Hutu fanaticism – Habyarimana's commune is nearby – have to do with the locals' reaction to me? Were I an uninformed tourist, relaxed and outgoing, would the Gisenyi folk respond to me quite differently? That is possible; being informed – therefore prejudiced – has its disadvantages. But all that said, there is a darkness, a grimness, an unease in Gisenyi that must surely transcend the individual visitor's attitude.

I took a new route away from the centre and on one stretch of road was almost asphyxiated by the most dreadful stench I have ever encountered. I had to breathe through my mouth – feeling waves of nausea – over the next half-mile, which revealed the source of the stench. In Gisenyi's grossly overcrowded jail, the primitive sewage system broke down a year ago and has not been repaired. To my astonishment the high double-gate stood wide open without a sentry in sight and hundreds of prisoners were sitting in rows on the dusty ground in an enormous forecourt. Later, an elderly French journalist, who arrived at the Palm Beach last evening, explained laconically, 'Would-be escapees are shot dead. The cheapest security system.' I wondered then about the fate of the young man who leaped into the bananas.

Back by the lake, I saw that swimming is out for today. Last night's torrential rain flooded a nearby river and the inshore water is now extremely unsavoury – smelly as well as muddy and containing every sort of litter including turds.

Again I strolled to the border where a Rwandan UNHCR clerk was tactless enough to tell the snooper that 1489 returnees had crossed since morning. More were crossing as I watched, slowly walking home under that splendid avenue of acacia, now in full yellow bloom, which separates Rwanda and Zaire. These folk seemed poorer than yesterday's contingent, virtually their only possessions the clothes they wore and some poultry – two or three hens per family, tucked under people's arms. Given the uncertainties awaiting them, their cheerful demeanour astonishes. But that's Africa ...

This country is festering with rumours and to get hold of a fact is very hard work. Yesterday, government spokespersons in both Kigali and Kampala – backed up by Kabila – denied allegations that Rwandan and Ugandan soldiers have infiltrated eastern Zaire. But a Goma-based Belgian priest, with whom I dined this evening, last week saw with his own eyes ten Uganda-registered trucks, packed with soldiers, crossing into Zaire near Rutshiro, thirty-eight miles north of Goma. At least *that's* a fact.

Today Radio Rwanda quoted a Belgian foreign ministry statement: 'If reports of thousands of Rwandan troops in Kivu Province are confirmed, this would signify a violation of Zaire's territorial integrity and a totally unacceptable situation.' Paul Kagame, Rwanda's Defence Minister, promptly dismissed 'these stupid allegations' and added, 'Why not ask what the Belgian mercenaries are doing in Zaire? Brussels is trying hard to divert attention from those 280 mercenaries led by a Belgian citizen, Christian Taverniers, and backing Mobutu.'

Kuwait, too, has indignantly denied that it is 'helping Kabila's Tutsi rebels' – to me a brand-new rumour. And this evening the Zairean military command alleged that mercenaries from Eritrea, Ethiopia and Somalia are assisting Kabila, while 2000 heavily armed Ugandan troops are said to be camped around Bukavu.

To find out how things really are in Bukavu I must go there – or try to. My new plan is to compromise on trekking. In Rwanda at present one can't expect the hospitality offered in most African countries and to camp would be unwise, given the numbers of psychopaths still on the loose. Therefore I'll set out at dawn each morning, walk twenty miles or so, then hitchhike on to the next town with a hotel – Kibuye tomorrow, Cyangugu the next day. Already I've noticed how very tough are the soldiers manning the roadblocks near Gisenyi, and I can imagine their attitude to a lone *muzungu* trekker. So I'll deviously hitchhike to the turn-off for Kibuye, a few miles beyond the roadblocks.

GUESS WHERE? 24 JANUARY
Hitchhiking out of Gisenyi was easy. An aged Belgian nun, driving a minibus-load of handicapped children to Kigali, gladly picked me up and was disappointed to hear I didn't want to go all the way. She told me she belongs to the Sisters of the Assumption. On 26 April 1994 six Tutsi nuns from her convent were raped and murdered at nearby Birambo. In Gisenyi town fifteen nuns belonging to other orders were massacred. Within this prefecture scores of Tutsi priests were killed on the hilltops, usually by their own parishioners. A Belgian priest was also killed while trying to escape into Zaire with two Tutsi friends who died beside him at the border post. Yet the leaders of the Catholic Church in Rwanda refused to condemn the genocide and oppose its organizers – recalling the Vatican's attitude to another genocide.

Although the map shows a main road from Gisenyi to Cyangugu there is only a rough track, used by few vehicles. For the first few miles it climbs gradually and is lined with tin-roofed, mud-brick dwellings. The locals, while not exactly hostile, seemed deeply suspicious. Only small children smiled at me – which of course meant I was all the time being smiled at. This wide, sloping valley floor is so intensively cultivated – with much inter-cropping – that you couldn't grow an extra onion between the bananas, sweet potatoes, sorghum, cabbages, cassava, sugar cane, ground-nuts, coffee, beans. Beans are a staple food, for most peasants the main source of protein. While driving from Kigali we passed acres of a high-yielding variety, growing on awesomely steep slopes. When Matt told me his mission had funded extensive research to induce an indigenous variety to double-yield I couldn't applaud this agricultural philanthropy. Here, as elsewhere in the Poor World, 'experts' have done immense damage by disregarding peasant knowledge and experience and browbeating subsistence farmers into the use of new seeds and methods that frequently prove catastrophic. The promotion of this high-yielding bean is a classic case: it is also the bean most vulnerable to disease and fickle weather. Rwandan farmers wisely sow up to a dozen different varieties simultaneously, thus ensuring that even if misfortune strikes some will survive. And ensuring, too, a less monotonous diet, since each bean has a distinctive flavour.

When the road began to climb around the flanks of steep wooded hills I noticed myself relaxing; now all visible dwellings were left behind. I cannot – the fact must be faced – feel at ease among Rwandans. Up and up went the broad red track, coiling through the trees, many now in blossom, until Goma appeared very far below, away to the north, beyond the dark blue shimmering of Lake Kivu. The sky was cloudless, the sun hot, the breeze cool. I tried to forget the deeds done on these hills, to concentrate on the wondrous beauty all around me.

At intervals tracks led off the road, a few motorable in a four-wheel-drive, most narrow footpaths, all leading to hidden communes. Sometimes figures were visible in the distance, beyond a valley, busy in their fields. Here more men than is usual in Africa work beside their womenfolk; a consequence, I'm told, of returnees having quickly to restore abandoned, overgrown land. The minuteness of each plot makes the hillsides look like allotments. All land belongs to the state; only in towns can Rwandans buy plots as building sites. Some 60 per cent of families have the use of less than one hectare (two and a half acres), normally divided into five or more widely scattered plots – and half the cultivable land is on gradients of over one in ten. In Rwanda each square kilometre of farmed land must support more than 450 people, a figure that is rising rapidly. This circumstance surely helped the organizers of the genocide as they plotted to turn the Hutu peasants into mass-murderers. But to say so out loud is wildly – in some circles unforgivably – non-p.c.

Until about 1.30 I met no one, either awheel or afoot; then a Land-Rover overtook me and stopped. Inscriptions on both sides recorded that UNICEF had donated it to Rwanda's Department of Health. The young Kabale-born Tutsi in the front passenger seat – Augustin – is a child-welfare officer and was on his way to check up on vaccination programmes in three communes and deliver 'supplementary feeding for under-fives'.

'Let us help you,' Augustin urged, opening a back door. 'You are coming to a roadblock, you will have problems on foot. And here is not safe, there is fighting at night in the forest.'

I sat in and asked, 'Who's fighting whom?'

'Our RPA are fighting the militia,' Augustin stated flatly – his bluntness almost startling me, so quickly have I become accustomed to Rwandan evasiveness on such issues. He introduced me then to the driver, Marc, a tall, burly, unsmiling returnee from Bujumbura – middle-aged, a genuine '59er. Augustin himself is small, slight, quite fair-skinned with a high forehead and a neat little moustache. He went on, 'Too many militia came back from the camps very well armed and in good health with money saved. That's the main thing the UN's done for Rwanda. Now they've merged into the communes. Everyone knows who they are but even the people against them fear to identify them. They're getting themselves organized into small units to hunt Tutsi survivors and destabilize our government. And in this area it's easy to get recruits, so many hate the RPF. Why do you walk in such a dangerous place?'

When I had explained myself Augustin advised, 'Don't say to the roadblock you're a writer. They'd think that means writing reports to Geneva about RPA "infringements of human rights" and "arbitrary arrests" – they've had too many foreigners with notebooks.'

Soon we turned a corner and saw the roadblock – a piece of string (not rope) stretched between two thin sticks stuck in the soft earth. Four soldiers, their AK-47s ready for action, were sitting on the verge looking purposeful; they seemed like hardened campaigners. The captain wanted to see my passport, to know why I was in a government vehicle, by whom I am employed, where I meant to spend the night ...

'I'm taking a taxi from Kayove' – Augustin's first stop – 'to Kibuye,' I lied.

'There are no taxis from Kayove,' said the captain – then he suddenly seemed to lose interest in me and waved us on.

'You can't get to Kibuye today,' said Augustin. 'There's no traffic, you must come back to Gisenyi with us. Or stay with my friend Callixte – he's clinic supervisor – and go on to Kibuye in the morning if you still want to.'

When we turned onto the Kayove track it felt as though the Land-Rover were climbing a wall. At walking speed we juddered through a patch of dense forest, the trees meeting overhead. Then the engine noise brought a reception party of dozens of small children. They encircled the vehicle, laughing and clapping, before running ahead of it, leading us onto the flat, open hilltop with its stunning views of other hills and valleys. Marc parked beside the health centre's storeroom and shouted at two young mothers who had appeared around a distant corner, ordering them to unload boxes. Augustin told me to wait near the vehicle; soon he'd be back with Callixte.

Kayove's health centre is outwardly impressive – well built, well maintained red-brick buildings hidden by forest from the rest of the 'parish'. The fifty-bed maternity hospital is long and low. In the opposite clinic are a consulting room, a dispensary, a radiography room (not functioning), a staff room, two day-care wards (empty today), a padlocked storeroom – all leading off a deep verandah, its walls hung with big bright AIDS-education posters. Nearby is a row of well-kept latrines, essential to cater for the hundreds of mothers and infants who converge here from miles around on vaccination days. Originally, rural health-care facilities were mission-funded, then the government came to contribute about 50 per cent of the running costs. The structural restorations needed post-genocide (massacres occurred in and around many health centres) were funded from abroad. However, the standard of health care has been declining since Rwanda's peasants joined those other millions of Africans who are the voiceless victims of a World Bank/IMF Structural Adjustment Programme (SAP).

I took an instant liking to Callixte, a handsome, sad-looking young Goma-born Tutsi who is successfully studying English by courtesy of the BBC World Service. He lives with his Bujumbura-born wife, Emerithe, and their eight-month-old daughter, Florence

Gratias, in a tiny brick bungalow at the forested edge of the compound. Emerithe, a nurse, also serves as Kayove's resident doctor.
In 1991 Rwanda had one doctor per 27,000 (or so) inhabitants –
when Britain had one per 659. In '97 Rwanda has even fewer doctors; many were killed, many others participated in the genocide
and are now prospering as exiles.

When Augustin and Marc had driven off to another commune,
Callixte showed me around. In the maternity hospital only twelve
beds were occupied. 'Ten years ago,' said Callixte, 'no empty
beds!' We glanced into the kitchen annex where two women were
cooking beans, rice and matoke (provided by the patients) on an
improvised wood-stove. 'Here was a fine gas-cooker', Callixte
gloomily recalled, 'until the looting that April.' Numerous offspring of the (untrained) nursing staff were wandering between
the buildings. 'Lucky they are,' commented Callixte, 'what
patients can't eat they get.' The toddlers seemed afraid of me;
their older siblings begged for sweets.

In the consulting room Emerithe was applying her stethoscope
to the chest of a terrified old woman lying wheezing on a three-
legged couch, propped up by bricks. When Callixte had conferred
with his wife (she speaks no English), he invited me – begged me
– to stay the night. 'Please be with us! Very early tomorrow the
Gisenyi–Kibuye bus is on the big road. For you I can stop it.'

Elated, I agreed to this plan; we could argue about bus transport versus trekking when the time came. Callixte carried my
rucksack to his little home and left me in the living-room while he
went to get the burgomaster's permission for a *muzungu* to stay
overnight in the commune. This was a cramped, dreary room, the
furniture sparse: a plastic-topped table, three metal camp-chairs, a
huge old horsehair armchair with hernias – and on the floor in
one corner a new expensive trannie-cum-cassette-player, the better
to hear the World Service. Three bullet-holes disfigured the ceiling. The arrival of Florence Gratias, in the arms of a teenage aunt,
brought on another bout of grandmaternal nostalgia.

When Callixte reappeared – walking slowly up the path, crest-
fallen – I foresaw a re-run of my Pierre experience near Gatuna.
And so it was. The burgomaster had refused permission, 'for security reasons'. I must return to Gisenyi with Augustin. It is said the

Hutu militia are targeting expats in this area – and their residences, offices and vehicles – to undermine 'the new Rwanda'. Last night in Kibuye a Dutch priest was attacked in his home and badly wounded; he is not expected to recover. A youth was at once despatched to the main track to stop the Land-Rover and ask Augustin to pick me up.

While we waited, Callixte admitted to being afraid of living in Kayove. 'They tell us, all must pretend not to be afraid and try to live well together – all Banyarwanda! But fear is there.' He laid a hand over his heart. 'In this commune more than a thousand were killed – the graves are near, I can show you if was time.' I asked why he and Emerithe had accepted jobs in this notoriously anti-Tutsi prefecture. He sighed and said, 'In Rwanda we could get no other jobs. And in Burundi and Zaire is violence even worse, now.' Then he began visibly to tremble. Dismayed, I reached across the table and held his hands, tightly. Last week, he told me, between thirty and thirty-five Tutsi 'survivors' were killed together in a commune near Kibuye town. (Precise figures are always elusive.) I understood then my own disquiet. This morning, trekking through all that beauty, trying to forget the deeds done on those hills, I accused myself of being morbidly obsessed by the genocide, failing to locate it in the past, allowing it to overshadow all my reactions to Rwanda. But it isn't in the past. The evil continues here and now, no longer a major drama, yet in its disruptive intensity no less because those massacred at one time, in one place, number thirty-five rather than 3500.

When the Land-Rover arrived Callixte invited everyone to drink tea, but Augustin was edgy. 'We need to get home before dark,' he insisted.

Not far from Kayove purple-black clouds suddenly gathered, then sank to envelop us in a thick mist. Marc slowed and Augustin exclaimed, 'I hate this!'

'But with a sensible driver it's safe,' said I soothingly.

'It's now the militia get going,' muttered Augustin. 'They're at home here, they know the terrain, the RPA are outsiders.' When we came to the roadblock it was unmanned. Instead of driving through the string, Marc got out and tenderly lowered it, then returned to replace it – a demonstration of loyalty to the state which Augustin seemed to regard as superfluous.

Ten minutes later we heard rifle-fire not very far away. Augustin and Marc argued in Kinyarwanda. I told myself it was all happening off the road, down in the forest on our right. Marc won the argument and speeded up in defiance of the mist. Augustin said to me, 'I told you they use the weather. We'd be safer now not moving. They can hear a vehicle and go for it.'

I decided that trekking back to Kigali from hilltop to hilltop – my fantasy en route to Gisenyi – was really rather a bad idea.

'A few days ago,' said Augustin, 'three Tutsi were murdered in Gisenyi town, one an off-duty RPA officer.' (The major had already told me this.) 'The bandits who killed them came out of the forest here.'

'How d'you know?' I asked.

'People see more than they shout about,' replied Augustin.

Back in Gisenyi, just before sunset, I called on the residence of an Irish NGO; Declan and Malachi were due to return today from a consultation at their Kigali head office. I found them packing up, having been ordered to leave Gisenyi immediately and not to sleep tonight in their residence but in the Meridien hotel – provided with armed guards specifically to protect expats. Rather peevishly I demanded, 'Why all this panic? What goes on?'

They explained it all started with the Spaniards ... On 18 January, the day before I crossed the border, three Spanish medical workers – two men and a woman – were shot dead in their Ruhengeri residence by persons unknown; a badly injured American colleague has since lost a leg to gangrene. At that point a penny dropped. The Gatuna immigration officer who so agitatedly waffled on about heavy rain and dangerous traffic had had something else in mind. Remembering the disdain with which the young Tutsi officer viewed me, I reckon she regarded expats as expendable.

It seems odd that I've been six days here, talking to many Rwandans and a few expats, yet have heard about these murders only now. I'm beginning to realize that the Rwandans are an exceptionally reticent people. And perhaps the expats assumed I already knew. Obviously Matt hadn't been told or he would have mentioned the attack while discussing Ruhengeri's particular problems after our stop in the town to buy a load of matoke.

The French journalist, François, was not surprised to see me back on the Palm Beach terrace. 'When they told me where you were heading for, I didn't think you'd get far.'

7

BAD TIMING

Last evening I discovered that François is quite a kindred spirit. He has been familiar with this region all his life – as a child he lived in Bukavu – and his present quest is for 'facts' about the killing of those thirty-odd Tutsi near Kibuye. 'Poor devils! "Survivors" no longer ... The militia see the genocide as unfinished business. That's the inevitable result of no one challenging the culture of impunity.' François is also investigating the motive(s) for the recent beating-up near Ruhengeri of a team of expat HRFOR monitors. And he is working on a series of articles about an aspect of the genocide that he believes should not be allowed to fade into obscurity – French government support for the organizers. That topic – one of the bees in my own bonnet – monopolized our conversation.

François was a twenty-year-old, working in Kinshasa, when the elected Patrice Lumumba was assassinated and replaced by the unelected Mobutu in 1960. 'A reliable chap,' said François of Mobutu, 'happy to co-operate with the West in destabilizing his neighbours, especially Angola.' However, in 1991 several of Mobutu's Cold War allies, including France, suddenly saw a need for 'democracy' in Zaire and ditched the dictator. France then concentrated on backing Habyarimana & Co. in the FAR versus RPA war. Quai d'Orsay denizens frequently expressed their concern for 'the principles of territorial integrity and national sovereignty in the Great Lakes region'. Yet in 1992 and February 1993 700 soldiers of France's élite Rapid Reaction Force intervened decisively to check RPA advances – advances which, if not impeded, would have stymied the genocide. And in 1993 alone FAR received US$10 million worth of French military aid. (For a minuscule country mainly populated by peasants living in dire poverty!) This 'aid' included training the 'Zero Network' death-squad led by – among others – Mme Habyarimana's three brothers. Zero Network's existence was exposed in October '92 by two Belgians – Professor Filip Reyntjens and Senator Willy Kuypers – who recognized it as a harbinger of genocide and said so at the time.

When the killing started in Kigali the French Embassy's Tutsi staff were locked out, left to their fate – certain death. However, the infamous Mme Habyarimana, her children, her equally infamous brother Seraphin Rwabukumba and some forty leaders of the MRND were rescued and cherished by the French government, which simultaneously refused political asylum to the five small children of Prime Minister Agathe Uwilingiyimana, one of the earliest victims of the genocide.

In Paris on 27 April 1994, while the killing was at its most frenzied, President Mitterrand, Prime Minister Edouard Balladur and Foreign Minister Alain Juppé officially received two of its organizers, the 'Foreign Minister' of the interim government, Jerome Bicamumpaka, and the fanatical Coalition for the Defence of the Republic leader Jean-Bosco Barayagwiza. Meanwhile France was still delivering arms to the FAR and continued to do so until June. Also, its Zairean stance was shifting again. On 9 May 1994 Mitterrand's special counsellor for African affairs, Bruno Delaye, told Gérard Prunier (temporary adviser to the Ministry of Defence), 'We want Mobutu back in, he cannot be dispensed with and we are going to do it through this Rwanda business.'

By mid-June most of the killing was over. And France's 'humanitarian intervention' – Operation Turquoise – began. This was prompted by rivalries within the then hybrid French government and by Francophone alarm when President Mandela tried to persuade Africa's Anglophone nations to take action. Re-enter our old friend, General Dallaire. As UNAMIR's commanding officer he was aware of and enraged by France's covert arms deliveries to FAR and suspicious of the motives behind Operation Turquoise. By then the poor man must have been beyond the end of his tether.

Said he, 'If they land in Kigali to deliver their damn weapons to the government I'll have their planes shot down.' In the end, Operation Turquoise did save a certain number of Tutsi lives – though not the 'tens of thousands' claimed by Mitterrand. It also gave protection to many thousands of FAR and *interahamwe* militia, enabling them to make their well-armed way, in safety, to the refugee camps. And for a time it considerably muddied the political waters, as it was intended to do.

'We [France] didn't cause the genocide,' said François, 'but probably without our interference it couldn't have happened. The constant backing of a Great Power encouraged the organizers.' Not a cheering thought for a Frenchman.

Malachi and Declan arrived then, on their way to the Meridien, looking exhausted after hours of packing up their home and office. They advised me to return to Kigali, stay with friendly expats in their secure compounds and see how the situation develops. This prospect pleases me not. Especially as all this post-Spanish-murders panic seems a bit excessive, an overreaction. However, at present there's little alternative so tonight I am staying in John Walton's bungalow with two of his colleagues, Gavin and Sandra. Luckily my present frustration had been half-expected, even as I planned – or wisely didn't plan – this mini-journey. Now I must settle for what's on offer, a view of NGOs in action on the hilltops. By the time my Rwandan visa expires on 18 February it may be possible to enter Kivu Province.

This morning, much to my annoyance, I found myself infected by the above-mentioned panic. When offered a lift to Kigali in an Italian NGO vehicle, driven by a charming young water engineer from Milan, I felt I'd be safer in a taxi packed with Rwandans. On the back seat of the minibus I was squeezed between a middle-aged man very obviously dying of AIDS and a youngish leper who had lost all ten fingers and half his nose before being diagnosed and treated. At five of the six baggage-check roadblocks en route (three more than when Matt and I drove down) the soldiers callously insisted on the AIDS patient being dragged out to queue with the rest of us, though he was travelling alone and unable to stand without support. His family were awaiting him in Kigali with one of those woven hammock-like rural stretchers. Two young women – probably daughters – burst into tears when they saw him.

During the journey, I pondered the standard NGO reaction to perceived 'danger'. Declan and Malachi were not scared, did not want to retreat from Gisenyi leaving their Rwandan colleagues as the only targets for whomever might have a grudge against foreign NGOs. But dead aid workers raise no funds back home – quite the contrary. They are not seen as martyrs in a good cause but victims of the inefficiency or poor judgment of their directors. Which in fact makes sense; most Rich World interventions hardly merit the description 'good causes'. Rwanda's present chaos is not simply 'an African problem' which kindly expat humanitarians are trying to alleviate. As France's contribution to the genocide illustrates, it is part of an immensely complex inter-continental problem.

THE SAME, 26 JANUARY

Despite its population (roughly 450,000), Kigali has the merit of seeming not like a city – more like a series of large villages spread higgledy-piggledy on several hillsides overlooking broad valleys. Mount Kigali (almost 6000 feet) is obvious but not dominant; other surrounding hills are only slightly lower. There was nothing here in 1907 when the Germans decided to install a civil administrator and develop a trading centre to improve their commercial prospects in Central Africa. (They had been allotted Rwanda/Burundi as part of their East African territories at the Berlin Conference in 1885.) Because the valleys were then malarial swamps, the Banyarwanda had avoided permanent settlement nearby, though Tutsi herds grazed the slopes. Later, under the Belgians, the small industrial district of Kimihurura burgeoned on the main reclaimed swamp. Today, however, fewer than 300,000 Rwandans are involved in the national economy's monetary – as distinct from subsistence – sector. Which perhaps explains why the busy commercial centre still has the aura of a provincial town rather than a capital city.

Wide, well maintained motorways connect Kigali's rich districts. The traffic is heavy, smelly and reckless; crashes are numerous and often fatal. The plethora of expat vehicles, each with its conspicuous logo, is mind-boggling – and alarming. International aid missions based here provide much of the urban wealth; very little aid money trickles away towards the rural areas where live 93 per cent of Rwandans. Today I noticed several vehicles newly stripped of their logos and inscriptions, preferring to seem *not* expat property. Also, some of the identifying notices at the entrances to NGO offices and residences have been taken down.

Kigali's middle-class communes are connected by steep, rutted, dusty tracks and not much troubled by motor traffic. Substantial bungalows (some colonial, some built by Rwandans since Independence) stand in ample, tree-shaded gardens, usually surrounded by high walls; their sturdy gates are opened only when the carefully polished family car departs or arrives. Every family who can afford it now employs an askari.

In the poor communes, precipitous narrow footpaths squeeze between two- or three-roomed shacks housing families of eight, ten, twelve or more. Tiny shops and wayside hawkers cater for local needs. The banana-beer shebeens do not advertise themselves but are detectable by anyone seriously interested in banana beer – one tenth the price of commercial brews, equally alcoholic and reputedly much better for the health. (Though the last opinion is disputed by expats who have watched it being made on the hilltops.)

On semi-rural slopes (Kigali's equivalent to leafy suburbs) stand a few large burnt-out dwellings, formerly the homes of rich Tutsi and already half-smothered by resurgent bush. Otherwise, apart from bullet holes on some exterior walls and many shell-damaged roofs, little visible evidence remains of the events of April–July 1994. Rwanda's physical rehabilitation has been surprisingly rapid – or perhaps not surprisingly, given the millions of aid dollars provided post-genocide. The country – and the capital in particular – was then completely devastated, with a severely traumatized population, no police force, no civil administration, no functioning economy, no educational or judicial system, no electricity or water supply, no medical care, no public transport.

In August '94 UNAMIR II arrived and was, naturally, made to feel unwelcome after the failure of UNAMIR I. In March '96 it was thrown out – or, as the diplomats put it, 'UNAMIR II retired at the request of the Rwandan government'. However, it had by then achieved much more than its predecessor. The Secretary-General's Special Representative, Shaaryar Khan (successor to the futile Booh-Booh), drew up an inventory of UNAMIR II's good deeds, over and above its official mandate:

It rebuilt 14 bridges, repaired 13 roads, made Kigali airport operational again, provided all necessary equipment to restore the telephone system, treated 1600 patients a day at its medical unit, vaccinated 62,000 people and supplied medicines and trained hospital staff all over the country. It also transported a million refugees and displaced persons; distributed food, seeds, tools and cattle; lessened prison overcrowding by building extensions for 20,000 inmates and relocating 10,000; cleared over 1400 mines and disposed of more than 1500 pieces of unexploded ordnances.

It is nice to be able occasionally to say – 'Three cheers for the UN!'

This morning I called to the local headquarters of a large and globally powerful NGO. My letter of introduction was from their head office, where a fund-raising officer had urged me to 'write something' about their Rwandan projects – a suggestion I feel ambivalent about, though it would be interesting to observe said projects. Weaving my way between nine of their four-wheel-drive vehicles parked in the forecourt, I entered a colonial-era mansion and found all the expat staff absent – 'unavailable for now', away at some NGO indaba hastily convened by the UN to debate the security situation. I left my letter and a contact number with a languid young Rwandan woman, sitting alone amidst a herd of computers in a large, comfortably furnished office.

Security problems aside, some NGOs are at present in deep trouble with the government, having failed to obtain work-permits for their expat staff-members as they agreed to do last year. So Isa informed me over supper in her bullet-pocked bungalow in Kicukiro – not far from the airport, where there was much fighting during the battle for Kigali. This was one of Isa's reasons for resigning from a British NGO and taking a translating job in a European embassy. She commented, 'Too many NGOs treat our government with no respect, behave like they were God Almighty. Like we should be so grateful to have them here they can pick and choose which laws to keep.'

Soon after the RPA victory, more than 200 aid agencies arrived in Rwanda – then a fund-raising winner. The majority, Isa complained, were unfamiliar with the country (often unfamiliar with Africa) and either ignorant of or misled about the background to the genocide. 'Mostly they zoomed in on the displaced-persons' camps – nearly all Hutu. They spent hardly any time or money on the survivors or the returnees – nearly all Tutsi. That made the RPF mad angry. And they gave no end of trouble to our new government departments. The people taking over were in a muddle anyway – no offices or equipment or money. And trying to learn as they went about how to run a country. Then they had to turn round and try and organize and dovetail all those NGO projects, a lot of them only half thought-out. Here we'll never have a good feeling between our officials and the agencies. We can't forget how fast most expats got themselves safely out when the killing started – no attempt to help friends and colleagues, people they'd worked with sometimes for years.'

Isa's husband, a prominent Hutu moderate, was murdered in Kigali in mid-April '94. She and her four children, aged ten to eighteen, had already fled to Butare where the genocide was delayed for a fortnight by a courageous *préfet* who refused to obey MRND orders. They were sheltered by an equally courageous elderly Hutu couple whose three sons were FAR officers, among those directing the genocide. Isa believes she and her children survived because a blind eye was turned on the septuagenarian parents' 'disloyalty'. However, when killer-teams were sent to Butare from Kibuye and Ruhengeri, the fugitives had to be concealed behind a false partition built overnight in the kitchen and ingeniously food-stained to disguise its newness.

Last year Isa adopted Albert, now aged three, the only surviving child of a Tutsi friend whose husband and five other children were slaughtered. Albert's mother committed suicide on the first anniversary of their deaths. 'She thought she was doing fine, then suddenly she couldn't handle the memories.' Such suicides, especially among women, are not uncommon – though they are not always acknowledged as suicides. Mercifully Albert was (or so it seems) too young to be affected by his mother's death. He is a most engaging child, composed and polite and affectionate;

throughout the evening he insisted on feeding me fistfuls of Bombay Mix.

According to Isa's sister – visiting from Gisenyi, where I first met her – 'little combats' are a regular occurrence now in the hills between Gisenyi and Cyangugu. ('Little' combats, during which two or three hundred are killed? But I suppose if you've experienced genocide that *is* 'little'.) Said Isa, 'Your timing is bad. You should've come before all this returnee militia hassle started. Then you could have walked safely through any prefecture.' I dare say she's right; when Rachel and Andrew lived here in '95 there were no such 'security problems' – at least not for *muzungus*.

27 JANUARY

At my present base, an NGO residence, I have a fellow guest. Nganga, a thirty-year-old Kenyan (Kikuyu), is simultaneously doing his Ph.D. – subsidized by a British university – on childhood trauma and setting up remedial units to help street children in Tanzania, Kenya and Rwanda. This 'interfacing' between the academic and humanitarian worlds bothers me. Nganga graduated in Britain with a first-class degree in psychology and is immensely congenial, a special person – compassionate, sensitive, thoughtful. But his conversational English has become painfully jargon-deformed, and one can see him sliding into the abyss of well-paid research, which will do little if anything to help those being 'researched'. A fortune is being spent on flying him from Nairobi to London to Dar to Kigali – and back again ... In other words, he has been absorbed into the fast-expanding 'humanitarian industry' without realizing quite what's happening to his career.

When I spoke of my feeling that the children murdered in '94 were luckier than the traumatized survivors, Nganga didn't disagree. In twenty years' time how many Rwandans will remain disabled, emotionally and/or physically, by their childhood experiences? Numerous details of what children witnessed, endured, were forced to do and voluntarily did are given in the African Rights report *Rwanda: Death, Despair and Defiance*. This book is so harrowing that when Andrew tried to read it, while living in Kigali, he failed – gave up halfway. Later, I struggled through to the end, with great difficulty. Rachel, watching me struggle, wondered

– 'What's the point?' But I believe there is a point. Deeply disturbing as are the minute details of the genocide, we do need to confront them, to remember them and – spurred on by our remembering – to put pressure on the 'international community' to fund
the Rwandan government's effort to punish, proportionately, the
organizers and perpetrators. When the media reported some of
those details people were shocked and revolted. But in the public
consciousness such reports soon merge into the morass of other
gruesome disasters that regularly snatch at fragments of our attention. The outside world's reluctance to focus on the details and
consequences of Rwanda's genocide is one of the reasons why
most of the chief organizers have escaped punishment while
100,000 or so Hutu (including children) rot in jail because they
have done the actual killing – often under duress – or are suspected of having done it.

Nothing more clearly defines the particularity of genocide than
the deliberate seeking out and killing of children – especially male
children – not only *en famille* but in hospitals, schools, orphanages, homes for the handicapped. Millions of children, world-
wide, are bereaved and traumatized by wars and natural disasters.
After an earthquake or a bomb attack they may find themselves
lying beside or under their parents' corpses – I shall never forget
the stricken small children I met in Cameroon, survivors of the
Lake Nyos gas explosion. In such circumstances, however, they
are incidental victims. In Rwanda, once the killing started, all
Tutsi children of an age to understand language knew they were
targets. And countless Hutu children witnessed their own fathers
– sometimes their mothers, too, and their older siblings – killing
their friends and playmates. Such experiences, as Nganga noted,
do not merely leave scars. A scar marks the place where a wound
has healed. In many cases the wounds inflicted on Rwanda's child
survivors are unlikely ever to heal.

Is the West's indifference to this genocide partly racist? Images
of children seeing and hearing their parents being hacked to
death, of spears being thrust through babies on their mothers'
backs, of babies being flung into rivers by their mothers to save
them from the other sort of death, of toddlers being beheaded or
disembowelled, of seven-year-olds having their arms chopped off,

of eleven-year-olds smashing five-year-olds' skulls – such images are of course dreadful, but perhaps insufficiently shocking because this is what Europeans have been conditioned, over generations, to expect of Africans. Yet we know there is nothing specifically 'African' or primitive about genocide; the country that produced Dürer, Beethoven and Goethe also produced the gas-ovens that eliminated six million Jews and other 'undesirables'. Nganga dryly remarked that very likely the impersonal high-tech Nazi method strikes some Westerners as less barbaric than the chopping up of one individual by another with a machete. Although the end result is the same, the European way might somehow seem tidier, more discreet ... He could have a point there. Many journalists became oddly obsessed by the killers' using agricultural implements – and, later, by the refugees' bare feet. They seemed not to realize that both phenomena are simply a measure of where this country is at, economically. Most Rwandan peasants habitually go barefooted, and if they want to kill a goat, or a bullock – or a person – they use bare steel, just as our own ancestors did before the invention of gunpowder.

Thinking on from there, is it fair to see a difference in degrees of culpability between the credulous, illiterate Hutu peasants – cunningly brainwashed and by tradition submissive to authority – and the thousands of educated Germans (and others) who collaborated to make possible the Holocaust? Not to mention all those Germans who for years knew what was going on but pretended not to notice. Or am I now, as Nganga hinted, being racist in a convoluted way, tending to blame Africans less because I expect Europeans to be more capable of defying a criminal régime?

We asked ourselves then, can there be such a thing as an understanding of genocide? Does anyone understand the Holocaust? Knowing why and how it happened doesn't really enable 'normal' human beings to comprehend the level of depravity involved. Or perhaps, as Nganga suggested, we don't want to understand, are afraid to understand – because genocide exposes what we prefer not to know about ourselves as human beings. It's reassuring to imagine a clear line separating 'normal' people from genocidal Turks, Germans, Rwandans. But given the combined pressures applied by the organizers of Rwanda's genocide, how would each of us react? Can we be certain we would continue to behave like 'normal' human beings?

Early this morning I had a disconcerting experience, provoked by my own stupidity. While walking on a footpath beside a dual-car-riageway – its lanes separated by shrubs – I noticed that there was, unusually, no other pedestrian in sight. Here was my chance to photograph an isolated mini-skyscraper, spectacularly damaged during the battle for Kigali and poised on a cliff-edge. As I aimed my camera a red car, speeding towards me along the far lane, slowed abruptly. The driver glared at me and yelled, angrily shaking his fist. Hastily I lowered the camera – photograph untaken – and walked on, vaguely wondering why so many Rwandans are paranoid about photography. My thoughts were on something quite different when the same car stopped beside me, the driver having turned at the nearest gap in the hedge, half a mile away, to pursue the offending expat. He emerged, his face ugly with rage – otherwise an unremarkable forty-ish man wearing a neat suit. Saying nothing, he struck me violently on the side of the head with the flat of his hand: so violently that my neck is stiff and sore this evening. By then there were several pedestrians nearby but none reacted in any way to this surely uncommon incident. As my attacker drove on to the next turning point I rubbed my head gently and called myself a fool. Elsewhere, I would now be attempting to analyse that encounter. In Rwanda, I accept it as one more conundrum.

That was a bad start to the day but later on Fate compensated me. By now I have a favourite writing-corner in a secluded and inexpensive Ethiopian restaurant far enough off a motor road to be comparatively fume-free. In its open-air bar, decorated with Ethiopian Airline posters of Gondar and Lalibela, the aroma of ersatz injara and wat drifts from the kitchen and bougainvillaea tumbles over a ten-foot-high wall. Here the more adaptable and price-conscious expats consort after work with their Rwandan friends. And here Pius approached me this afternoon, as I closed my notebook and took off my specs. He already knew about my thwarted journey; a few days ago his friend the restaurant-owner listened sympathetically to my tale of woe.

Pius was born three years after his parents fled to Uganda in '59. In January '95 he 'returned', a fluent English-speaker with not a word of French. 'Naturally I wanted to live in my own country but at first it felt like some foreign place.'

'And now ...?' I asked.

Pius was silent for a few moments, eyes downcast, frowning slightly and, it seemed, making some decision. As our Primuses arrived he said, 'Now, it's different. I know I'm needed. In Kampala I worked eight years for a paper, writing in English. But here I can write in Kinyarwanda and there is a big task for me, doing anti-propaganda. Why did we have a genocide? What made it possible? It's not normal. And it can't happen suddenly. Rwandans must try to understand it, nothing can be healed without understanding. The killers, the survivors, the witnesses – everyone needs to know why it became possible. People should be thinking and talking about this, looking for the true explanations. Not just struggling on, trying to live as if it hadn't happened. When I came first many wanted to talk and talk about what they saw and suffered – to describe the most terrible events – it was their therapy. That was good. Now they have gone silent – and not because they're healing. I know it's now nearly three years ago, they have had time to cry. And I hope all did. Maybe those who didn't killed instead. But I shouldn't say such things – it's too easy for returnees to talk. We weren't involved, we didn't personally suffer except the way every Rwandan suffers still from the evil of it.'

I said, 'Maybe the survivors have only enough energy left to struggle on, none to spare for asking "Why?" Anyway they must think they know the answer. And the killers and their accomplices have their own set of answers.'

'But they're all wrong!' said Pius. 'They know nothing about the tangles in the background, for so many years the truth was hidden from people here. Without studying at Makerere, talking to scholars, how could I know about our past? Before the colonists we were isolated, accepting it was OK for 15 per cent to rule the rest. Then the Europeans came to abuse that set-up for gain, putting Tutsi and Hutu into a confrontational position. So when the Hutu got independence and power they persecuted us and went totalitarian. Then they felt their power threatened by

the international community and went berserk and we had genocide. Easy to organize with most Hutu still ignorant and fright-
ened and full of memories of Tutsi cruelty. Many of the peasant
killers were victims, too. In a way, even the organizers were victims. You can trace the blame back to the Belgians and the Tutsi
chiefs corrupted by them.' Pius paused, 'Are you bored?' he asked,
suddenly anxious. 'Maybe you know about all this?'

'I'm riveted,' I reassured him. 'Doubly riveted because it's coming from a Tutsi. Let's have another Primus.'

Pius beckoned a waitress and continued – 'I've heard a few foreigners saying it's all wrong to associate the war – the RPA invasion – with the genocide. They want to keep those two events separate. I see why, politically it makes sense. It's emotionally they're
wrong, not knowing what makes our peasants tick. It's too soon
to judge about the political bit, nothing has shaken down yet, we
can't see how sincere the RPF are about power-sharing. So far I
believe in them, I think most are good guys. Only you have to be
suspicious about the effects of power on personalities. But without the "invasion from Uganda" I'm certain genocide could never
have been organized, there wouldn't have been enough fear
around. More pogroms like before – yes, surely, but that's different. And all those Hutu refugees, they were terrorized by propaganda about Tutsi soldiers taking revenge on them. Which of
course some are doing now though we don't hear much about it.
The RPA couldn't keep up to Kagame's Ugandan standards when
they had to recruit from Tutsi survivors and returnees from
Burundi and Zaire. Maybe you get irritated by clichés but they're
true. Violence breeds violence. Past Tutsi violence bred the genocide.' Pius stopped and studied my face, then chuckled. 'You're
shocked! You're thinking I'm trying to excuse the genocide – me,
a Tutsi! You're off your nest, I can see!'

I admitted to being off my nest; actually I haven't been on it
since crossing the border. But I denied thinking that Pius was
'making excuses'. Looking for explanations is another sort of
activity. I added that what most deeply shocks me, in Rwanda
now, is the 'culture of impunity' – a tiresome sociologist's buzz-
phrase yet useful in this context.

'That ties in', said Pius, 'with what I'm on about. It's true many who set up the genocide and many killers seem carefree. No remorse, no fear of punishment, seeing Rwanda's history justifying what they did. I mean the propaganda version of history they were fed on. Unless we can get to answer that "Why?", countering the propaganda, how can we have reconciliation? The RPF sound like hypocrites when they preach "we must all be Banyarwanda together". False history and then the genocide have fixed everyone in a distorted mould. That's why I say outsiders are needed. Only people who escaped that mould can break it for others and help them start again, facing facts.'

I was moved by Pius's face-the-facts mission and said so. But privately I remained unconvinced that it could achieve much, even were he working with teams of kindred spirits. Not that I doubt his commitment to his ideal or his intellectual ability and honesty, an honesty too rare on this scene. He concluded that the genocide has muzzled plain speaking, indeed has made it dangerous. Given three-quarters of a million dead Tutsi, references to past Tutsi cruelty, to their repression of and contempt for the Hutu majority, are certain to be seen as making excuses rather than looking for explanations. 'But', said Pius, 'nothing venture, nothing win!' And on that we clinked glasses.

Walking back to my NGO base, I wondered how the different categories – survivors, killers, accomplices, passive witnesses – are in fact coping, inwardly, with the aftermath of genocide. A many-layered question, when asked by a European.

One hears it argued that Africans possess a capacity we lack to transcend such horrors – are able to get on with life *now*, forgetting what happened *then*. This may be partially true, in relation to some disasters, tragedies, bereavements. But I cannot believe it applies to present-day Rwanda. This is an eerily subdued country. People don't communicate normally. Most Africans are ebullient, uninhibited in their social exchanges, openly affectionate or antagonistic or argumentative – it all hangs out. Not so here. In taxis, bars, marketplaces, restaurants, in queues at the bank or super-market, conversations – whether personal or commercial – seem curiously controlled, taut. Because Rwanda is such a tiny country, with quite a good public transport (minibus-taxi) system, people cannot be sure of finding anonymity in another place, leaving behind their genocidal roles. There is a widespread awareness of who did what, and to whom what was done. The genocide organizers were cunning. By forcing so many to kill, by spreading the guilt throughout the population, they forged a bloody link of loyalty between the Hutu. Thus were countless thousands deprived of the possibility of claiming, afterwards, that they had been anti-genocide – though left to themselves they might never have raised a hand against a Tutsi neighbour.

The submissiveness of Rwanda's peasants goes back a long way. Jean-Jacques Maquet, the French anthropologist, noted the absolute power of the traditional Tutsi kings:

Inferiority is the relative situation of a person who has to submit to another in a defined field. But dependence is inferiority extended to all spheres of life. When the ruler gives an order, he must be obeyed, not because his order falls into the sphere over which he has authority, but simply because he is the ruler.

In 1974 Major-General Juvenal Habyarimana imitated the kings by founding the MRND – the Mouvement Révolutionnaire National pour le Developpement. No other political party was permitted and membership was compulsory for every Rwandan. No one could change their place of residence without good reason; all ID cards had to show their owner's address. Within every MRND cell keen spies (keen for promotion) observed activities on each hill. In Gérard Prunier's words, 'Administrative control was probably the tightest in the world among non-Communist countries.' The want of remorse that at present so worries outsiders is surely connected to this 'culture of control'. Countless peasant killers were psychologically incapable of *not* obeying commands.

29 JANUARY

This evening Nyanya is euphoric. A fax arrived from Andrew. On 29 September (or thereabouts) Rose will acquire a sibling. I became so over-excited I invited two friends to celebrate with me in Kigali's up-market Chinese restaurant and spent more in a few hours than I would normally spend in a month.

2 FEBRUARY

Today Sandra and Gavin invited me to accompany them to a Sunday luncheon party in Ruhengeri prefecture, at a tea estate run by old friends of theirs from Sri Lanka. Twenty miles short of Ruhengeri town we turned off the main road and passed through a straggling trading centre, its mud-brick stores all locked up and looking semi-derelict, many bullet-pocked with shell-damaged gables or roofs. Then we followed a wide valley of extraordinary beauty that wound between low wooded hills and high rounded mountains – the latter meticulously terraced, every inch cultivated. Pedestrians thronged the narrow bumpy dirt-track, the young women wearing brilliantly patterned wrap-around skirts and carrying tall woven baskets on their heads. They walked in single file with that marvellous supple grace too often lost in early middle-age when decades of over-exertion in the fields bring on rheumatism. This is Rwanda's most densely populated region: the 1991 figure was 820 people per square kilometre of cultivable land.

Next came a long, steep climb, the track curving around a series of mountains, each higher than the last, the views increasingly frustrating to this would-be trekker imprisoned in a motor vehicle. We were now close to both the Zairean and Ugandan borders, traversing the last corner of Rwanda to be brought into the Tutsi kingdom.

At the entrance to the tea factory-cum-residential compound we encountered abnormally tight security; expats living on this remote hilltop are extremely vulnerable to anyone running a 'kill foreigners' campaign. Although Gavin's vehicle was expected, we had to wait while the askari checked the registration number with our host. And fifty yards farther on another double gate was elaborately locked.

Kali Alles, who manages this estate, gave me a conducted tour of the factory, pointing out countless bullet- and shell-holes; most have been patched up but those on the very high roof are too difficult to reach. The Alles's garden is a vivid botanical cornucopia overlooking a score of lower hills, their tints varying with distance. As we sat on the verandah drinking iced beer and talking of books and music, then eating a work-of-art curry, it was difficult to remember that here is not Paradise but a district where everyone's nerves – locals' and foreigners' – are now permanently on edge.

We left in time to get home before dark; these days no expat travels after sunset. On the way, several extra roadblocks and many racing military vehicles puzzled us. I had a supper appointment with NGO friends and immediately on entering their living-room my hostess's expression warned me that the news was bad.

This morning in the commune of Kampanga, twelve miles north of Ruhengeri town, and less than twelve miles east of where we lunched, a Canadian priest was killed while saying Mass. He was shot at close range, when it seemed his killer was about to receive Holy Communion. The man then fled down the length of the church and disappeared. No one tried to capture him, which is fair enough given that he was armed and homicidal. One of my fellow-guests knew Fr Picard, a sixty-one-year-old White Father from Quebec. He had lived in Rwanda for thirty-four years, stayed with his parishioners throughout the genocide and saved a dozen or more Tutsi lives. Probably the motive for his murder was to get rid of a witness, someone who might recognize and denounce the ex-FAR and *interahamwe* killers among the returnees. Those men prefer to return to their own communes where their reputations are enough to terrorize the peasants into silence. But someone of Fr Picard's calibre could not be so easily silenced.

Later: A radio message has just come through from the UN, ordering all foreign aid workers not to stay overnight in Ruhengeri but to commute from Kigali. Everyone advises me to forget Bukavu. But I haven't quite given up hope.

8

'THE MADAME IN THE VEHICLE'

Rwanda presented me with, inter alia, a professional ethics problem. Various aid workers were hospitable, informative, helpful – even allowing me to accompany their local staff on day-trips to hilltop projects. Inevitably I have reservations about some of those projects, but I must avoid ungratefully embarrassing any NGO by identifying it. Therefore this chapter, though based on my daily notes, is not a chronological transcription of my journal.

A Rwandan might be identified thus: Aphrodis Emmanuel Munyurabatware from the cellule of Nyakibingo in the sector of Ruharambuga in the commune of Kirambo in the prefecture of Gikongoro. In 1960 Rwanda's chiefdoms and sub-chiefdoms were replaced by eleven prefectures, each administered by a *préfet* and *sous-préfet*, based in the main town. A burgomaster and councillors, appointed by the government, control each commune. Communes are divided into sectors, each supervised by a councillor. Junior officials (*responsables*) oversee the smallest units, cellules of ten or so homesteads (*rugas*). There are no villages; a commune is made up of hundreds or thousands of *rugas* (a hut or huts in a small, usually hedged compound) scattered on several hillsides. On a high flattish hilltop stands the commune office, a long, one-storey, solidly constructed building flying the national flag. From here the burgomaster and his councillors administer their territory. The communal police are accountable to the burgomaster; all over Rwanda, during the genocide, they supplied the *interahamwe* with weapons, transport and every sort of encouragement including free beer. Because the national gendarmerie was completely politicized – merely an arm of the MRND – there was no police force available when the RPF began to govern in July 1994.

At some little distance from the commune office, dispersed over the hilltop or on slightly lower ledges or connecting saddles, is the parish: a large Catholic church, possibly one or two smaller Protestant churches, two or three schools, a health centre, perhaps a (doctorless) cottage hospital, sometimes – depending on a commune's size and accessibility – an imposing convent and/or a seminary. All parish buildings are European-style; many were the scenes of massacres. They symbolize the wealth and power of the Catholic Church, which by 1930 had secured a tight grip on Rwandan society, its authoritarianism bringing nothing new to the peasants' lives. But now things are changing. The leaders of all the Churches disgraced themselves before, during and after the genocide and Christianity may find it hard to recover its old influence – despite the heroism of a minority of nuns and clergymen.

When the First Hutu Republic took the baton of power from the Belgians in 1961 it ran on without faltering. The Catholic Church vigorously supported the new government and its parishes continued to prosper, as they did after Habyarimana's bloodless (almost) coup of 1973. At first his dictatorship made little impression on the majority, yet as time passed it did bring certain benefits for everyone. In 1962 the Republic's per capita income was the third lowest in the world. By 1987 Rwanda had overtaken sixteen countries, medical care was steadily improving and school attendance had risen to 62 per cent.

For decades Rwanda was the international donors' model protégé. The foreign aid workers then tripping over each other in Kigali found the country very agreeable indeed: clean and neat, stable and well-organized. Habyarimana was admired for eschewing any messy experiments with democracy or (God forbid!) socialism. The hard-working peasants knew their place and kept to it. Those Tutsi who had refused to run away, despite the pogroms, were allowed to be economically active though discriminated against politically. When Rwanda suddenly became a butcher's yard too many expats couldn't believe that the MRND and its allies had planned what was happening.

During the previous five years, outside influences had been pushing Rwanda towards economic disaster. By 1987 coffee was bringing in 79 per cent of the nation's export earnings. Two years later coffee prices plummeted on the world market, though not in our shops, and Rwanda – among several other small countries, but more than most – was devastated. Immediately after came the World Bank/IMF SAP, already mentioned. By 1993 Rwandans were asking how often the world's poorest populations must 'structurally adjust' to still worse poverty while the richest imposed globally applicable rules to suit themselves. This abrupt and severe increase in rural hardship, combined with faction-fighting among the rapacious Hutu political élite as their 'cake' shrank, contributed significantly to the moral collapse that left space for genocide.

Over the past two years UNICEF has registered almost 26,000 family reunifications, yet more than 94,000 'unaccompanied children' (their official designation) remain in 'centres' or foster-care. These centres, supported by foreign aid, are not called 'orphanages'; that is too defeatist. Of course many children know their parents are dead – often they have seen them being killed – but the under-fives can give no indication of why they were found astray as toddlers or picked out of some ditch as babies. Others only know that in the general panic they somehow became separated from all their family. Some NGOs run specialist teams of 'tracers' (Rwandan workers) who are now searching for relatives with renewed energy, feeling that since the mass return in November '96 their chances of success are greater. Tracing is a formidable task, demanding limitless persistence as clue after clue at first looks promising, then proves to be false.

Like most humanitarian endeavours, this one is fraught with complications. By now many children – in a centre for more than two years – have, inevitably, become institutionalized. Their lives are secure, ordered, hardship-free; they have three meals a day, water comes from nearby standpipes (perhaps even from taps), adequate clothing is provided, schooling is provided, a bunk-bed is provided for each child (or one between two toddlers). Their minders are, on the whole, kindly and there is a town as setting for their social life, limited though it may be. Among the older age group – say ten to fifteen – this institutionalization can cause severe readjustment problems, especially if they are being reunited with recently returned relatives who may themselves be having readjustment problems. Life is tough on the hills. Food must be cultivated by the sweat of one's brow – and if meals happen twice a day you're lucky. Water must be carried long distances up muscle-taxing gradients. Fuel must be collected from the forest. Bed is a pile of banana fronds on a mud floor (probably damp in the rainy season), and you share a thin blanket with two or three others. Garments are scarce and ragged and – because of the water problem – filthy. School may be too far away or too expensive – anyway an extra mouth to feed means extra limbs are needed to cultivate. Also, there are no bright town lights (only firelight after sunset, and that not for long), no taped music being played in bars, no casually pitying expats to stand you a fizzy drink ... Some teenagers soon run away from rigours they can't cope with – often physically can't cope with, life in a centre having so softened them.

One morning I set off in an NGO vehicle with two young Hutu women tracers, a Tutsi driver – a '59er returnee from Zaire – and Annette, a slim, silent, expressionless fourteen-year-old who had seen no member of her family since May '94. Now a 'found' aunt, her dead mother's sister, had agreed to give her a home in a sector of a commune bordering on Burundi. She wore the centre's uniform, a simple sky-blue frock, freshly washed and ironed, and a pair of blue plastic sandals to match. Her luggage was a heavy wooden trunk of Belgian provenance, stuffed with donated garments and toys and knick-knacks. I thought it strange that she came alone to the Land Cruiser, dragging her trunk behind her. Strange that no friends were there to see her off, wish her well – it was early, before school time.

The track was very rough and on the town's outskirts Annette, sitting in the back between the tracers, suddenly vomited all over them. As they mopped up, Louise, the English-speaker, explained, 'She wasn't in a vehicle for two and a half years, since the truck from a camp in Tanzania.'

The Land Cruiser climbed slowly up and around one hill, two

hills, three hills. On the second and third I noticed something puzzling: much fertile land uncultivated. All over the slopes and level ledges wild vines are choking banana groves, coffee bushes have grown to trees, weeds and grasses stand four feet high, there is an abundance of grazing but no cattle or even goats. Given the land shortage, and endless talk about Tutsi returnees having problems with Hutu squatters, I had visualized every plot being taken over. Pre-'59, many Tutsi lived in this prefecture, so they and their progeny could hardly be accused of squatting had they resettled hereabouts in '94 on their return from Burundi after the RPA victory. Later, an expat who, unusually, speaks Kinyarwanda, told me he intuited that post-genocidal vibes had deterred such resettlements. And Hutu from the grossly overcrowded hills near Kigali feared to take over these abandonded *rugas* so close to the Burundi border. However, one can now see, dotted over the slopes, small patches of newly-dug brown earth where some recent returnees from Zaire have begun their struggle to reclaim the land.

On the third hill we were overlooking Burundi, a mile or so below us, and a quarter of the way down we could drive no farther. A narrow pathway ran through banana groves, some plants liberated from weeds and vines but many dead or dying. For twenty minutes we saw nobody and passed only one tiny *ruga*. On most hills Rwanda's overpopulation is not evident; invisible people beaver away far from the paths.

The second pathside hut was Annette's aunt's home: a three-roomed mud shack, its tiny windows unglazed but wooden-shuttered, its roof of red-brown tiles. (These are a pleasing Belgian innovation.) The door was padlocked so we sat and waited. Then abruptly Annette stood up, rushed around a corner and could be heard vomiting again.

'It's nerves,' remarked Louise.

Soon after, a youth emerged from the bananas, barefooted, ragged, dripping sweat. Yes, he knew where his mother was working, he'd fetch her. Half an hour later she came toiling up the steep slope below the hut – small, thin, worn-faced, a December returnee from a Tanzanian camp. She hesitated, stared silently at the tall fourteen-year-old with burgeoning breasts, well-groomed hair, a smart frock, new sandals. This was not the eleven-year-old peasant child she remembered. Then she stepped forward and briefly embraced her niece: a shy embrace but intense. At once Annette's expressionless mask was discarded. She smiled and wept and as they embraced again I chanced to notice their hands – similar hands, but the aunt's work-coarsened, Annette's sleek from easy living.

Much talk followed but we were not invited into the hut. Then came form-filling in triplicate; each copy of the document had to be signed by Annette, her aunt, Louise and a witness – an elderly emaciated man summoned from that other pathside *ruga*.

As we all strolled back to the vehicle half-a-dozen small children and a toddler (terrified of me) appeared out of nowhere and tagged along. All these recent returnees were relatively healthy on their arrival home, said Louise. They are no longer so.

The toddler has ringworm all over his head. A four-year-old's hands and forearms are covered in monstrous warts. Other small children have open sores and angry-looking rashes. How, I wonder, are the adults adjusting, after so long in well-run (albeit militia-bullied) camps? One has to be careful not to exaggerate the 'comfort' of the camps, yet they did provide regular food supplies and more and better medical care than the indigenes living around them could ever hope for.

As Annette's cousin strained to shoulder that heavy trunk I noticed its patchwork of faded labels; it had often travelled by sea in colonial times. There were none of the lingering farewells we would indulge in, though the tracers were obviously fond of and concerned about Annette. Wordlessly she walked away, without a backward glance, into her new – but really her old – life. Her aunt's home is a two-hour trek from the hilltop amenities.

We drove then to the next hill to check on the well-being of a nine-year-old boy reunited with his maternal grandparents three months ago. This did not involve descending all the way to valley level; these twin hills are, as it were, joined at the navel. Hereabouts no vehicle can go above cycling speed, which slightly lessens my frustration. Soon the Land Cruiser had to be abandoned again and our walk took us almost to the bank of the frontier river. In this border area the driver was not too happy about being left sitting unarmed in a stationary vehicle that might tempt any anti-NGO militia who happened to be around. In Burundi stolen vehicles are easily and quickly 'transformed'. Or they might simply burn it ...

The boy was not in his grandparents' *ruga* – or anywhere around. The grandparents were evasive; so were the three men repairing their thatch. Gently but firmly the tracers probed: at which point I saw why they go on such missions in pairs. Together they can to some extent represent 'authority' as a lone African woman could not do in a *ruga* full of men unless she was very exceptional. I tactfully left them to it and walked down to throw a stone into Burundi across the narrow river – not that I've anything against Burundi, just to prove it was a mere stone's throw away.

Eventually it transpired that the missing boy was so seriously disturbed that his grandparents (who themselves seemed quite disturbed) couldn't cope and transferred him to an uncle on the other side of the hill. It was hard work finding uncle, to-ing and fro-ing up and down and around that hill from *ruga* to *ruga*, seeking directions from stressed-looking people who viewed us with some suspicion. Uncle is a sullen, hard-faced character. He prevaricated at length before admitting that the boy had run away; one felt he did not regret losing him. Did the child really run away? In any event, he has disappeared and there is nothing to be done about it. An NGO has tried to help him and can devote no more resources to a search very unlikely to succeed. The sun was setting – slipping into a crimson cloud-lake – as we got back to base.

Next morning, soon after dawn, we were off again in another direction with a different driver, a Tutsi survivor. Soon we passed a mass grave marked by a new monumental gravestone. I would have photographed it but for the fact that among those 7000-plus lay our driver's parents, paternal grandfather, four siblings and numerous nephews and nieces. He survived because he was trading in Burundi at the time.

We drove far to find a family of five orphans, reunited with a maternal uncle last September. Normally follow-up visits happen after a month or so but this routine was disrupted by the November/December returnee crisis.

Approaching this *ruga*, I could sense my companions' apprehension – and they had reason for it. The eldest boy, aged fifteen, ran away to Kigali. Uncle rejected the fourteen-year-old because he was lazy (fate unknown). The eight-year-old has gone to his grandmother and the two girls, aged ten and twelve, have been retained but were working too far away to be summoned. Or so Uncle said; he was being aggressively non-co-operative.

'We can't ask too many questions,' explained Louise. 'That way we could annoy people. For tracing to succeed, we depend on help from the whole community.'

Next stop: Granny's remote *ruga* to find the eight-year-old. A two-hour search took us along some alarmingly narrow tracks, never meant for a vehicle, overlooking a deep valley where communal rice was being sown. (Most valley floors are not cultivated in family plots.) Then the driver very slowly forced the Land Cruiser through jungly vegetation so dense that the windows had to be closed to protect us from thorny branches. Here I suggested, 'Isn't it time to walk?' Louise and Felicité demurred, complaining of aching legs after the previous day's two brief ambles. However, the jungle soon won and we left the vehicle two miles from Granny's squalid hut-shed.

At one end of the dwelling, decaying vegetable refuse was piled high and hens scratched and pecked all over it. Beside that pile, on a tattered straw mat, a young woman lay naked under a threadbare, filth-encrusted grey blanket. She was delirious with malaria, tossing and turning, moaning and trying to throw off the blanket – kept in place by a tiny girl with hideously burn-scarred legs. A missing gable wall left the structure open to all weathers, and Rwanda's nights can be very cold. For the visitors low stools were brought from a pitch-dark inner room. On an unsteady bench against one wall sat six little boys – including our quarry – using machetes to peel manioc taken from a mound at their feet: hard work for small hands. None can afford school fees. Granny was draped in scraps of fabric so worn you couldn't guess at the garment's original identity. A small woman, haggard and slightly wild-eyed, she had an abscess on one ankle. A middle-aged man joined us, his right arm missing from the shoulder and his left hand from the wrist.

('A survivor,' whispered Louise, 'they left him for dead.') Two women followed; before realizing that some of the boys were their sons I had assumed them to be in their late fifties. Both looked slightly Tutsi in different ways; they are in fact 'Hutsi' – half-and-half.

This indaba continued for nearly an hour. The eight-year-old, a cheerful-looking lad, gave long answers to the tracers' questions and seemed genuinely content to remain with Granny. I could see why; as he spoke she looked at him with love. She has lost her only daughter, his mother – she needs him. Despite that *ruga*'s acute poverty, he is lucky.

As we returned to the vehicle, Louise observed that to her generation increasingly frequent intermarriages had made the Tutsi/Hutu distinction seem irrelevant in many communes. Left to themselves, Rwanda's peasants didn't have the inbuilt prejudices of, for example, most Northern Irish, to whom intermarriage has been anathema – and potentially dangerous. The Rwandans do share a common culture. 'We are all Banyarwanda' is not merely an expedient RPF slogan, though there is an understandable tendency to dismiss it as such. Consider the gathering in that bottom-of-the-pile *ruga* – Granny a Hutu, the maimed man a Tutsi, one 'Hutsi' woman the widow of a Tutsi, the other wife to a Hutu who joined the *interahamwe* and became a killer of Tutsi. Louise, who filled me in on all this, succinctly summed it up: 'Our genocide didn't come from what was inside people, it came from what leaders put into people.'

I am comforted by many accounts of Hutu adults now helping parentless Tutsi families, giving them emotional support as well as practical assistance. As we went jolting along the main track, Louise pointed down one slope towards a solitary speck of UN blue amidst a patch of beans, cabbages and baby banana plants. In that tarpaulin-roofed bender live six Tutsi orphans, aged four to sixteen, who are successfully feeding themselves, with some guidance from Hutu neighbours, off their family plots. Their hut was looted and burned but they hope soon to build another with NGO aid. When the eldest sibling, a sixteen-year-old girl, was traced to them last month they rejoiced to have a surrogate mother.

On one hilltop we passed a trendy modern basilica, painted

bright blue; it is bullet-marked and surrounded by weeds, all its windows and doors sealed with tin sheeting. 'It must stay closed,' said Louise, 'thousands died in there.'

Here as elsewhere, only small children showed friendliness towards me, though the Land Cruiser is well known and the tracing team's mission understood. Several adults uneasily asked Louise, 'Who's the madame in the vehicle?' She explained to me, 'Some will be fearing you're an HRFOR monitor!'

The last *ruga* on our list, quite close to the town, was also inaccessible by vehicle. Halfway up an overgrown precipitous slope ten people occupy a tiny hut that seems about to slide into the valley. These returnees from Tanzania are severely malnourished, the worst case a two-year-old boy not yet able (or not wanting?) to walk and responding to no stimulus. His father is too feeble to stand without help, his bag-of-bones grandmother was slumped in a corner of the hut. A little family land is available but no one has the energy to clear and cultivate it; all depend on a few banana plants urgently needing attention. 'We'll organize an emergency feeding programme,' said Louise. 'Supervised, or some neighbours might grab their rations. After a month on high-energy biscuits they should be able to fend for themselves.' I wondered if she was being over-optimistic.

Most indabas take place outside the huts; sometimes stools are provided, sometimes not. I got the impression this was a measure of how welcome the tracers were, or how much resented for their nosiness.

Rwanda could do with many more goats. There is ample grazing, the bovine population having been so drastically reduced, and goat meat would provide desperately needed protein for children – though one has to admit it's more likely adults would eat them. I wish too (when in a maternalistic mood) that someone would try to persuade all Africans to drink goats' milk, one of the staple peasant foods in so many countries. Louise shuddered at the thought. 'But it smells!' she protested.

During the genocide thousands of Tutsi homes were burned, shelled or otherwise demolished. Thousands of abandoned Hutu homes were soon appropriated by returning Tutsi exiles; more than 400,000 had returned from Uganda, Burundi and Zaire by November '94. House-building was therefore high on the RPF's 'Government of National Unity' agenda and for obvious reasons was a 'project' that greatly appealed to NGOs. (Photographs of smiling families moving into their new homes – provided by kind people like you – are a fund-raiser's delight.) For practical reasons the government favours villages as a feature of the new Rwanda. If you want to provide piped water and sewage for everyone – maybe even public telephones and electricity, one day – it makes sense to create compact villages. But the Banyarwanda have never lived in villages and, despite their traditional subservience to Authority, are resolutely refusing to do so now. (Incidentally, nearly 70 per cent of the rural population had access to safe drinking water pre-genocide, an achievement unmatched elsewhere in Africa.)

In one commune I was shown 192 dwellings built scarcely twenty yards apart, as specified by the Housing Ministry. These were completed two months ago but 191 remain empty. The other is occupied by a tragic young woman and her apathetic toddler. She is the Hutu widow of a Tutsi; he and their three small children were killed in her presence. Then she was gang-raped: the toddler is the result. Logically she too should have been killed; for genocidal purposes the wives of Tutsi counted as Tutsi. Looking at her I wished she had been killed. She never speaks, doesn't try to survive – neighbours bring her food once a day. But with what's left of her humanity she loves that toddler. When I appeared – a strange apparition, to her disordered mind threatening – she seized the little fellow and clung to him and stared at me with a mad pathetic defiance.

I'm not sure I'll want to renew my visa at the end of one month in this country.

Later my companion – Casimir, a '59er from Uganda, now an aid worker – explained, 'It's not only that people are against the new idea of living close together. Coming back from the camps they're afraid of being obvious targets for anyone wanting revenge – with those shiny roofs and beside the motor-track. It would be too easy to attack and wipe out villages and get away quickly. Most will only feel safe living in the old way, hidden on the hills, hard to get to. I say to them, "Wouldn't you be safer in a group, not just one *ruga* by itself?" But they can't see it that way, maybe they've too many memories of group massacres. Crowding into churches, schools, hospitals, commune offices didn't save the Tutsi. Many survivors don't understand how the refugees were forced to go to camps by the organizers. They think all who fled killed. But I tell them I believe the killers are the ones who didn't come home, ran away instead with their families into the middle of Zaire.'

It is disconcerting to see so many empty new houses when all over the nearby hills are two-man-tent-sized benders, made of interwoven sticks and banana fronds, roofed with the UN tarpaulins given to each returning family and often sheltering up to eight people. More than 35,000 returned to this particular commune in November and December.

Tin roofs are given to NGOs by the UNHCR, which imports them from Nairobi at considerable expense. The government opposes this arrangement, arguing that a valuable local skill (tile-making) is being lost, and anyway tiles are cheaper – in fact cost only the makers' time and energy, plus firewood for baking. And wood could be bought from the government's own plantations, thus circulating aid money in Rwanda instead of spending it in Kenya. Now, of course, tiles are coming to be seen as inferior, old-fashioned – and some people are demanding tin instead of wooden doors. The UNHCR insists that, given the need to house thousands rapidly, tin roofs make sense. There is, however, no shortage of labour here; Rwanda swarms with jobless young males. The only real advantage of a tin roof is for rain-collection, yet none of the 'Shelter Programmes' I have seen includes guttering – not an expensive extra, nor is the tar-barrel to go with it. All these shining metallic sheets are so offensive I wince each time we come upon a rash of them – and they won't look much better when rusted. In contrast, the long-lasting red-brown tiles merge perfectly with the landscape.

In another commune we visited a site on which a score of returnee men are working quickly and cheerfully to build themselves new homes with well-made, sun-dried mud bricks. Casimir's NGO is arranging to transport their tin roofs from

Kigali and is itself paying for the wooden doors and tiny shutters, to be made by a local carpenter. Some WFP boffins are considering a scheme to provide these men with free food while they build, and Casimir voiced his doubts about this. 'Is it sensible? Look how they are now, they must have food enough or they couldn't work so hard at such heavy labour. If the WFP comes along with hand-outs they could begin to think they should get wages too – instead of working voluntarily, independently. That way you set up more of this dependency we're cursed with. Why not leave them as they are, happy and proud to be building their own homes? Anyway most donated food is sold at high prices to buy banana beer. Or sometimes – not so often – to buy more palatable food.'

Topographically this was an unusual site, a long, level, grassy ridgetop, the nearest thing I have seen to a plateau in Rwanda. 'Here used to be many cattle,' said Casimir. 'Tutsi cattle – none left. Most cattle were killed too, then eaten. People enjoyed many big feasts in those days. The ones not killed they took to the camps, loaded in FAR trucks. You've heard looting was part of the plan? That was smart! Permission to loot – official encouragement to loot – got thousands joining the *interahamwe*. Very poor idle young men. Then they were given beer to make them keener to kill. Often rich local businessmen donated beer – their contribution … Everything was looted from the Tutsi – and from the Hutu "enemy". Money, livestock, household goods, clothes – everything. And immediately the confiscated land was used or "rented out" by the commune's officials. You were asking me about the neglected land – I think it was neglected sometimes because it was Tutsi-owned, making people superstitious about using it. A few Hutu have admitted to me they felt that way.'

Casimir confirmed that many survivors survived simply because they could afford to pay off the *interahamwe*. The maimed man I met in 'Granny's' *ruga* was one such. He promised to tell two *interahamwe* where his cash was hidden if they took him to hospital; an arm and a hand had to be amputated but he kept his life at the cost of a mere RF10,000.

To me this aspect of the genocide seems peculiarly dreadful; another proof that the killings were far from being 'an upsurge of ancient tribal hatred'. The bought-off militia were betraying their 'cause'; they should have disdained all cash offers and got on with the killing. Their failure to do so concentrates the mind, very unpleasantly, on the economic impetus behind the genocide. Most Tutsi peasants were no better off than their Hutu neighbours, yet what little they had could be possessed by their killers. Is it reasonable to deny, as some do, that overpopulation made easier the organization of the genocide? A frightening thought, when one looks ahead, globally.

Elsewhere, I visited a housing project specifically for parentless children – a modest project, run by a small NGO.

Over-emotionalism is not one of my flaws yet among those children I more than once came close to tears. For a young family to be orphaned is under any circumstances tragic – but normally, in Africa, a supporting network of relatives and friends remains. For many of these Tutsi orphans, there is nobody left. Everyone they or their parents were close to is dead. The combination of their utter destitution and their joyless, haunted faces shattered me. And their terrible aura of hopeless loneliness was accentuated by their physical isolation as they struggled to build new homes on remote plots.

The first family on Angeline's list (five children, the eldest a girl of fifteen) lives thirty minutes' walk from the motor-track. Their present home is a leaking round thatched hut no bigger than many African poultry-huts – barely high enough for me to stand up in. Their possessions are: one battered dechi-type saucepan, one ladle, one blanket (donated) spread on banana fronds. Nothing else. Not even one spare garment between them. They use pieces of wood as hoe-substitutes. Theirs is a Catch-22 situation. They are too small and frail to cultivate the three family plots and must remain too frail while they are so malnourished. Neighbours sometimes help but themselves have little surplus time or energy. The building of their new three-roomed shack has been delayed because the young man hired by the NGO to do the job – he comes from the nearest *ruga* – fell ill two weeks ago. Now he is back on the job, helped by several small boys enlisted as voluntary labour. An unexpectedly urban note was struck by a cocky young man wearing new blue jeans, a striped anorak, a green baseball cap and trainers. He sat on a camp stool cradling on his lap a giant ghetto-blaster with its aerial fully extended. Happily this machine was not working. When we arrived he remained seated and ignored us. In turn Angeline and Eugene – her team-mate, also Hutu – ignored him. He is this cellule's *responsable* and takes it upon himself to 'supervise' NGO-funded building in the hope of being able to extract a 'fee' from some naïve foreign aid worker. 'He should be in prison,' Angeline said afterwards. 'He was a killer.'

For these simple dwellings, the raw materials are elemental: earth, water, wood. The earth is dug on the spot, a few yards from where a framework of thinnish bluegum poles has been erected; these poles are shoulder-carried from the nearest plantation. (Every commune has its state-owned plantation.) A hoe to dig the earth and an axe to cut the poles are the only tools used. A major task on most sites is the fetching of water to pour into the mound of earth, which is kneaded like dough – but rather more vigorously – until its consistency is precisely right. Then large wodges are slapped into oblong spaces between the poles, starting from ground level. A final smooth coating of mud is often applied to the floors and exterior walls. But that's optional; if you're too weary and underfed and demoralized to bother you just move in as is ... The end product looks crude, yet observing the young builder in action I could appreciate how much skill is involved. He worked intently, his hands sensitive, moulding and balancing each wodge of mud as it went into its space. This was no dreary mindless job like driving a crane to construct a prefab skyscraper. The 'primitive' dwelling was his creation, its worth and durability entirely dependent on his personal skill. He looked absorbed and content – a man enjoying job-satisfaction.

Two months ago the NGO gave five goats (two half-grown) to this family. When Angeline asked to see them it transpired they are being looked after by the *responsable*'s mother, Domina, allegedly because they might be stolen from the children. There was something wrong with this story; the fact that the children lack the strength to cultivate does not mean they are incapable of herding and caring for five goats – ample grazing is available on their own plots. An agreeably long walk took us halfway round the hill, then steeply down to Domina's *ruga*. She is a widow, with a harsh voice and hard eyes. In a filthy cramped corral close to her tiled whitewashed dwelling she keeps a cow, a yearling bull and a calf. We crossed the small reeking-of-ammonia yard where Angeline yelped with dismay as her dainty court shoes sank into liquid manure; they will never be the same again. The goats were confined in a pitch-dark lean-to, the door padlocked. Reluctantly, Domina opened it. They all looked poorly, especially the younger ones; a bundle of fodder – coarse grass, freshly cut – lay on the pellet-strewn floor. I diagnosed an urgent need for sunlight, lest they develop the equivalent of rickets. At once Domina picked up the note of criticism in my voice and became openly hostile. The usual long discussion did not take place. Crisply Eugene told her that when the children's house is complete the goats can be stabled at night in the tiny hut, and that's where he expects to find them when he returns next week.

At noon, when we stopped between sections to share a thermos of tea, the silence was broken only by birdsong – a veritable orchestra of birdsong, but on these field-trips binoculars are of course *verboten*. Their use might confirm the worst suspicions of commune officials or soldiers about the spying role of NGOs. Here we were looking down on a thousand feet of almost sheer cultivated land, rising directly from a wide, flat, marshy valley. 'How do people dig and plant and harvest on such gradients?' I wondered aloud.

'This slope below us', said Eugene, 'in past times would not be used for crops. With cultivation the soil is loosened and soon you have bad erosion. The soil is our only wealth, we have no minerals. We should be using much more terracing, but with us it's not a traditional skill. Before, our farmers took care to rest their land. Now it must all be in use all the time and is losing fertility. The EU and other funding agencies try to make us use chemical fertilizers – they arrange demonstration plots to show us how much more we could grow. But our farmers are wise and have doubts. They see their soil hasn't enough organic material to take in much of those artificial fertilizers – they leach away. More animals giving more manure would make more sense. Those demonstration plots taught our farmers more than the EU experts and advisers ever learned!'

'Anyway,' said Angeline, 'UNICEF calculated ten years ago that the average annual farming family's income was £187. It's surely less now. Even if chemicals worked, who could pay for them? Our government doesn't have the foreign exchange to hand them out free.'

'These problems can be solved,' said Eugene. 'I believe in our farmers. They have to be very smart cultivators – and they are! If they're not pushed into doing stupid things they'll come up with solutions.'

En route to the next commune we passed two large level plots conspicuously uncultivated amidst miles of flourishing bananas, sweet potatoes, manioc, beans, tomatoes. Obtusely I asked why so much fertile land has been left to the weeds. I should have realized that these are mass graves, as yet unmarked. Some communes have by now erected massive headstones recording the date(s) of the massacres and the approximate number buried together – 6000, 7000, 8000 ... In Kigali, on the first anniversary of the start of the genocide, 100,000 bodies – collected from temporary graves in the city and surrounding communes – were ceremoniously re-buried.

The present population of this commune is over 46,000, living in ten sectors. Since November, 8442 have returned. The burgomaster is very proud of his exact figures and I don't doubt them, given the Rwandan heritage of efficiently run commune offices. This Tutsi burgomaster is a returnee from Zaire, and Angeline commended his dedication to the peasants' welfare and his unusual willingness to free NGOs from red tape.

We spent the afternoon driving many miles to check on the welfare of goats donated to four orphaned families still living in their parents' looted homes. Such families are exceptionally numerous in this commune, where many children stayed on the hills while both parents worked nearby in Kigali, returning at weekends to cultivate. Of these four families, two were concealed by Hutu neighbours until the militia moved on, impatient to get to the next looting point. The other two hid in the bush and were lucky. 'Here they didn't use hunting dogs and were not so thorough about killing children,' said Angeline. 'I don't know why.'

In some communes, in other prefectures I have visited, only ten or fifteen Tutsi survived out of twelve or fourteen thousand.

We found all the goats in excellent condition; three had recently reproduced, the rest were heavy with kid. Descending from these hills, we sould see the northern shore of Lake Muhazi very far below; on the map this long narrow lake looks like some strange, many-legged insect. Reeds grow densely around the edges and pollution from a nearby 'unregulated' sugar refinery has killed most of the fish. This was once a popular Belgian mini-resort complete with a little quay for pleasure boats and a small guest-house and bar/restaurant, now closed. Nearby is an enormous four-storey red-brick seminary, grimly prison-like and still in use though it looks deserted. There is little sign of life around the hilltop parishes in this area. We passed several vandalized wayside shrines with empty niches where once stood the Sacred Heart, the BVM or some 'protector' patron saint who had failed to protect.

Next morning Donatile and Floride, both Tutsi medical workers, escorted me to other hilltops. This was a day with a halo around it. Giti, the first commune visited, prides itself on being one of the two communes (out of 143 in Rwanda) unstained by genocide. Marking the 'border' stands a large new notice showing a sketch-map of Giti and proclaiming in Kinyarwanda, French and English: 'This commune did not commit genocide.' Our Giti-born driver told me the burgomaster deserved all the credit 'for saving his people from sin'. One would have expected some more complicated explanation. But there is ample evidence, from all over Rwanda, that the 'success' of the genocide did indeed depend on the local authorities' encouragement and co-ordination of the killers.

Here, as elsewhere, the main tracks are lined by cleverly coppiced bluegums, the new shoots tinged rose-pink and wine-red. In one section a labour-gang of some 200 ragged men and women were digging long trenches to plant more trees – 'donating' free labour to the state. This form of tax (*umuganda*) already existed and was hated in pre-colonial times. The Belgians and their Tutsi surrogate rulers abused it even more ruthlessly, and after 1961 it was abandoned – then revived by Habyarimana in 1974. (His new régime also demanded a water tax, a health tax, a market tax and school fees, the last optional.) *Umuganda* quickly became central to the MRND's methodical development of Rwanda. In theory, each

peasant (of both sexes and all ages over fourteen) had to contribute only two days a month or a half-day a week. However, the
government was soon claiming that Rwanda's public-spirited citizens felt such enthusiasm for improving their country that they
were volunteering to do extra time – a lot extra. *Umuganda* maintained the motor-tracks and footpaths; built commune offices,
health centres, schools and prisons; cleared the bush for enormous
forestry plantations; dug trenches for gravity-fed water systems
and for drainage and anti-erosion ditches. The burgomaster and
councillors decided what needed doing and when and by whom.
(The burgomaster was a government appointee, his loyalty to the
MRND unwavering.) One consequence of *umuganda* is a country
visibly better off environmentally than its neighbours, with far
superior public buildings in the rural areas.

The Churches, donor institutions and foreign NGOs praised
umuganda. They saw it as a sensible use of an underemployed
population and as proof that the industrious peasants deserved
Rwanda's annual US$20 million of aid money. Few foreigners
bothered to scrutinize *umuganda*'s 'voluntary' component, yet by
the mid-eighties this system was, blatantly, forced labour and
becoming more so – more forced, more laborious – and increasingly being exacted to cultivate Big Men's farms. In 1990, when
Habyarimana reluctantly agreed to the formation of opposition
parties, the MRND's grip was loosened slightly, and there began a
boycott of all *umuganda* tasks that were of no immediate benefit
to the peasantry, like the repairing of motor-tracks used only by
the personal vehicles of the élite.

Then, as Gérard Prunier records, the genocide led to

a 'rural' banalisation of crime. Killings were *umuganda*, collective work,
chopping up men was 'bush clearing' and slaughtering the women and
children was 'pulling out the roots of the bad weeds'. The vocabulary of
peasant-centred agricultural development came into play with horrible
double meaning.

Now *umuganda* is being used (and probably abused) by the
new government to help reconstruct this devastated country.

As Donatile remarked, communal life is all high tension at present. Even by Rwandan standards the prefecture of Rural Kigali

has become alarmingly overcrowded, because so many Tutsi returnees settled here in 1994 believing it to be the 'safest' region. Also, the recent Hutu returnees arrived too late to plant and will need donated food (not always available) until next season. In most cases they have yet to repossess their land, now being used by others – often Tutsi. The arrangement is that those who have cultivated plots may retain them until after the next harvest but must then give them back to the original owners. An apparently equitable arrangement, but it may not seem so to those on the 'giving back' side. Inevitably there will be disputes about the definition of 'original' owners; that could mean the Tutsi families who were terrorized into exile a generation ago. In Floride's view, everything will depend on the burgomasters' determination to make this plan work and enforce law and order while it is being implemented. Thus far – all my NGO minders tell me – there has been surprisingly little overt friction. The consensus seems to be that most Rwandans have no stomach for further violence.

In a large health centre-cum-small hospital, recently restored by my minders' NGO, most of the beds were empty – as in Kayove and for the same reason. In many communes excellent work is being done by nutrition officers. Here a Tutsi returnee from Zaire teaches women and girls how to balance a family's diet even if the food available is very limited, how to cook without losing nutrients, on what to wean babies, how to cater for old people when they have lost all their teeth. Behind the health centre rabbits are bred and children taught how to look after them and adults brainwashed to overcome their distaste for eating them. Donatile longs to see every family keeping rabbits; a healthy young doe can be bought for about RF850, a buck for less and away they go ... But then he sighed and referred to the old problem of peasant conservatism – which certainly contributed significantly to the famine death-toll in Ireland 150 years ago, though it's not now p.c. to mention this.

In all the sixteen health centres I've visited, AIDS-education posters (USAID-funded) are prominently displayed, conveying their messages through graphic picture-stories with the minimun of text. In Kigali, AIDS is now the major cause of death; by 1990 33 per cent of the city's sexually active population tested HIV-positive. No one can give me a more recent figure, but it is feared the returnees from the camps will spread the infection on the hills, where the 1990 figure was 3 to 5 per cent. Otherwise, the main causes of death are malaria and intestinal and respiratory diseases. For reasons nobody understands, malaria has increased rapidly during the past fifteen years and spread to altitudes where it was previously unknown.

Many other clever and colourful health-education posters decorate the walls of long verandahs where, on infant vaccination days, scores of mothers queue for hours. The stern white-coated doctors – very obviously 'authority figures' – process the babies as though they were inanimate objects, never glancing up at a mother's face, concentrating on bottom after bottom after bottom. By now I've observed three such queues and been dismayed by their quietness, apart from the indignant yells as the needle goes in. It isn't natural for a gathering of African women to be so unsmiling and silent. Each women carries an exercise book carefully wrapped in cellophane: her baby's medical record. At a small table, a few yards from the doctor, sits a clerk who fills in the details, stamps the date, signs the entry – and away goes mama.

Rwanda has thirty-four hospitals and 188 health centres; 80 per cent of the population lives within three miles of a 'health facility' of some sort. But nearness to a facility is small consolation if you can't afford to use it. And, despite Rwanda's remarkably rapid reconstruction, no hospital or health centre is functioning now as it was before the quadruple disaster of collapsed coffee prices, the SAP, civil war and genocide.

Overlooking one health centre from a nearby ridgetop is a long, red-brick, two-storey seminary – now derelict, all its windows broken, its doors removed, every fitting looted, the floors and walls still darkly stained. I didn't ask, 'What's the story?' I don't want to hear any more of those stories.

On most hills we have to walk a little distance and it worries me that my young Rwandan women minders find these paths so difficult. Sometimes a male has to help them up – or down, if the incline seems perilously steep. A generation or two of motorized urban living has cancelled out all the ancestral centuries of coping with such slopes.

In another southern prefecture Fonsie was my minder on two day-trips to border communes. Mbarara-born Fonsie is energetic, competent and diplomatic – diplomatic, that is, when dealing with local officials who are trying to cheat his NGO. I'm not sure his attire is very tactful; a Museveni T-shirt is unlikely to win him friends among the militia-influenced returnees.

These communes' Shelter Programmes use *umuganda* labour. On level ground beside a little stream work-gangs pack mud into moulds cut from scrap metal, then turn the bricks out to bake in the sun. Next they are head-carried to the building site some three miles away where skilled men, paid by Fonsie's NGO, construct the houses. I shall always remember watching 150 brick-laden men and women processing silently along a tree-shaded track in single file, their bare feet making no sound on the red earth. Fonsie has no qualms about *umuganda*. 'In a poor country,' said he, 'there is no other way to get things done. And peasants need organizing.'

We drove on then to a plantation where another work-gang was cutting poles, closely watched by two commune overseers. The poles must be carried five miles. 'You have to be careful here,' explained Fonsie, 'or they try to cut extra poles and slip them to friends. Wood is valuable.' I said nothing but thought it might be quite a good idea to give the workers a pole each at the end of their day's work. But then, I have never understood about economics.

Fonsie's NGO is also dealing with returnees resistant to becoming village-dwellers. In this region, he said, many families don't want to settle and furnish new homes until reunited with relatives still missing. They wish to be free to move off in any direction at a moment's notice should a clue materialize and are reluctant to leave homes unguarded. One local burgomaster is trying to persuade everyone to move simultaneously into a village by suggesting that there should be a big party, with limitless banana beer, to celebrate their taking up residence – a party of course thrown by the NGO involved. I am puzzled by this novel resistance to the will of Authority. Perhaps it's a healthy sign that a mould has been broken – one of the moulds that so worried Pius. Or if not broken, at least cracked.

How are the returnees affected by the sight of so many ruined, burned, demolished homes among the overgrown crops? Their own and others ... Some of the '94 Tutsi returnees from Burundi vengefully attacked deserted Hutu *rugas* in their region and looted whatever the refugees had left behind. Several of my NGO minders have commented on the 'alarming apathy rate' (Fonsie's phrase) among the recent Hutu returnees, especially the women. 'It seems', said Fonsie, 'as if they were able to avoid dealing with memories in the camps. Then back where it all happened they're re-traumatized, can only sit around looking at the weeds – and wouldn't you be the same!'

I suppose it is possible that *umuganda*, as work-therapy, will incidentally help some of those returnees. If left to themselves they might continue to 'sit around', looking anguished, crumpled, enervated. In Kigali I met an expat who has trained fifteen women to provide counselling services on the hills. This group finds that the Tutsi survivors, and those Hutu who did not flee, are by now less traumatized – on the whole – than many recent returnees. They helped each other, as soon as the genocide was over, to recover from shared horrors – talking at length about their experiences, however dreadful, and hugging and consoling each other over cups of tea or coffee or bottles of beer. In contrast, many refugees remained under the influence of those who had instigated them to kill and were kept in a state of terrorized confusion. The government has been attempting to provide for them a calming atmosphere, a safe psychological space in which to regain their emotional balance. But for some this may never be possible.

Fonsie and Pierre (the driver) thought we should picnic at a 'famous tourist spot' on the prefecture's highest hilltop. This long narrow ridge overlooks Burundi on one side, very far below, and a deep forested valley on the Rwandan side. One can't imagine many tourists using the approach track in its present state, but here the Belgians planted a long avenue of cypresses and set up three attractive little thatched rondavels with half-walls of bamboo. Two magnificent golden-brown eagles with white tail-feathers were circling nearby below eye-level – then soaring up, gliding over the ridge, again swooping low. Fonsie agreed that here I could safely take photographs, but he was wrong.

Soon I had enraged two men, drinking Primus in another of the rondavels, by seeming to aim the camera at them – when in fact I was aiming (unsuccessfully) at an eagle. The Rwandans' camera-phobia is unique in my experience, outside of Muslim countries. These men were, it transpired, VIPs: the prefecture's RPA commanding officer and the commune's burgomaster, both Tutsi. The former, a returnee from Burundi, was an unpleasant character, stupid and arrogant, immensely tall but beginning to put on flesh. He recently took great umbrage because Fonsie declined to give him a lift in his NGO vehicle. He failed to appreciate how dangerously compromising it could be were a particular NGO to be associated in the popular mind with the RPA. Moreover, there is a strict government ban on NGOs giving lifts to any Rwandan under any circumstances.

These omnipresent NGO vehicles – large, powerful, polished, costing at least twenty years' worth of Rwandan wages – contribute hugely to the expats' present 'image' problem. Most citizens remain unaware of the government ban and can't read the typed notices, in Kinyarwanda and French, stuck on the vehicles' back windows. It can only seem heartless – positively cruel – when expats and their Rwandan colleagues, travelling in almost empty vehicles, refuse to help frail old women or malnourished children as they toil uphill loaded with water or firewood.

Descending to the parish, not far below, we were followed by the CO's military jeep. An *umuganda* gang was returning from a work-site and marching purposefully towards the large open space outside the commune office, where they joined hundreds of others sitting on the ground. 'This is a good burgomaster,' observed Fonsie. 'Here he comes to discuss with everyone the commune's needs and projects. He has brought Museveni's ideal from Uganda, he understands how village councils work. Here that idea could help reconciliation but our people need time to get used to it. They're only used to burgomasters as dictators. Museveni's village assemblies, electing their own committees with real responsibility for decision-making – to Rwandans that's a strange notion.'

In this commune Fonsie had to deal with a young *responsable* who had either got his sums wrong or defrauded a carpenter. We all sat in another rondavel, at one end of the trading centre, beside the roofless ruin of a fire-blackened dwelling once substantial.

The aggrieved carpenter had been awaiting us but it took forty minutes to locate the *responsable*, who arrived looking half-scared, half-defiant. Three other men became verbosely involved and during this lengthy indaba I strolled down the track questing about for banana beer. These hilltop trading centres, their rows of little shops and stalls free of any commercial advertisement – even for Coca-Cola – remind me of communist countries before the free-market virus attacked them. Even among beer drinkers, there is little nicotine addiction in the communes, apart from the elders' long pipes, popular among both sexes and smelling rather like my mini-cigars. In general Rwanda seems more cigarette-free than the average African country, probably because most people can't afford to smoke – though Rwanda grows some tobacco. Or perhaps because the previous puritanical régime discouraged smoking? No doubt BAT – inspired by its board member Lady Thatcher – is even now planning to change this healthy situation.

Driving back to base (the carpenter paid, the *responsable* chastened) we talked about one of the main sources of dissension between the government and foreign NGOs. The former resents well-qualified Rwandans being lured away from its service by NGOs offering much higher salaries; but there's a certain illogic here, as Fonsie pointed out, because the government also advocates expat experts being replaced by skilled Rwandans. And the pool of skilled Rwandans is at present very shallow.

'Why', I asked Fonsie, 'was the old régime so on-the-ball about health care and so neglectful of education?'

'It's easier to dictate to ignorant people,' said Fonsie, 'and the Church ran more than half the health centres. That's why family planning didn't take off until the Pope's visit in 1990. Before that, our bishops were forever rabbiting on about "natural methods". When the Pope left the "evils of contraception" out of his sermons here the bishops got the message. They've kept quiet since and allowed their health-centre staffs to give advice and gadgets. They haven't said the gadgets are OK, they just pretend not to notice. Already that's making some difference, though not enough.'

Rwanda's population has gone from two million in 1940 to more than seven million today, with ten million expected by 2002. Which makes the educational scene all the more scary, since agriculture cannot possibly absorb such an increase. Pre-genocide, some 60 per cent of children attended woefully inadequate primary schools, barely 6 per cent went on to the secondary level and less than 1 per cent graduated from a university.

Next morning – in the same commune – George, a young Canadian, invited me to accompany him to a health centre-cum-thirty-bed-hospital restored by his NGO. (The militia looted most health centres and hospitals and in many cases damaged them structurally.) After various unforeseen (by George) delays, this work was to have been completed the previous day. And so it had been, but the shoddy workmanship and blatant cost-cutting infuriated George. Also, extra space has been devoted to storage and there are only twenty-four beds – the contractor's arbitrary modification. Poor George felt thwarted and guilty because his contract had ended and he was going home next day, leaving an important task unfinished. I watched him coping well with his anger and being consoled by the driver-translator. 'Be happy, George,' said Jean. 'These men are bad fellows, you have worked your best, now I'll fight with them.'

As yet, only the dispensary is open; there a semi-literate nurse-assistant prescribes simple remedies and gives injections. What most bothered me were the scores of hypodermic needles dumped on the grass at the edge of the compound with several small children, including the nurse's, playing nearby. When I drew these to Jean's attention and he reproved her she merely looked puzzled.

Later, George revealed the details of his travail. This was a complicated story, involving three building contractors whom he suspects of working in cahoots though ostensibly they are rivals. One can see how tempting it must be for the locals to take advantage of young, inexperienced expats. Especially when dealing with contractors on the make, no amount of dedication compensates for an aid worker's wetness behind the ears. In most jobs, new recruits learn while subordinate to senior staff. In the fast-expanding aid world, NGOs often give a huge amount of responsibility – an unfair amount – to young people who may never before have left home. Older people are not, on the whole, willing to live for long periods in places like Rwanda, Angola or Mozambique.

As an NGO protégée I have of course been witnessing the worst of rural poverty and post-genocidal misery. However, it has cheered 'the madame in the vehicle' to observe also how many families have 'got it together again' in less than three years – their plots well tilled, their homes in good repair, their donated clothes sometimes verging on the fashionable, their children certainly not starving. My Rwandan minders, being intimate with the communes they operate in, are able readily to distinguish between the returnees and others. Some returnees are among the more affluent families, for reasons into which, I am advised, one does not enquire. This belies a large, brightly coloured poster (touching evidence of the RPF's striving for reconciliation) that is displayed in most schools, health centres, commune offices. It depicts a border crossing point – on one side a bare hill covered with UNHCR tents, on the other a forested hill overlooking a village of identical new tin-roofed dwellings. An emaciated, ragged, barefooted refugee family has just passed the barrier pole, small bundles on the parents' heads. They are being joyously welcomed by a well-fed, well-dressed, well-shod commune family who live – we deduce – in one of those new homes. The text is in Kinyarwanda, French and, significantly, English: 'Banyarwanda, welcome Home, in peace let us rebuild a new Rwanda.'

9

THE TURNING
OF THE SCREW

En route from Kigali to Butare one seems to be descending, but in fact this is the higher city and at night perceptibly colder. Around Gitarama the landscape becomes more conventional; the hills are less steep and no longer separated by those distinctive wide flat valleys, though banana groves and bluegum plantations continue to dominate. The road surface is flawless and the young Muslim at the wheel of our minibus drove carefully, unlike most Rwandans. As usual in this well-disciplined country, only the legal number of passengers were carried. Again I noticed their silence and an unexpressed yet discernible hostility to the expat. This was a cheap taxi; the non-stop service costs a little more. But I prefer (frugality apart) the slower pace of vehicles that stop frequently to drop off and take on – or to readjust the roof load, or allow people to buy potatoes or charcoal from wayside vendors.

We passed several 'Shelter Programmes', hundreds of mud-brick homes being built with UNHCR aid – as numerous conspicuous notices proclaim – on land cleared by gangs of prisoners from the many commune jails, each holding three to four hundred genocidal suspects. When a convoy of three UN vehicles came towards us the youth in front of me leaned out to shake his fist at them while shouting something abusive. The UN will never be forgiven for their 'desertion' of Rwanda in April '94. Moreover, aid workers in general are seen as 'professional humanitarians', here to profit from other people's misfortunes. This is only partially unfair. In many countries one meets expats who are in one way

154

or another misfits back home and see aid work as offering an escape, besides having a certain glamour and allowing more scope for the uncriticized use of limited talents. However, most of the aid workers I've met here are dedicated individuals – several of them astute and conscientious enough to have become quite quickly disillusioned and troubled by the futility of their present mission.

Butare considers itself to be – and is – a cheated city. As 'Astrida' (so named in honour of the Belgian queen) it was colonial Rwanda's administrative centre. It was also the country's intellectual and spiritual (or perhaps I should say ecclesiastical) centre, complete with cathedral. In 1961, when 6000 people lived in the village of Kigali, Butare was the obvious choice as capital of the new Republic of Rwanda. But politics intervened. This region was associated with the liberal opponents of President Kayibanda's clan, based in Gitarama, and so the President decided to create a new city that would owe all its loyalty to the new régime. The stated reason was 'Kigali is more central' – a laughable excuse, given the size of Rwanda.

Throughout this comparatively tolerant and tension-free prefecture, Tutsi used to form an uncommonly high percentage of the population. In April '94 Butare had Rwanda's only Tutsi *préfet*, Jean-Baptiste Habyarimana, who heroically refused to do his 'duty' by helping to arm and co-ordinate the killers. As word spread that Butare remained 'safe', tens of thousands of terrified families took refuge in its communes. The *préfet* then toured the hilltops, welcoming them, guaranteeing their safety, organizing feeding programmes and first-aid tents. He insisted on senior military and civilian officers accompanying him to several parishes, and through the force of his personality and the proper use of his authority he restrained the *sous-préfets*, burgomasters and councillors from unleashing their killers. It is astounding that one man was capable of protecting a prefecture for twelve days while all around genocidal madness convulsed the country.

On 18 April the government replaced Jean-Baptiste Habyarimana with a Gisenyi FAR officer, Colonel Tharcisse Muvunyi, and a civilian administrator, Sylvain Nsabimana. The deposed *préfet*, together with his wife and two children, was murdered that evening. On 19 April, in the Parish of Karama, at least 38,000 were killed; more than 12,000 died together in the church. In the Parish of Cyahinda a carefully planned military attack, also beginning on 19 April, slaughtered at least 20,000. Groups of five or six hundred tried to escape into Burundi across the Kanyaro river at various fording points but were macheted by the *intera-hamwe* – babies being chopped up in front of their mothers before being flung into the water. Throughout April and into May the killings continued in every Butare commune. In the end, this prefecture was the scene of some of the worst massacres; the coming together of so many Tutsi, during that period of illusory safety, simplified things for the killers.

Now I find it strange to remember that during the worst of the genocide I remained oblivious to what was going on, being so absorbed in the excitement and joy generated by the birth of the new South Africa. But as the world rejoiced with South Africa, hundreds of thousands were being torn asunder by South African fragmentation grenades, sold by Pretoria to the Kigali régime in 1992. These were the favoured mass-killing weapons as FAR troops, gendarmerie and communal police exterminated men, women and children packed into churches, convents, schools, hospitals, commune offices.

Nowadays, according to my Kigali friends, Butare feels much less tense than the capital: but this morning it didn't feel so to me. On arrival I wandered around for an hour or so, testing the vibes and appreciating the non-urban atmosphere – almost small-town-ish. Then, outside the Groupe Scolaire Hospital, I stopped to ask a white nun the way to an NGO residence. She proved to be Irish, though with a Belgian order, and has lived here since 1964. Even as she lowered her Toyota van's window I could see that she was suppressing anger. The security guards at the hospital gates wouldn't admit her to visit a priest badly injured yesterday in a car crash. At present no expats, they said, were to be allowed through these gates. Not even an elderly resident nun speaking fluent Kinyarwanda – virtually an honorary citizen of Butare and among the few whites who did not run away in April '94.

Later I tried to visit the university, promoted as one of Butare's tourist attractions, but a friendly security guard – a Ugandan returnee – explained that 'just for now' no expats are allowed on the campus.

Taking liquid consolation in the Chez Nous hotel's open-air bar I met Ahmed, a Sudanese Muslim who since 1985 has been working with various NGOs in East Africa. A man of exceptional perspicacity and wit, he is the sort one wishes could become a life-long friend. (That is the main disadvantage of the travelling life: meeting kindred spirits only briefly.) We considered the fate of Rwanda's 'accused' prisoners, said to number 100,000 by now. Within the larger prisons the appalling conditions have caused an unknown number of deaths and the loss of many limbs through gangrene. However, Ahmed is dubious about the statistics; it seems some are imprisoned for only three, four or five months while some informal investigation is being conducted. (Or while some relative is collecting a certain amount of cash?) A minority are now being tried by the Special Tribunals set up in each prefecture, but obviously the majority can never be given conventional legal treatment with the very limited resources available. Their 'human rights' are therefore of great concern to some outside observers, but the HRFOR monitors one sees zooming around all over the country can do nothing about this particular 'violation'.

Said Ahmed, 'If they were seen to be making progress in that area somebody would kill them. And it's my opinion they don't have the know-how. That's surely a job for Rwandans, specifically. Without belonging to the culture they've no way to get at the truth.' Like others I've listened to, Ahmed despairs of Rwanda's justice system. 'It's chaotic, almost to the point of non-existence. And right now you can't blame the government for that. They haven't the personnel or the funding to pull it together.'

Then Ahmed told me about Jean-Paul, a 'Hutsi' (Hutu father, Tutsi mother) employed as a driver by his NGO since August '94, popular with all his fellow-workers and completely dependable. Two months ago a Hutu sister-in-law 'accused' him and he has been in jail ever since, living on a bucket of rice and beans brought to him every Wednesday by his devoted wife – Wednesday being 'feeding' day. (What must that unrefrigerated food taste like by Tuesday evening?) Jean-Paul's expat employers are allowed to visit him twice a month and find him astoundingly philosophical; he says he can't believe an innocent man will be convicted in the new Rwanda. His wing of the jail is not a horror-pit and he gets plenty of fresh air and exercise, being marched out every weekday morning to make bricks. Meanwhile the accusing sister-in-law is cultivating his land and doing nicely, thank you.

A disquieting story. However, Ahmed is more sceptical than his European colleagues, more aware of all the possible combinations and permutations. No one disputes Jean-Paul's reliability, amiability, respectability, popularity and so on. Yet it remains quite possible that he was a killer, that his sister-in-law's accusation is justified.

'But why so long delayed?' I wondered.

Ahmed shrugged. 'Could be lots of reasons – like someone's died who would have killed her if she'd accused before. Genocide leaves a very dirty tangle.'

It does seem unlikely that Jean-Paul was a trained death-squad killer. But, as Ahmed pointed out, you can't slaughter 800,000 people in less than three months without recruiting thousands of 'amateurs' who revert to normal when the frenzy is over. At least apparently revert to normal – and maybe actually? Is there a parallel here with troops returning from a war during which they ruthlessly killed as many as they could of those they had been told were 'the enemy'? (The gratuitous bombing of Dresden's residential districts slaughtered thousands of helpless men, women and children.) Most ex-soldiers, though by no means all, readjust easily enough to civilian life. But in Rwanda that is a tricky parallel, never to be extended to the organizers of the genocide who knew they were setting up something very different from war.

Ahmed and I plan to meet again tomorrow. I find him much more on my wavelength than most African Christians. I remember speculating about this in Cameroon, when staying with Fulani families. Does it mean that in Africa Islam has taken root as Christianity has not (and cannot)?

4 FEBRUARY

Butare is very proud of possessing the National Museum, a gift from Belgium's King Baudouin I, opened in 1988 and covering 2700 square metres. Designed by M. Lode Van Pee, it lies (fortunately) below road level as one approaches from Kigali. Let my guidebook (*Rwanda Today*, by Jean-Claude Klotchkoff, 1990) describe it:

A superb architectural achievement, incorporating brick, glass and wood in futuristic forms ... this building is made of sun-dried clay bricks like those manufactured by Rwandan peasants. By playing with the palette of colours of this traditional material – from ochre to beige to tea-rose – the architect embellished the facade with geometric motifs which evoke rustic mats and baskets. The museum is composed of pavilions with pointed roofs, and recalls the straw huts still seen in the Rwandan countryside.

Undeterred by all that, I entered – and for hours was enthralled. So were my few fellow-visitors: all young men, looking like students, moving silently from room to room singly or in pairs. It must be good for their morale to see how much beauty was created by their forebears – and happily still is, in some areas – using wood, earth, vegetable dyes, papyrus and eleusine fibres. Photographs taken between 1910 and 1970 show men and women wearing their own minimal garments made of bark, skins and woven vines. Even in cool Rwanda, Africans don't really need the absurd amount of clothing now worn in imitation of Europeans, including heavy jerseys, woollen balaclavas and – the ultimate status symbol! – padded anoraks with hoods.

A replica of a royal thatched hut (the outer walls also thatched, the interior walls bamboo partitions) is thirty feet high with an elaborate porch – truly a work of art, constructed of stooks of tall grasses, forest branches and woven creepers. What must the loss of those skills do to a people's self-esteem?

I paid my respects to the memory of Major-General Rwigyema, standing in front of his crayon portrait – hanging between life-size photographs of the Presidents Kayibanda and Habyarimana and the present President Bizimungu. Evidently there is no photograph of the unfortunate Rwigyema, the RPF's most popular and inspiring leader, killed on the second day of the October 1990 invasion from Uganda. He was the only RPA casualty that day.

A student accompanied me back to the town; he had spent hours taking notes in the geology room. Corneille is a survivor, one of those Tutsi saved by Hutu neighbours who knew they were thus putting their own lives at risk. All three generations of his family were killed, either on their hill or in Kigali. His Hutu friends hid him in a shallow grave in the soft earth of a banana grove, scattering loose withered fronds over a small ventilation hole. For six days he lay there, being given just enough water, at irregular intervals, to sustain life. Urination had to happen *in situ* and that was, he said, the worst of it – even worse than the immobility. When disinterred, by night, rashes and sores covered his thighs and lower body. By then there were, apparently, no Tutsi left alive in that commune – only heaps of putrefying corpses – and the death-squads had moved on. Yet Corneille remained in danger; some local Hutu, their cunningly aroused hatred still glowing white-hot, would have needed no further urging to kill him. His friends concealed him in their *ruga* for two months, a time of extreme tension. The possibility of being detected and 'pointed out' often felt like a probability.

Such survival accounts – and they are numerous – sound like gruesome parodies of *Boy's Own* adventure stories involving incredible feats of stamina. Every sort of stamina: physical, mental, emotional. Yet the Tutsi survivors – bereft of all or many of their family and friends, their possessions looted, their homes and careers destroyed, their businesses appropriated – have received from agencies far less sympathetic attention and material help than the Hutu refugees and 'internally displaced persons'. Also, the RPA soldiers, who had stopped the killing, went unpaid until December '94, while the ex-FAR, the *interahamwe* and other killers were being sustained in various camps by the UNHCR. Nor were the Tutsi survivors' very real security concerns appreciated by the 'humanitarian community'. On 15 January '95 HRFOR published its Operational Plan in which 'the most vulnerable elements of Rwandan society' were defined as 'refugees and IDPs'. This prompted an angry vice-rector of Butare University (Dr Emmanuel Bugingo, who lost his wife and most of his friends and Tutsi colleagues) to demand, 'And where was the concern of the UN for human rights during the genocide? Where? What human rights, whose human rights?'

The participation of so many doctors and nurses in the killings should not, I suppose, surprise anyone who knows anything about the Holocaust. Twenty doctors on the staff of Butare's University Hospital have been identified by name in *Death, Despair and Defiance*, and there is no shortage of witnesses to provide detailed evidence against them. They include Dr Seraphin Bararengana, a surgeon and younger brother of President Habyarimana, and Dr Bruno Ngirabatware, a younger brother of Stanislas Mbonampeka, former Minister of Justice. Twenty-six members of the staff of the University Centre for Public Health were also implicated as leaders of the death-squads. These include five doctors and Therésie Nyiramisago, a younger sister of President Sindikubwabo, head of the interim government in charge of Rwanda at the time of the genocide. Between staff and students, more than 900 were killed on the university campus – many of them Hutu but, as 'intellectuals', suspected of disloyalty to the Hutu Power ideology. Usually their children, living in the university's residential district of Buye, were also killed. Gérard Prunier records:

On the campus of Butare University, a Hutu teacher whose Tutsi wife was in an advanced state of pregnancy saw her disembowelled under his eyes and had the foetus of his unborn child pushed in his face while the killers shouted 'Here! Eat your bastard!'

Butare's Groupe Scolaire Hospital provided seven identified genocide organizers, notably Dr Jeanne Nduwamariya, whose habit it was to go to roadblocks around the city and taunt the *interahamwe* for their failure to kill certain named 'wanted' women. She formed a deadly trio with Pauline Nyiramasuhuko, the Minister for Family and Women's Affairs, and Simeon Remera, wife of a prominent local politician. Her husband was (maybe still is) Dr Jean Chrisostome, then Butare's Regional Health Director, notorious for his extremism. He had raged against the Arusha Accords and frequently publicly denounced Butare's *préfet*, Jean-Baptiste Habyarimana, as 'an RPF accomplice'. One of Dr Chrisostome's Tutsi colleagues left her job after being similarly labelled; when the killing began he led the *interahamwe* to her home and she and her son were murdered. Her severely wounded daughter remains incapacitated. Dr Nduwamariya departed for Gabon in July '94 to become a gainfully employed exile.

Butare is, indisputably, the ecclesiastical capital of Rwanda. Nuns swarm, many of them very young, and so do priests – less obviously. The massive brick cathedral remains by far the largest building in this pleasingly undeveloped town. It is in an architectural category all its own, with windows showing some remote Gothic influence and a hint of the Byzantine about its west door. The austere interior comes as a pleasant surprise: pale brick walls, a very high arched ceiling of dark beams and bamboo, a simple stone altar. Queen Astrid of Belgium laid the foundation stone shortly before she died in a motoring accident in 1935. Four years previously the Catholic Church had finally vanquished paganism when the resolutely anti-Christian King Yuhi V Musinga was replaced by the hand-picked (a Belgian hand) King Mutara III Rudahigwa, who soon proved himself a satisfactory puppet. Or so it seemed at the time. The reality was rather more complicated.

Since 1899 the Catholic Church had been present and active in Rwanda but for a generation its few converts came from amongst the poorest of the poor. Then suddenly, in 1927, thousands began to clamour for baptism. They had seen the light and it showed them that under the Belgians' reformed administration becoming a Christian must be the first step to joining the new élite. By 1994 Rwanda was routinely described as 'the most Catholic country in Africa'.

My guidebook (consistently slanted to placate the MRND) gives one revealing quote from *The Evangelization of Rwanda* by Abbé Felicien Muvara: 'In 1959 the Belgian trustee administration and the Catholic Church, by giving strong support to the Hutu élite, dealt the Banyiginya monarchy a death blow. By doing so, they sped up the foundation of the Republic.' The Catholic Church (and all other denominations, in a grisly display of ecumenism) continued to give 'strong support to the Hutu élite' – before, during and after the genocide. Even non-Christian outsiders like myself have been shaken to discover the extent of their complicity with Hutu extremism. Given their influence, the senior churchmen could without doubt have put a brake on the killing machine. Every Sunday in every parish their message was heard; only they had the means and the power to counteract the foul

RMC propaganda and the rabble-rousing communal officials. Why did they not intervene? Because with very few (and not very potent) exceptions they were 'Habyarimana's men'. The Catholic Archbishop of Kigali, Vincent Nsengiyumva, was also a successful entrepreneur, a close friend of the Habyarimana family and a member of the MRND central committee until December '89. At the beginning of June '94 the Anglican Archbishop of Rwanda, Augustin Nshamihigo, and the Anglican Bishop of Kigali arrived in Nairobi to give a press conference and announced that they were there 'not to condemn but to explain what is happening in Rwanda'. Mark Huband of *The Observer* commented, 'Even the most senior members of the Anglican Church were acting as errand boys for political masters who have preached murder and filled the rivers with blood.'

Of the 192 clergymen killed, few died in defence of their parishioners; they were killed because they were Hutu moderates or Tutsi. A minority of priests, nuns and pastors opposed the genocide; another minority enthusiastically collaborated with its organizers while the majority simply sat on the fence. In the Rwandans' hour of need, their Christian Churches gave no leadership, abandoning them to the civil authorities. Despite its imposing superstructure, the Catholic Church had provided no moral foundation on which the ordinary Rwandan could stand steady while rejecting the concept of genocide. Instead, it had contributed to the moulding of a population who believed it was right to do what they were told to do. The result, now, is demoralization in its original sense. After the event, genocide makes you think; why did you go along with it? Subsequent developments have proved that it wasn't necessary to slaughter all Tutsi to preserve for the Hutu what had been gained by the 1959 revolution. So now there are many Rwandans adrift in an ocean of guilt, doubt, shame, denial, bewilderment, cynicism – and resentment of those who led them into hell.

There was only one person in the cathedral this afternoon – a young man lying stretched out, face down, at the base of the altar, gently knocking his forehead on the floor and muttering what sounded like the same frantic prayer over and over again. I don't think he registered my presence.

Were Evelyn Waugh alive and in Africa he could base a sequel to *Black Mischief* on the antics associated with 'the Burundi sanctions'. These date from August 1996, when a bloodless military coup reinstated Pierre Buyoya as President of Burundi. (Not much else is bloodless in present-day Burundi, where the internecine annual death-toll is about 50,000.) Although the Buyoya régime is not recognized by any country, the UN has never ratified the sanctions imposed by neighbouring states, which are themselves among the leading sanctions-busters.

Late each evening, when Butare is abed, one can hear the convoys of petrol tankers and articulated trucks revving up their engines before rumbling off to cross the border. A little earlier, some of the sanctions-busting planes have passed overhead, beginning their descent to Bujumbura ninety miles to the south. They come from all directions – Belgium, Dubai, Angola, the Congo Republic – and are unafraid of over-flying the sanctions-imposing neighbouring states. Some are gigantic Antonov transporters; NGO workers visiting from Bujumbura report the Burundi army was never before so well equipped, and the capital's thriving French restaurants continue to be well supplied with fine wines and the very best of French cheeses and patés. Meanwhile Burundi's main exports, coffee and tea, travel unhindered to Dar or Mombasa.

Black Mischief indeed, but unfunny for Burundi's impoverished Hutu majority and not very funny either for the middle-class urban Tutsi – as Ahmed observed, when we met again this evening at Chez Nous. He is working at present near one of the main smuggling ferry-points and often sees rice, sweet potatoes and manioc being sold cheaply to Rwandans by Burundians desperate for cash with which to buy petrol and other imported goods (mainly imported from Kenya). He occasionally visits Bujumbura and since August has observed the price of those foods more than doubling. 'They could soon have famine,' he said sombrely, 'and they've run out of medical supplies and some seeds and all fertilizers. That's lethal, like in this country 90 per cent are farmers. And guess who's raking in the loot? The Tutsi élite could wash their shirts in champagne! It's always the way with sanctions, I've seen it happen before. For those at the top, prices and profits go up –

up into the stratosphere! I can't get on with the Burundi Tutsi. If the Rwandan lot were the same in the old days, I'm not surprised they ran into trouble.'

At sunset, while returning to my NGO residence, a touching coincidence cheered me. Walking along Butare's pleasantly decrepit main street, I heard shouts of 'Mama Rosa! Mama Rosa!' Turning, I saw a beaming young man, hawking Bukavu mobiles, running towards me – a November returnee. He was full of detailed enquiries about the real 'Mama Rosa' and about Rosa herself, who plainly has made a lasting impression on her Bukavu circle.

Two days hence I should be within sight of Bukavu, looking at No. 19 across the lake. Sandy – my hostess here – is driving down to Cyangugu and will be glad of company on the way. Her NGO has decided to pull its expat team out of that area, for security reasons, and they will need help with their packing up. A dismal occasion for them; they are unanimous and emphatic about wanting to stay on, but the decision cannot be theirs.

Sandy and Serge are a splendid young couple, by far the most effective aid workers I've met in Rwanda. They have a hunch that one faction within the government, known to be eager to get rid of foreign NGOs, may not be too upset by the recent expat murders. Incidentally, the original account of the Spaniards' murders, given in a UN news-sheet, has proved to be a fabrication. Presumably it was circulated to disguise the fact that the RPA guards who shot at the robbers-turned-murderers, as they were escaping with their loot, did not behave very sensibly. Only when the soldiers appeared did the robbers turn back and kill the Spaniards. Why did the UN swallow what was fed to them, without checking?

In Ruhengeri town, last week, an NGO security guard was murdered while on duty. When his young widow, with their first-born on her back, appealed to the NGO for a little financial assistance she was told they couldn't be responsible for any of their staff's dependants. 'How to lose friends and antagonize people,' commented Serge.

Sandy gave me a copy of a report published on 31 January by HRFOR, which has recently become less indifferent to the plight of the survivors. According to the report, Hutu death-squads murdered at least 227 survivors in 1996 and are now threatening many Tutsi in their homes on the more remote hills of Ruhengeri, Gisenyi and Cyangugu prefectures. Several cases of poisoning have been reported – a family's food contaminated and every member dying. The UN is now urging the Rwandan government 'to take measures to protect the survivors from the militia'. This must cause much governmental foaming at the mouth. It reveals the UN at its most crass.

Today government spokesmen are publicizing the unoriginal theory that Fr Picard's killer was one of the recently returned militia. They have announced that after the Spaniards' murders the RPA killed more than eighty people in a 'crackdown' in the forest of Ruhengeri prefecture. 'But did they', wondered Sandy, 'crack down on the right people?'

In Ruhengeri town it is believed that the lone gunman is a Tutsi survivor, well known locally, who lost his mind during the genocide and was released not long ago from a psychiatric ward.

This evening a friend of Serge's called during supper, a tall, slim, dark-skinned young man, with a narrow face, fine features, a rather haughty expression – the very prototype of the colonists' 'superior Hamitic Tutsi'. He told me he was born and grew up in Kinshasa, where his father ran an import business.

I asked, 'Are all your family here now?' – assuming them to have been among the many who hastened home from Zaire when the RPF took over.

'Only my aunt is here,' replied Aloys. 'My parents and three brothers and two sisters were killed in the genocide.' He made that statement almost casually, showing no trace of emotion, as I might say 'I'm flying home on the 15th of March.'

I haven't yet learned how to deal with this situation when I'm taken unawares. I looked at him, the look presumably conveying my reaction, but found myself incapable of speech. To have simply said, 'I'm so very sorry' or 'How awful for you!' would have seemed almost offensively banal. Yet those same words would have sounded natural, adequate, acceptable had his family been killed in an earthquake or air-crash.

Afterwards Serge explained that this family had returned in '91 when Mobutu's rejection by the West adversely affected father's business. Aloys survived because he had gone to Mulindi in March '94 to join the RPA.

5 FEBRUARY

Although Butare experienced more than its share of genocidal horrors, it does now feel less stained and shadowed than Kigali. 'The spirit of place ...' Perhaps that's at work, a tradition of tolerance reasserting itself, exorcizing the evil that took over in '94.

This morning, in the old colonial suburb, I walked along wide tree-lined avenues, their surfaces softened by pine needles. Here large gardens – some given over to maize or beans – surround well-kept bungalows and important-looking villas, a remarkable number occupied by NGOs and various UN or EU agencies. I was searching for Juliette's home, Juliette being a young university lecturer eager to talk to me about Donatilla Mujawimana. Had Sandy not identified her as Tutsi I'd never have guessed; she is among the many whose appearance contradicts the stereotype. As the askari admitted me, she emerged onto the verandah – a plump, short, golden-skinned twenty-five-year-old who inter-braids auburn false hair with her own and wears heavy make-up and long flowing gowns.

Juliette brewed coffee in a large bright kitchen – shared with three other young lecturers – while telling me about herself. (She already knew quite a lot about me, having read my autobiography.) Father was a '59er, a businessman based in Kampala where Juliette was born. Most of the family returned to Kigali in '92, when increasing Ugandan hostility towards the Banyarwanda in general was making things uncomfortable. Juliette, however, remained behind to study economics at Makerere University. In '94 her mother decided to spend Easter with her. 'She arrived on 3 April, very worried, saying things were terrible in Kigali – terrible tension.' On 11 April Juliette's father and two younger brothers were killed. Within the next week her three married siblings, their spouses and five of her eight nephews and nieces were killed. Like Aloys, she stated this in a flat, matter-of-fact voice, looking away from me towards the hibiscus outside the kitchen window. Then suddenly her expression hardened and she spoke through clenched teeth. She hopes the organizers of the genocide will be tracked down, extradited, tried in Rwandan courts and immediately executed, without giving Amnesty or HRFOR or anyone else time to protest. I can see her point.

We took our coffees to the verandah where climbing roses – pink, white, yellow – entwined the pillars and we were overlooking an ex-lawn planted with cabbages and onions.

For two hours Juliette talked. The case of Donatilla Mujawimana is, in a sense, straightforward, but there are extraneous complications from which the outside world can – and must – learn lessons. On 21 April 1994 Donatilla, a poor Hutu peasant married to a Tutsi, was raped and publicly sexually mutilated in Kayenzi commune, Marenga sector, Kayonza cellule in the prefecture of Gitarama. Although thousands of Tutsi women were repeatedly raped and gang-raped – sometimes over a period of weeks – before being killed, this is the only known case of a Hutu woman being raped during the genocide. Donatilla had recently married and moved to Kayenzi commune, and it is assumed her attacker mistook her for a Tutsi – or perhaps didn't care, only wanted revenge for her husband's escape from the *interahamwe*. She remains semi-invalided as a result of the frequent beatings inflicted on her by the rapist while she was confined to a neighbour's house. And her left foot is permanently deformed. She was examined by Dr Maurice Bucagu, a gynaecologist and obstetrician, at his Kigali clinic. He reported:

The left inner labia is the site of a lesion scar of about 2 cm long, situated half way between the clitoris and the fourchette, oblique from top to bottom and from left to right ... The vulva has been scarred by a lesion which would correspond to an incision by a sharp object, for example scissors or a knife ... There is still today a post-traumatic inflammatory oedema of the left ankle.

That was on 9 November 1996, when African Rights arranged a full medical examination for Donatilla. 'Otherwise', said Juliette, 'she could not have afforded it. These are very poor peasants.'

On 20 March 1996 Donatilla, accompanied by her husband Gerard Gatanazi, her stepson Abiyingoma Habyarimana, now aged thirteen, and another witness, Scholastique Nikuze, travelled by taxi to Kigali and in Muhima police station accused Joseph Ruyenzi of rape and sexual mutilation. On the morning of 30 March Ruyenzi was arrested, a file having been completed and presented to the public prosecutor's office and a warrant written out by Gaetan Ntibiringirwa, who observed all the correct procedures. At the time of writing Ruyenzi remains in Kigali Central Prison.

I asked, 'Why was he not accused much sooner?'

Juliette stared at me with something akin to contempt. 'Can you not imagine what an ordeal it was to accuse him? To give such details to a tough bunch of gendarmerie? In Europe you've specially trained policewomen and counsellors and help-lines and so on for rape victims. Here we don't. But our feelings are the same. And the mutilation – can you imagine yourself describing that to those men? She could never have done it without Gerard's support and the evidence of her stepson and witness. For ages Gerard himself was traumatized, by her ordeal and his own while being hunted. He needed time to get to a state where he could accuse. What made it all worse for him – the two families were old friends. Ruyenzi's parents lived close to Gerard's *ruga* and his mother was godmother to Gerard's mother.'

Juliette told me about Joseph Ruyenzi's background; her information was based on personal knowledge, with some of the details provided by a recently published African Rights report on the case. In 1994 Ruyenzi was a teacher, a prefect of studies at a Nyabikenke college, and as such greatly respected by the youth of his home commune, Kayenzi. Both there and in Nyabikenke he had been known since 1990 as a Hutu Power extremist, a political activist who worked closely with senior commune officials, some of whom preceded him to prison – as did two of his brothers and several other relatives. When the genocide started he became one of Kayenzi's militia leaders and was relentless in his pursuit of individual Tutsi who, like Gerard, had eluded the death-squads and were in hiding. One such, Noel Habyarimana, tried to take his family to the 'safety' of the bishopric of Kabgayi. At a road-block his wife and six children were murdered; he escaped by a fluke and took to the bush. Ruyenzi then paid three *interahamwe* for the use of their hunting dogs to track him down but he escaped again, this time thanks to the quick thinking of a Hutu neighbour. In Kayenzi many Hutu hid Tutsi, usually children. To find these, Ruyenzi announced that Caritas, a Christian NGO, was seeking families who had Tutsi 'lodgers' to give them food rations and cash. The gullible Hutu obediently gave lists of their 'lodgers' to those who were allegedly distributing Caritas goodies. At once the militia toured the sheltering *rugas*, killing all the Tutsi including three babies.

I asked another of my silly questions. 'Why did anyone trust Ruyenzi, at that stage?'

'Because of his status,' replied Juliette, impatiently. 'They were very simple people, and he had authority as an educated man, a teacher in an important school, from an influential family.'

As the RPA approached Gitarama, Ruyenzi moved to Cyangugu, returning to his parents' home in September '94. He then went job-hunting in Kigali, where Radio Rwanda employed him in January '95 as a Kinyarwanda news-reader.

'Radio Rwanda is government-owned and -run,' said Juliette. 'It's too easy for killers to get away with it and settle in good jobs in Kigali. Will the Tribunal ever find anyone brave enough to give evidence against Ruyenzi? Donatilla and Gerard have had to move, they daren't stay in Kayenzi. Ruyenzi's family are intimidating everyone who could testify against any of the ones in prison. They're sure they can safely murder witnesses, that's what "the culture of impunity" means. If no one will smash it we can have no justice. I know exactly who killed my family. A lot of us do. But we can't find justice.'

At some stage Ruyenzi had joined the League for the Promotion and Defence of Human Rights in Rwanda (LIPRODHOR), which forms part of the Collective of Human Rights Leagues and Associations (CLADHO). In April '94 the chairman of LIPRODHOR was Innocent Mazimpaka; he, too, has been accused of rape during the genocide and has been defended by both LIPRODHOR and CLADHO.

Within two days of Ruyenzi's arrest Amnesty International had launched a campaign on his behalf, issuing one of its Urgent Action letters in which he was described as a 'journalist' – though a news-reader is not a journalist and previously he had worked only as a teacher. The Amnesty letter referred to 'government victimization of journalists in Rwanda' and urged its members to demand 'information on the charges against Joseph Ruyenzi' and insist that he be 'given access to legal advice'. It suggested that his arrest might be linked to 'attempts to exercise his right to freedom of expression as a journalist'. But neither then nor later did Amnesty produce any evidence that Ruyenzi ever tried to put together or broadcast programmes offensive to the government. And Ruyenzi himself has stated that he sees no link between his arrest and his Radio Rwanda work.

Amnesty International, the world's largest human rights organization, has a well-deserved reputation for helping the helpless by focusing public attention on the misdeeds of oppressive governments. But in this case its Central Africa Team's shameful irresponsibility caused Donatilla – whose name was never even mentioned by Amnesty – much extra grief and hurt. Moreover, Amnesty undermined her credibility within Rwanda, where peasant women have no status and virtually no legal rights and are unlikely to be believed if such an honoured organization is seen to be on the side of the accused. Amnesty's Urgent Action letters are circulated globally, taken seriously by the media and acted upon by countless mini-organizations concerned about human rights. Ruyenzi soon became an international hero/victim, a 'prisoner of conscience'. Letters poured in to the goverment's Office of Information and into President Bizimungu's office from Canada, Japan, Britain, India, Australia, Germany and elsewhere, all pleading for him to be 'fairly treated' and protesting against his 'being abused for distributing information about Rwanda'. One indignant American journalist wrote:

He has committed no crimes. He has been arrested without a charge. He has been sent to Kigali Prison, which already holds four times as many prisoners as it was built to hold. And why is he there? Solely for exercising his right to free speech as a journalist.

I hold no brief for the present Rwandan government; very likely human rights are nowhere near the top of its agenda. That, however, is beside the present point. On 30 March 1996, when Joseph Ruyenzi was arrested, Amnesty knew as much as I did about him, and since it rejected the true explanation for his arrest, given by the Director of the Office of Information, it should have undertaken its own independent investigation of the case. Instead, it continued to run its damaging campaign until 1 July '96, when Ruyenzi was removed from the Urgent Action network. Even then Amnesty failed to admit its error and counteract the misinformation it had spread around the world. Yet on 30 March it had communicated to the Rwandan government that 'unless impunity in Rwanda is brought to an end, human rights abuses are likely to continue'.

Meanwhile Reporters Sans Frontières (RSF), the French organization dedicated to 'preserving press freedom', had also become involved. On 1 April it issued a statement claiming that Ruyenzi had been 'arrested by soldiers from the RPA, reportedly charged with participating in clandestine meetings and there has been no news of his whereabouts since his arrest' – all of which was pernicious nonsense. On the same date RSF wrote to President Bizimungu:

Reporters Sans Frontières is informing you of its extreme concern over the matter of Joseph Ruyenzi and requests you to instantly do everything in your power to identify the place where he is currently detained and, unless he is charged, to obtain his immediate and unconditional release.

Not until mid-May did RSF try to establish the facts. Yet it has its own correspondent in Rwanda, the editor of a Catholic newspaper, Fr André Sibomana – based in Kabgayi, close to Kayenzi. However, unlike Amnesty, RSF did finally acknowledge its mistake in another letter to President Bizimungu (5 July) admitting that an inquiry 'enabled them to collect damning testimonies against Joseph Ruyenzi'.

'The worst thing for Donatilla and Gerard', said Juliette, 'was the local media reaction to all this international fuss. Some articles made it seem like Donatilla was lying so Ruyenzi must be innocent. She's still miserable and humiliated about this. If you could see them now you'd cry. They've lost their home and their land and are living off corners of other people's plots. They'll never get back their physical health. Donatilla suffers terribly with every period though she was normal before – a very strong young woman, walking miles. She'll never again have the strength for farming but she's qualified for nothing else. She can't carry anything on her head, all the massue blows left it so sensitive.' (A massue is a nail-studded wooden club.) 'They used it too on her breasts and feet. Gerard has to do all the farming and fetch the water and most of the work at home. But he was badly beaten before he escaped so he's never well. Donatilla is just waiting for AIDS, like all the other rape victims who survived. The only thing they've left is loving each other very much.'

Juliette then offered me lunch but I seemed to have lost my appetite. As I was leaving she lent me her copy of the African Rights report – *Joseph Ruyenzi: Prisoner without a Conscience.* 'In there', she said, 'you can read all the details I couldn't talk about.'

Walking back to the town centre, I found myself seething with rage. Not about Donatilla's case in particular, but about the general lack of concern among outsiders for such survivors, coupled with their tenderness for prisoners like Ruyenzi. Linked to that is the ease with which exiled (fugitive) genocide organizers deceive those around them – are taken at face value, made welcome, helped by being given good jobs in various African countries and in France, Belgium, Canada, Scandinavia and who knows where else. The case of Innocent Mazimpaka, LIPRODHOR ex-chairman, illustrates this 'denial syndrome' at its most scandalous. In April '94 he was employed by a Dutch NGO, the Netherlands Development Organization (SNV). His younger brother, Fabien Rugwizangoga, was burgomaster of their home commune of Gatare in Cyangugu prefecture. Gatare's Tutsi population on 6 April was 12,263, of whom twenty-one survived. Mazimpaka used SNV vehicles to transport death-squads and grenades and to *drive into* groups of Tutsi by way of showing onlookers how they should be treated. He planned and led the 11 April Parish of Hanika massacre, a quasi-military operation that led to the deaths (usually slow) of between 3500 and 4000 Tutsi who had taken refuge in the parish church. And that was only the start of it ... Why then did SNV continue to employ Mazimpaka, giving him a job in their Benin office? And when he was accused of genocidal crimes why did they try to defend him by distorting the evidence?

What is going on here? And how much of what is going on has to do with the sheer superficiality of the West's concern about an African genocide? Leading to an unwillingness to spend time, energy and money on establishing the truth and punishing the guilty. Also, as Gérard Prunier reminds us, 'Events not seen on a TV screen do not exist in contemporary Western society. And TV coverage of the genocide was not available, given the technical near impossibility of catching killers in the act.' But there must be more to it than that. One can discern complicated reasons for the widespread reluctance, outside Rwanda, to accept that the genocide was organized by those who had all the advantages of education, money, power and the respect of the peasantry. Can the average outsider cope with the horror only by labelling it 'primitive savagery', thus distancing it from 'our world'? It is, apparently, too much for us to stomach that the criminals are those Hutu a visiting foreigner would most comfortably consort with. With that, there goes a shying away from detail. To study, for instance, the not exceptional brutality of Donatilla's rape and mutilation means confronting the sort of pornographically violent behaviour that would have delighted the Marquis de Sade. Perhaps it's natural for most people to shy away from such details.

6 FEBRUARY

At present we are all more tense than we realize. Yesterday afternoon I called in to Sandy's office to fetch a book and my heart gave a little lurch when I saw her face – very pale, her eyes strangely blank. She had just heard by radio that about three hours earlier – it was then 5 p.m. – five HRFOR monitors, travelling in two marked UN vehicles, had been murdered in the Nyungwe forest some forty miles from here. They were a Cambodian, an Englishman and three Rwandans who had spent the previous night in Gitarama and were en route to Cyangugu.

Only when Sandy joined me at sunset, at the end of her ten-hour day, did she explain that Graham Turnbull and Sastra Chim-Chan were friends of hers and Serge's. They had been planning to attend Graham's Kigali engagement party this weekend and to help him and his Ugandan fiancée write out the wedding invitations.

Later, more details came by radio, some too gruesome to be recorded here. One of Sandy's Kigali colleagues was also driving to Cyangugu yesterday, to help the departing team move out, and half an hour after the ambush he came on the scene. The UN vehicles had turned off the main road to visit a commune prison two miles up a dirt track. In the forest they were fired on and surrounded by more than thirty men; there are conflicting reports about whether or not some or all of them wore uniforms. One driver survived, seriously injured but conscious and able to give evidence. Then he died on the plane that took the bodies to Kigali from Cyangugu airstrip. Had he been able to stay in Cyangugu hospital he might have recovered, but he was refused admission; the authorities feared an attack on the building to eliminate him as a witness. Clearly the RPA are considered incapable of protecting a hospital – not very reassuring ... It's assumed the ambush was carefully planned; many in the commune would have known in advance about this HRFOR prison visit, which had to be prearranged with the burgomaster.

Sandy's field director forbade her to drive anywhere today – not that either of us felt like taking that route through the Nyungwe forest. This evening the three evacuees from Cyangugu arrived to stay here overnight. They are in a state of shock, bemused and grief-stricken. The Cyangugu NGO community was small, and Graham and Sastra were close friends of theirs. They spent Christmas together, co-ordinated their days off to do things together, truly enjoyed each other's company. The trio were utterly devastated at the thought of Graham's fiancée arriving in Kigali today, looking forward to the reunion on Saturday. Sastra's wife, too, was looking forward to a reunion; he would have been flying home next week at the end of his Rwandan contract. Heartbreaking – and yet, I thought, what a tiny drop this is in Rwanda's ocean of misery.

The UNHCR have become quite hysterical and seem to be assuming totalitarian powers over the NGOs who work with them; all expats have been ordered to abandon their projects and hole up in Kigali 'until the situation becomes clearer'. Surely this is a tactical error, giving in to whatever faction (a moot point) wishes to rid Rwanda of foreign NGOs.

My new plan is to taxi to Gitarama tomorrow morning, stay the night at another NGO residence, then obediently take refuge in Kigali. At noon today the government broadcast a 'request' to all foreign nationals not to enter the prefectures of Ruhengeri, Gisenyi, Kibuye and Cyangugu, where the RPA are about to embark on a 'crackdown' against ex-FAR and *interahamwe* 'infiltrators'. Bye-bye Bukavu!

GITARAMA, 7 FEBRUARY

This morning Bess, my Gitarama hostess, together with representatives of all other NGOs based here, attended a two-and-a-half-hour security meeting with the prefecture's senior RPA and gendarmerie officers. The expats were assured that they are valued in Gitarama and must stay and will be cherished by the security forces. Bess's residence is to have a military guard from sunset to sunrise, and a strict 7 p.m. curfew has been imposed on all aid workers, expat and Rwandan. This evening Bess's young Egyptian colleague was harshly reprimanded for arriving home eight minutes late. And quite right too; if the Rwandan authorities are expected to take NGO security seriously, then those being protected must be seen to take it equally seriously.

It was also proposed that in future military vehicles should escort NGO vehicles on their tours of the hills. A tricky proposal, threatening to compromise NGO neutrality, given the deep distrust existing between some returnees and the RPA. And perhaps a counter-productive proposal; the RPA is now influenced to an unwholesome extent by fanatically anti-Hutu returnees from Burundi, mostly in the officer class. And many of the recent young conscripts are ill-disciplined Tutsi survivors, who cannot reasonably be expected to operate impartially should events bring about any confrontation with their 'fellow-Banyarwanda'. As Pius said to me in Kigali, 'Our army is not a swarm of angels.' In this country it's impractical for NGOs to work under armed protection; if they don't feel safe on their own, they must go home.

Bess reckons the RPA commanders in each prefecture know when a particular NGO is at risk and will usually provide what protection they can. But my fellow guest, recently evacuated from Ruhengeri, disagrees. In that town she had disquieting experiences at NGO security conferences; it seemed the local RPA viewed expats as a nuisance, rather than as people who should be encouraged to stay around by being given more protection than the rest of the population.

Going walkabout this morning, a rough track took me steeply up from Gitarama's uninspiring colonial town centre towards a large hilltop market. En route I came upon a busy district of old arcaded shops, stocking no more than the bare essentials, with tailors of both sexes busy on the verandahs and hawkers sitting beside their mountains of beans or flour, displayed by the wayside on UN tarpaulins.

Here an elderly barefooted woman, small and thin and sharp-featured, suddenly rushed towards me, laughing shrilly, and slapped me very hard on the back. When I extended a hand she seized my forearms, stared intently into my eyes – a crazed, unblinking stare – then hugged me with manic strength, pinning my right arm to my side, and wouldn't let go. Her face was anguished, her speech a hysterical babbling. The stench from her ragged shift and ravelling cardigan was overpowering. Flinging her head back she began to howl and pant, tightening her grip on me until I feared for my ribs. All around us, everyone stopped everything to stare and laugh. With my free hand I gently stroked her forehead and her tangled, dirty hair: there was nothing to be said, even if we had shared a language. Gradually she calmed down, released me – then flung herself on the ground and began to sob silently. As I walked on, the spectators, still laughing, broke into excited comment on the incident. I felt, and still feel, beyond commenting. Except to note the odd fact that an incident of this nature could stimulate among Rwandans something approaching vivacity.

Later I was told Alphonsine's story, well known in Gitarama. A Hutu married to a Tutsi, she saw her own brothers – three of them – hacking her husband to death. Her eight children, aged from three to twenty-five, were killed. This was not a mass slaughter; three times within a month the *interahamwe* – always including her brothers – came to her *ruga* seeking her hidden children. She pleaded with her brothers at least to spare their three-year-old nephew but they beheaded him in her presence. A resourceful woman, she had successfully smuggled two grandchildren (a baby and a toddler) to a distant friend's *ruga*, after her husband was killed but before their mother's death. (Even amidst the prevailing terror, this was an unusual ploy – to separate a nursing baby from its mother.) At the end of May, the doctor who was among the local genocide organizers called a public meeting and announced that order had been restored, the *interahamwe* disbanded and everyone could come out of hiding. Next day, when Alphonsine fetched her grandchildren from their refuge, they were murdered at a roadblock – as were all the other Tutsi who had believed the doctor. She tried to hang herself but failed. Then she went mad.

KIGALI, 8 FEBRUARY

We left early for Kigali; Bess and her local staff had to attend a 9 a.m. security conference called by their own NGO. On Monday they must attend a general conference for all NGOs that shelter under the UNHCR umbrella; they are to be given 'personal protection' advice by a security expert from the British Embassy. How much of all this panic is inspired by a UN overreaction? How real is the risk to any individual, percentage-wise? Or is that a silly question? This morning Bess quoted a veteran aid worker of her acquaintance whose motto was: 'Unless engaged in saving lives, don't risk your own' – which makes sense. Certainly few lives are being saved in Rwanda by the present activities of all those NGOs and EU and UN agencies, now numbering 180.

Soon after the Spaniards' murders the government issued a soothing statement: 'Goodwill prevails between Rwandan officials and NGO workers despite the co-ordination problems, which are to be expected when there are so many organizations doing the same work. Those problems are not the fault of the individuals at the various NGOs, but of their respective headquarters which sent them out on overlapping mandates.'

That statement also criticized the new UNHCR refugee integration plan. 'It turned out that the "plan" was a fund-raising tool sent only to donors.' No wonder people question UNHCR statistics, such as the totally implausible claim made on 24 January that 'Hundreds of thousands of Rwandan refugees and displaced persons are trapped within Eastern Zaire.'

On the way to Kigali our driver told us, 'Within a few days they'd identified the killers of the Spaniards. Three ex-FAR soldiers – and they'd a friend, a local security guard, who let them into the Medicos del Mundo compound. Two of them soon died in custody. It's the quickest way to deal with people like that.'

10

A DILEMMA WITH
MANY HORNS

Towards the end of World War II Winston Churchill referred to it
as 'a crime that has no name'. Soon after, it was given a name by
Raphaël Lemkin in his book *Axis Rule in Occupied Europe*
(1944). Lemkin combined the Greek 'genos' (tribe or race) and
the Latin 'cide' and declared that 'genocide' means 'the destruction of a nation or of an ethnic group'. Its aim is the complete
(never selective) extermination of a group, each victim being killed
simply because she or he belongs to that group. It requires meticu-
lous organization and it has to be a collective act, for reasons both
practical and psychological. In Alain Destexhe's words, 'The
specificity of genocide does not arise from the extent of the
killings, nor their savagery or resulting infamy, but solely from the
intention: the destruction of a group.'

Our century has endured three genocides: the Turks against the
Armenians in 1915, the Nazis and their allies against the Jews, and
the Hutu extremists against the Tutsi. In 1948 the UN General
Assembly approved the Convention on the Prevention and Punishment of the Crime of Genocide. Article I states: 'The Contracting
Parties confirm that genocide, whether committed in time of peace
or in time of war, is a crime under international law which they
undertake to prevent and to punish.' This explains why the US
government and the UN at first refused to recognize as genocide
what was going on in Rwanda; had they done so they would have
been obliged to intervene. Instead, the 'international community'
drove its humanitarian machine onto the scene after the event –

with a shameless fanfare of publicity trumpets.

The UN's military failure in Rwanda has had a sequel in the failure, to date, of its judicial intervention, the International Criminal Tribunal for Rwanda, established on 8 November 1994 by Security Council Resolution 955 and based in Arusha, Tanzania. The ICTR's mandate confines it to judging events (physical acts) that took place in Rwanda during 1994 and prevents it from investigating either the extensive, long-term preparations and propaganda campaigns that preceded the massacres or the collusion with *génocidaires* that took place outside Rwanda after 1994. These restrictions infuriate the Rwandan government (and others) because their genesis is so obvious. They serve to protect from the ICTR spotlight both the French government's collaboration with the *génocidaires* and the Security Council's lethal passivity. Among those who thirst for justice to be seen to be done, the ICTR arouses both derision and anger. In June '95 its six judges were appointed for a four-year term, and its budget for '96 was US$36 million – yet so far it has indicted only twenty-one people, thirteen of whom are in detention while the others remain at liberty. It complains of being understaffed, having scant resources (!) and being 'unsuitably based' because Arusha has 'poor communications and complicated logistics'. A recent report on the ICTR by the UN Office of Internal Oversight Services (mark the UN's bureaucratic fecundity) described it as 'slow and ineffective' – a laughable understatement. Even by UN standards, its gross incompetence and reeking corruption are breathtaking. Galvanized by this report, Kofi Annan, the Secretary-General, sacked two senior officials, Mr Honoré Rakotomanana, Deputy Prosecutor, and Mr Andronico Adede, Registrar. In September '96 the outgoing Prosecutor, Judge Richard Goldstone of South Africa, remarked that 'bureaucratic tussles' were among the Tribunal's main problems, as recruitment had to be carried out through the UN. Also, 'sufficiently qualified staff' were in general unwilling to work either in Arusha or in Kigali, where the Prosecutor has his main office.

Rwanda's jails and detention centres by now hold some 95,000 people, and daily the numbers increase as 'accused' returnees are arrested. On 30 August 1996 the Organic Law was promulgated in Kigali to deal with crimes committed between 1 October 1990 and 31 December 1994. It divides those accused of genocide and crimes against humanity into four categories:

1 The national organizers and those found guilty of 'incitement to hatred'
2 The local leaders, who arranged the distribution of weapons and grenades and transported the killer squads around the hills
3 Those who killed under duress, or caused serious physical injury
4 Those who looted, destroyed property, stole cattle – but did not kill

Recently, the crimes of rape and sexual torture have been moved from (3) to (1) in response to pressure from women's groups.

This categorizing represents a frantic effort to deal fairly with an evil minority (the genocidal leaders) and a credulous majority (their followers). Given approximately 800,000 victims, a figure not disputed, it has been estimated that there must be at least 80,000 killers, assuming ten murders each to be a reasonable average and including the few maverick Tutsi whose ferocity has become legendary, so keen were they to flaunt their loyalty to the MRND. (The relevance of this macabre estimate escapes me – and how does one arrive at 'a reasonable average' in such a ghastly context?) However, whether the killers number 60,000 or 100,000, they are too numerous to be dealt with in the normal way as 'murderers'. The abnormality of genocide extends beyond the deeds to judicial procedures and punishments. Another of the ICTR's perceived flaws is its inability to hand down death sentences. Of those awaiting trial here in Rwanda, 2000 or so are in Category 1, for whom the death sentence will be mandatory if they are found guilty.

Today I was shown an Amnesty International Urgent Action circular, dated 3 January 1997, requesting Amnesty supporters to 'express deep concern about the sentencing to death of Deogratias Bizimana (a nurse) and Egide Gatanazi (a commune official) after an unfair trial in the Kibungo High Court which lasted only about four hours on 27 December '96'. The circular continued:

The defendants had no access to legal council either before or during their trial. They were not given adequate time to prepare their defence. They were not allowed to summon witnesses for their defence or to cross-examine prosecution witnesses. It has been reported they were booed and prosecutors applauded during the trial, without any intervention by the presiding judge ... Most of Rwanda's judicial officials, including prosecutors and judges, have received only up to four months training. The impartiality and independence of many of the judicial officials is questionable, following statements by some judicial and government officials that defendants should not request legal counsel ... There are only sixteen defence lawyers currently practising in Rwanda ... Please appeal to the authorities to take all measures necessary to ensure that all trials taking place in Rwanda conform to international standards of fairness as required by international human rights treaties to which Rwanda is a party, including the International Covenant on Civil and Political Rights and the African Charter on Human and Peoples' Rights.

Reading this unrealistic rubbish, I felt angry. Demands such as Amnesty's are, in effect, attempts to protect genocidal criminals from the only form of justice (rough) now available in Rwanda. And the criminals are quick to seize on gullible allies and use their misplaced concern to the full.

What right do outsiders have to meddle thus? Neither Amnesty nor the UN nor any other branch of the international community can claim to be in the business of consistently upholding international law (as distinct from endlessly mouthing platitudes about democracy, justice and human rights); otherwise the genocide would not have happened. The UN had the right man (General Dallaire) in the right place at the right time. But they chose not to use him.

A few days ago Gerald Gahima of the Rwandan Ministry of Justice pointed out that no judicial system existed after the genocide. All those qualified to operate it had either been killed or fled into exile. He quoted somebody's bizarre calculation: to provide fair trials (or indeed any trials) for the numbers now in jail would take more than two centuries. Mr Gahima is adamant that all Category 1 prisoners must be tried but he hopes many others will avail of the 'Confession and Guilty Plea' procedure, provided for in the Organic Law; this guarantees reduced penalties in return for confessions. Category 1 defendants can also confess and plead guilty, and though the death sentence is mandatory they have a right to appeal within fifteen days. Many believe that this mandatory death sentence with a right to appeal constitutes a fudge, that in the end no one will be executed. According to the Organic Law's introduction, 'The exceptional situation in the country requires the adoption of specially adapted measures to satisfy the need for justice of the people of Rwanda.' Yet the first tribunal court did not sit until 27 December 1996 and to date only twelve cases have been tried, with eleven Category 1 defendants given death sentences and one Category 2 defendant given life imprisonment. For the mainly Tutsi government, and the newly established judiciary, and the Tutsi survivors, and the killers themselves and their communities, the post-genocide administration of justice presents a dilemma with many sharp horns – ethical, emotional, psychological, political, economic. Maybe a fudge is inevitable, though pregnant with peril.

10 FEBRUARY

The Mille Collines hotel has one thing in its favour: it is easy to find, on its shrubby city-centre hilltop. Today I braved its nastiness for the third time in search of an elusive Irish friend. At reception the usual queue, long and restive, was being dealt with by one smartly uniformed man, all his movements exaggeratedly slow. One feels his only pleasure in life is thus to torture impatient *muzungus*. Today, as before, he claimed never to have heard of my rather famous friend and his equally famous TV crew.

Hoping that Fergal might appear by chance, I sat in the middle of the vast foyer. Here the furniture is designed to prevent nonspending drop-ins from relaxing for a few hours; uncomfortable little stools with low backs accompany round metal tables too small to write on, their plastic tops feigning wood. Towering jungle plants occupy every corner; elsewhere are ferns, orchids, minipalms and weirdly contorted bushes that seem to be attempting some painful acrobatic feat. Gigantic illuminated advertisements for Sabena Airways decorate the walls; Sabena and the state are coowners of this hotel, originally built as a tourist trap. The golden ceiling has built-in lighting, the square pillars are mirrored, the souvenir shops expensive and second-rate. *Muzungus* mill around, their expressions anxious or ill-tempered or both. Most belong to an obvious category: UN, media, corporate. A few are indefinable, looking very rich and vaguely sinister. (Arms dealers? At present Kigali is their favourite Central African rendezvous.) It was not long after noon, yet elegant young women of all races and mixtures of races were prowling to and fro, the Africans usually the most elegant. The Mille Collines is Kigali's main expat brothel where business has not – I'm reliably informed – been noticeably affected by AIDS but condom sales are off the scale. It's odd seeing no tourists in a hotel of this type.

An Israeli journalist, waiting for his photographer, talked to me about failed peace processes. Then I became aware of a youngish man sitting at a nearby table, listening to our conversation. When I was alone he introduced himself: Melchior, who 'returned' from Uganda in August '94 to work for a small NGO devoted to Oldies. His wife ('she has a good UNICEF job') still lives in Kampala with their twelve-year-old daughter. 'Some old people', said Melchior, 'suffer most of all, seeing children and grandchildren dead. That makes their life meaningless, some do kill themselves.' I thought of Alphonsine ...

The Oldies' aid agency suddenly ran out of money, a not uncommon occurrence among the smaller NGOs. During some much-televised major emergency they can collect what seems like a lot of cash but too often they lack the skill to manage it prudently. 'So our old people had to say goodbye to their foreign friends, very quickly, and me and my colleagues – we've no more jobs. It's not good, everybody thinks aid workers have plenty all the time and we trust them, feel safe with them. Those old people got a bad shock, seeing this is not true. Now I get angry, seeing Health Department men driving round in the vehicle I used to drive. It's wrong how NGOs leaving must give all imported property to the state. As presents – big presents! Vehicles, computers, copiers, fax machines, filing cabinets, desks, cameras – everything not a personal possession!'

Melchior begged me to try to find him a job in Rwanda – or, better still, in Ireland. (This explains his frequenting the Mille Collines.) He showed me his ID card – 'You take my details.' Now he looks shockingly unlike the chubby man in the photograph; on first seeing him, his extreme thinness worried me. It could be hunger but I fear it's AIDS; this might explain his not rejoining his family on losing his job.

Having discovered my profession, Melchior eagerly suggested our collaborating on a book about Oldies and the genocide; he would act as my interpreter and guide. This was one of those pathetic plans so often dreamed up by Africa's educated jobless when they meet a writer. He wants to work on such a book himself but has no tape recorder or camera so how could he? Did I know anybody who might lend him those aids to authorship? I pointed out that both are unnecessary – in fact counter-productive. Then I gave up on Fergal and invited Melchior to lunch with me. As nobody in their right mind buys anything in the Mille Collines we strolled down to the Restaurant Metropole on the Rue du Travail.

This is a large, dimly lit, agreeably no-nonsense eating-place: bare wooden floor, bare wooden tables and benches, a choice of good plain food at reasonable prices – chicken, beef, goat, fish, potatoes, matoke, rice, beans. Curious glances followed the expat to a table at the back, as far as possible from the ghetto-blaster on the bar counter. Melchior chose matoke, goat and beans but couldn't finish his meal. Apologetically he explained, 'I'm not used to so much food at one time.'

Two middle-aged men in a corner had smiled a greeting as we arrived. 'They're Big Men,' said Melchior *sotto voce*. 'The tall one, he's Mr S——, the tribunal judge for his prefecture. The small thin one is an editor, very influential, teaching RPF ideas for our future.' When I asked, 'Are they Tutsi?' Melchior laughed. 'You shouldn't say that, we're all Banyarwanda!' It pleased me to see Big Men eating in the Restaurant Metropole. I said as much to Melchior who remarked, 'The best of our new leaders are poor because honest.' Soon after, the Big Men introduced themselves, using the novelty of my mini-cigars as an excuse. Both speak English – not fluently, but Melchior helped out. At first the conversation centred on me and the editor suggested an article, to be translated into Kinyarwanda, about why neighbours kill each other in Northern Ireland. Politely I declined this commission. Mr S——

nodded approvingly and observed, 'Too complicated for newspapers.'

To think of Mr S—— as a typical tribunal judge would be comforting but probably not very realistic. He impressed me as a man who is kind, imaginative, intelligent, with a dry sense of humour which must help to keep him sane despite his present job. Referring to the hideously overcrowded jails, now attracting so much foreign criticism, he reminded me that it was part of the *génocidaires*' overall plan to implicate the maximum number of Hutu. In many communes the role of the FAR soldiers was to stand by with their guns, supervising the use of machetes, massues and spears. When fragmentation grenades were thrown into crowded buildings not everyone died instantly; hundreds – sometimes thousands – had to be finished off with 'rural weapons', often on the following day. And it was usual for the organizers to arrange relays of killing teams, thus ensuring that no male in a commune could plead innocence.

In practice, said Mr S——, the Organic Law's categorizing makes life no easier for judges like himself who are genuinely striving to be impartial. It's impossible to prove, given such a welter of blood and fear and hate, that one peasant was acting under duress while another was enjoying himself. As for the commune officials, there is ample evidence that a number participated in the slaughtering with the greatest reluctance. Yet when compelled at gunpoint to 'do their duty' and put their people 'to work', some of those men became the most implacable hunters of Tutsi. This does not surprise Mr S——. He believes that having had to anaesthetize their consciences they literally went mad and sought to become 'champion killers' in an insane attempt to justify to themselves their overcoming of that initial reluctance. But how to deal with such people when they are standing in front of you, being judged? Not seen as abstract component parts of a genocidal machine but as individual human beings … Leaving aside the organizers, who can know how culpable any killer on the hills really was? 'That', said Mr S——, 'is between a man and his God.'

Recalling the two unbloodied communes, I asked, 'If those burgomasters could defy the organizers so successfully, why didn't others do likewise?'

Mr S—— had a plausible answer, but one that sidestepped my question. Two defiant men, he said, could be ignored because 'the work' was going so well elsewhere. A more widespread defiance would merely have altered the management of the genocide, causing it to become more 'military' – as happened to an extent in Butare prefecture – without reducing the death-rate.

I asked then how often uncomplicated cases come up, like the beheading of Alphonsine's three-year-old son. One man murdered that child in the presence of witnesses who have survived. If he were to be accused, and the witnesses were brave enough to give evidence, would that not be a straightforward case? Shouldn't he immediately be sentenced to, at least, life imprisonment?

Wearily Mr S—— explained that there are, as he sees it, no uncomplicated cases. What was that man's mind-set when he murdered? Probably he had been conditioned for years, through RMC broadcasts and otherwise, to regard as a mistake the sparing of infants and children during the earlier pogroms because so many of those spared became RPA soldiers. Therefore Rwanda's 'final solution' required the killing of all Tutsi males. (Some girl children were allowed to live; by marrying Hutu they would cease to be Tutsi.) To us this mind-set is incomprehensible. We cannot come to terms with its hideous, spurious logic, with an inhumanity totally negating everything that sustains normal societies, whatever their state of 'development'. Ever since July '94 academic outsiders have been busy analysing the genocide, holding conferences to consider it, writing papers to explain it, being intensely cerebral about it. Mr S—— commends those intellectual exertions but admits they are of little help to him as he tries to assess the culpability of the accused individuals standing before him.

The tribunals' hearings are open to the public and Mr S—— has invited me to observe him in action 'when the security situation improves'. But when will that be?

Usually I choose to travel in peaceful places; never before has a security problem hampered me. And being confined to a tense NGO community in a subcutaneously hostile city is undeniably infecting me with expat unease. Which is silly – but proof that most humans are herd animals, even if they like to think of themselves as sturdy individualists. Yes, aid workers do by now have some reason for unease. However, were I to go on my merry way across the hills it's unlikely any Rwandan would mistake me for NGO staff, a species well known for its aversion to walking. Be all that as it may, the decisive factor has to be John Walton's conviction that I should remain in Kigali, not even venturing to other prefectures by minibus. His letter of invitation obtained me my Rwandan visa and it would be unfair to put him in the position of having to worry about me – or, if the worst happened, feel guilty about me.

Each morning one wakens wondering what the day's horror will be. Last Sunday there was the *matatu* massacre, next day the bomb in the bus-station – luckily noticed and defused in time – and today in Kibungo an evangelical NGO's compound was fired on and looted.

Sunday's *matatu* ambush has shaken Rwandans as expat murders do not. Two vehicles, travelling in convoy from Gisenyi, were held up ten miles outside Kigali, where the descent from the high plateau begins, and the passengers ordered out – Tutsi this side, Hutu that side ... There has been no coherent report of exactly what happened next, but eleven Tutsi (some say thirteen) were shot dead and of those who tried to run away (both Tutsi and Hutu) twenty-six (or twenty-eight) are now seriously injured in hospital. Given the crucial significance of roadblocks and way-side mass-murders during the genocide, this ambush has put the hairs up on the backs of many necks. The killers (number unspecified) wore military uniforms but that surprises no one. Ex-FAR 'refugees' held on to their uniforms for use on Special Occasions.

I have recently been befriended by two mixed (Tutsi and European) couples with small children, and in both families the anxiety level has risen perceptibly since Sunday. Every room in each house is being 'alarm-buttoned', with a ten-minute response time guaranteed. It would, however, take less than ten minutes to kill and escape. The Tutsi partners are, physically, very obviously Tutsi. In one case the survivor husband knows who macheted his parents, but the Hutu witnesses, though willing at the time to identify the two men, are afraid, with good reason, to give evidence in public.

Jason often sees those killers around Kigali – for survivors a profoundly disturbing though quite usual experience.

Mixed marriages are much commoner in the NGO world than they were a generation ago. Cynics attribute this to AIDS, some expat men having abandoned the happy-go-fucky lifestyle and some African women now shrewdly insisting on marriage, refusing to be monogamous mistresses jettisoned when the male moves on. Yet many relationships remain recklessly casual; several of my young UN acquaintances have live-in partners (usually lissom Tutsi lasses) and no one pretends these alliances are other than temporary.

11 FEBRUARY

What does Kigali offer the likes of me, by way of diversion? Walking is the answer, this idiosyncratic capital being in fact a series of villages. Daily I roam over the hills, following rough tracks through semi-rural districts rich in bird-life and overlooking wide valleys – part bushy, part cultivated (maize), part papyrus swamp. Here the traffic fumes and noises are far away – far below, on the dual carriageways. Between small cellules, on ledges bulldozed out of steep slopes, stand numerous palatial new villas – many already occupied, others being built. All are well guarded, some by three armed men if the high surrounding walls have not yet been completed. Post-genocide Kigali is awash with money, the torrent of aid dollars augmented by the lavish spending of rich Tutsi returnees.

Long walks engender thirst and to reach my favourite city-centre 'pub' I cross a valley, then zig-zag upwards on narrow footpaths that wriggle through a slummy area of one-roomed shacks. Nowadays the Addis bar is subdued, suffering from a UN diktat forbidding aid workers to frequent any open-air bar, restaurant or café into which some passer-by might fling a grenade or two. This afternoon I was alone with my Primus until a gloomy young Ethiopian appeared. He has been working here for a year and complained bitterly that every fifteen days he and his compatriots must renew their visas at a cost of US$30. He has a theory that most Tutsi hate *muzungus* because they let the genocide happen. And most Hutu, he reckons, hate Ethiopians because MRND propaganda, imitating the colonial variety, convinced them that the Tutsi are of Ethiopian descent. I was glad when Pius arrived to deliver me from all this negativity, not that he was in a very positive mood today. Since the *matatu* ambush his mother has been begging him to return to Uganda – 'But I can't run away, I have my crusade here and the worse things get the more it's needed. Those militia, they're sure of support in hard-line areas – where the RPA have gone to crack down on them. And maybe all over the country they can stir things up. They're so clever at managing simple people's minds, with talk of Tutsi domination again. What we most fear is a Burundi-type situation developing – not formal war but regular small massacres. The expats are all in a heap now but for us this increased violence is much more frightening. They can up and run, like they always do, when the heat comes on.'

By now I feel I know Pius well enough to ask awkward questions. While a 'madame in a vehicle' I met five burgomasters and all were Tutsi: three returnees from Zaire or Uganda and two survivors. The latter expressed some opinions that made it hard to imagine them being genuinely acceptable to the ordinary Hutu folk of their commune. However, all five are reputed to be efficient administrators. Sometimes one's mind is invaded by thoughts so politically incorrect that it's difficult to articulate them. But I bravely asked Pius, 'When it comes to running the show, is it possible the Tutsi in general have something the Hutu in general lack? Could this be why 15 per cent were able to rule 85 per cent for centuries?'

Pius smiled, for the first time today. 'You look embarrassed,' he said. 'And the short answer is – I don't know. But I think it unlikely. I do know it's pointless looking back to colonial or precolonial times, in this context. Under our new RPF government the Banyarwanda have their first chance ever to live together as equals, having the same educational and economic opportunities. After a generation of fair competition we'll have the answer to your question.'

I took a deep breath and asked the really awkward question. 'How equal will equal be? The RPF is, essentially, Tutsi. It proclaims a Banyarwanda ideology and perhaps people like Paul Kagame are true believers. But how keen are most Tutsi returnees on power-sharing with the majority? Given their memories of pogroms and genocide – and a built-in superiority complex?'

'The Tutsi peasants had no superiority complex,' retorted Pius sharply. 'They shared poverty with the Hutu on the hills.'

'But now most Tutsi peasants are dead,' I said – feeling as I spoke a little wave of physical nausea. (Rwanda affects one like that.) 'And many of the 400,000 Tutsi returnees are educated and fairly well-off – some very well educated and rich. They're in a position to try to reassert themselves as a dominant minority. Thousands of the Hutu leadership class were either moderates and killed or extremists and killers – now exiles. So there's a big gap. And plenty of Tutsi to fill it. How much influence does the Museveni-inspired wing of the RPF have over the average Tutsi returnee?'

Pius smiled again – rather a forced smile this time. 'You ask too many questions too soon. We must wait and see.' He looked at his watch and stood up – 'See you tomorrow!'

12 FEBRUARY

This morning, an odd incident – more saddening than frightening. As I walked down a track away from the motor road – bananas on my left, maize on my right – three young men were coming towards me. I noted their faces hardening on seeing the *muzungu* but that's nothing new in Kigali. We passed each other and all three addressed me jeeringly in Kinyarwanda. I ignored them, then one man turned back and pushed me into the grassy ditch on my left. It wasn't a very vigorous push; I don't believe he intended me to topple over. But his companions applauded him – relished seeing the *muzungu* humiliated, scrambling out of a quite deep ditch with some difficulty. I can't imagine this sort of harassment happening anywhere else in Africa. Although a very unlucky elderly woman might be murdered, robbed or raped in some urban shanty-town, an incident involving jeering and jostling is unthinkable. Only in Rwanda is being a mama no protection. Expats are fair game – legitimate targets.

By now the air of Kigali is dense – sometimes foetid – with rumour. Rwandans and expats are agreed that it is peculiarly unnerving that the facts about various incidents remain so elusive.

Some say the HRFOR ambush was meant for a government delegation, also expected that afternoon in the commune. But this is unconvincing; UN vehicles are distinctive and Graham and Sastra could hardly be mistaken for Rwandans. However, if Big Men from Kigali were expected in that dangerous area at that time, why were there no RPA around? Or were there? Some people are convinced that the monitors were killed by the RPA who reportedly ran amok in that commune last month, murdering several recently returned Hutu women because they couldn't find their 'accused' husbands. Allegedly the burgomaster had requested HRFOR to investigate, specifying that he wanted Sastra Chim-Chan to be one of the team. It seems the Cambodian was known for his courageous reports – no diplomatic vagueness or sweet euphemisms or tactful omissions. (But there is no record of effective action being stimulated by any HRFOR report.)

The ambiguity surrounding the current violence is itself destabilizing. One knows, in Northern Ireland or Sri Lanka or Kashmir or Israel, why and how and by whom the battle-lines are drawn. Not so in the new Rwanda. Maybe the monitors were murdered by the *interahamwe*, maybe by a faction of the RPA, maybe by local officials resentful of outsiders probing their application of rough justice to real or suspected genocide killers. The government's silence fertilizes wild theories and scare stories – which can hatch out into powerful myths believed in by many and of use to anyone with an interest in keeping the pot of trouble on the boil.

Today one NGO field director remarked plaintively, 'If only we had more accurate information it would be easier to make rational decisions about where we go – or don't go – next.' He acknowledged that when the Hutu militia returned behind the shield of the refugees the foreign community should have foreseen 'destabilization' and planned accordingly.

As usual, the Americans are the most twitchy expats. They recall, shudderingly, last year's threat from a Nairobi-based Hutu Power group known as Palir (People in Arms to Liberate Rwanda). In June '96 Palir issued a communiqué urging all Hutu 'to stand up and fight the vampires who have taken hold of our country. To start off our combat on the right foot, we must attack every person or entity which helps in the consolidation of the power of the RPF.' Palir offers rewards to anyone who kills Americans resident in Rwanda; the sums are comparatively modest, by international standards: US$1500 for the assassination of the Ambassador, $1000 for any other US citizen.

The latest Palir communiqué, dated 23 January, threatens all expats. The Internal Resistance Front (FRI) of Palir makes the following announcement:

Its objectives are strictly military and target only positions of the army of occupation. At the same time, the FRI declines all responsibility for the injuries which may be sustained by those who work and live with the soldiers of that army. It is astonishing that expatriates calling themselves humanitarians live with the army of occupation where they are used as human shields. Since Palir is determined to track down every soldier wherever he may be, we can only counsel expatriates to keep their distance.

Since 1995 the US government has been an energetic and vocal supporter of the RPF régime – to the fury of France, which sees its linguistic empire dwindling as Rwanda is lured by dollars and sweet words into the anglophone camp. Complaining noises still come at intervals from the Quai d'Orsay: 'Why is America supporting a régime that took power by force, is dominated by a minority and uninterested in democracy?' Everyone knows the answer. Rwanda is America's newest puppet, fitting neatly into that row of other recently acquired puppets – Uganda, Ethiopia, Eritrea – who in November '96 were presented by the US with $20 million worth of military equipment to enable them 'to contain Islamist Sudan'.

13 FEBRUARY

Several NGO directors have recently arrived in Kigali 'to look at the security situation on the ground'. This afternoon I had a robust argument with one such character. When questioned about his agency's prolonged support for the refugee camps in Zaire his answers were those of a professional politician. Smoothly he pointed out that an NGO's duty is to be 'neutral', to provide succour all round. (An attitude praised in a recent UNESCO bulletin dealing with human rights: 'Political considerations must not be allowed to tarnish humanitarian actions in any way.') Less smoothly, I pointed out that this neutrality, post-genocide, amounted to an evasion of what had been going on in Rwanda. Genocide is not war, it is a crime under international law and the humanitarians' amoral stance was the last thing Rwanda needed. Now the RPF's struggle to establish some semblance of normality is being thwarted by those murderous militia who were among the beneficiaries of 'neutral' aid.

'But', protested the director, 'our job is to help all in need. It's somebody else's job to sort out the guilty from the innocent. And what happens if we hang back waiting for that to be done? What happens to all the kids? In some camps a thousand babies and more were born every month – no one can say they're guilty!'

Fair enough. In this case, the only 'somebody else' with the necessary authority was the UN, which lacked the will to intervene. No wonder the NGOs and the UN agencies do not form a mutual admiration society.

Humanitarianism has become big business, a useful safety-valve for a Rich World offering fewer and fewer well-paid jobs. Yes, there must always be an emergency humanitarian machine oiled and ready to go when disaster strikes: but 'emergencies' do not occupy most aid workers. With certain honourable and well-known exceptions, aid agencies concentrate on the effects of poverty while ignoring (often remaining unaware of) the political causes. They rally round the victims of corporate greed, people hungry and/or ill because of some cataclysmic drop in the price of a commodity (copper, coffee, cocoa or whatever), or as a result of communal pesticide poisoning or artificially created drought. Yet what such situations most urgently require are not palliative and too often inappropriate 'development projects' but loud political protests against GATT, the WTO's machinations and those SAPs so callously imposed on the poorest countries by the World Bank/IMF. However, 'charitable organizations' are forbidden to meddle in or even comment on matters political. This exposes them to many corporate viruses, and the symptoms of their consequent debilitation are plain to be seen. Ferocious funding wars lead to all manner of dirty tricks, dishonest advertising and exaggerations of the extent of a 'human tragedy'. And each strives to be always in the foreground, having its logo seen here, there and everywhere, getting most attention whenever the media or some visiting dignitary takes an interest in its area of operations. On balance, a sordid scene.

Thirty-three years ago, in India, I was shocked to observe how quickly fund-raising rivalries on the international stage percolate down to local scenes of action. There they can do much damage, both to personal relationships between NGO teams and to the cost-effectiveness of their obdurately non-co-operative endeavours. Even in the sixties, far too many NGOs cluttered the world; more than 200 were working with 85,000 Tibetan refugees. Already the waste of resources was scandalous. By now it verges on the criminal – such a duplication of offices, equipment, vehicles, staff, residences. And the high Kigali rents, paid in dollars to local landlords already affluent, are enraging Rwandans who do not earn dollars. The employing of house-servants, guards, gardeners and drivers spreads wealth – it is argued – throughout the community. But – it is counter-argued – the comparatively high wages paid by expats set a standard unrelated to the national economy and are therefore a source of future discontent and dissension.

Three years ago, in Mozambique, I first noticed how many new roles are taken on by the bloated aid industry when a country has disintegrated under the pressure of war and related miseries. This change is neatly summed up in an African Rights Discussion Paper, *Humanitarianism Unbound?*

In countries like Somalia and Mozambique, relief agencies play a crucial role in setting the international agenda. They may be the chief providers of public welfare, among the main sources of salaried employment and commercial contracting, but even more significantly they act as news agencies and diplomats. In short, relief agencies are expanding into a void left by the contracting power of host governments and the declining political interest of Western powers. But it is a void they cannot fill.

To an extent, this applies now in Rwanda, which may partly explain the government's lack of affection for NGOs.

Apart from the 'tracing programme', my glimpses of the various aid agencies' projects on the hills did not impress me. The motives and/or competence of many of the people who run NGOs from Rich World head offices need careful scrutiny but rarely get it.

When criticized, it is in the interests of all these agencies, as component parts of the same machine, to cover up for each other. Nor is criticism always welcome from field-workers who might venture to suggest, when they report to their head offices, that such-and-such is not the best way to achieve so-and-so. Some young people who arrived here full of enthusiasm were frustrated to find themselves in charge of costly but blatantly ineffectual projects; NGO workers are constrained, like the UN, by their mandates. Most of the local staffs are also admirable (certainly all my minders were) but in many cases are being insidiously corrupted by the futility of their well-paid jobs. To earn so much for doing so little is not good for anyone's morale.

Aid agencies that successfully fund-raised when Rwanda was the humanitarian flavour of the month can find themselves with earmarked money – not to be spent elsewhere – but without any idea how to use it sensibly. Then hare-brained projects are hastily devised, like giving goats to parentless families and paying for the construction of individual houses on scattered hills. Given the vulnerability of orphans to predatory neighbours, and the children's ignorance of goat husbandry, the creatures' welfare must be monitored. Therefore a massive, petrol-guzzling vehicle, complete with driver, sets off to spend two days checking twelve goats on widely separated hills.

As we drove round and round those hills, I fumed inwardly at the spending of so much on transport to inspect projects which themselves cost very little. A four-roomed, tin-roofed mud shack which will last about twenty-five years goes up for US$350, most of that being spent on the imported roof. You don't buy much petrol in Rwanda for $350. One man or woman on a small motor-bike, such as the *umuganda* overseers were using, could have done our tours of the goat-owners and house-builders at a fraction of the cost. Unfortunately, when vehicles are available people look for opportunities to use them. And for some young male aid workers part of the job's attraction is access to these powerful and vastly expensive four-wheel-drive Rovers and Cruisers. (What percentage of the aid industry's hard-raised funds is squandered annually, world-wide, on vehicles and fuel for needless journeys? Not to mention the drivers' wages. It bothers me that most aid workers think nothing of offering me – a tourist! – the use of their vehicles to go on round trips of perhaps twenty miles. They think I'm mad to walk when there are vehicles parked outside with idle drivers relaxing beside them.)

One hears acid comments about the ineptitude of small NGOs – 'Really they just get in the way, they don't know what they're doing.' Yet in crises some of these – too tiny to have far-away controlling bureaucracies – can achieve remarkable things on a shoe-string in a very short time. For instance, when the refugees flood-ed home the mini-agencies simply acted, fast, while the Biggies were contentiously communicating with their head offices and consulting outside 'experts'. (Is it not strange that towards the end of the twentieth century 'experts' are still being taken seriously?) However, the Biggies have the funding to stick with it in a particu-lar situation, whether wanted or not and whether 'doing good' or not. Whereas the minnows sometimes have to pull out abruptly (like Melchior's NGO) when they wake up one morning to an empty kitty.

14 FEBRUARY

Last night, in the small hours, I heard someone being murdered – nearby, beyond the wall of my hostess's small garden. The killing took what felt like a long time. It wasn't a shooting. I won't soon (or ever?) forget those sounds.

Pius and I were invited to dine this evening with a rare crea-ture, a Belgian born in Rwanda in 1929 who has lived here ever since, come hell or high water, refusing to be 'rescued' when the genocide started. Nowadays, because of the curfew, being invited to dinner means staying the night so I brought my sleeping-bag and had thoughts about sleeping on the verandah, as in Bukavu. But Hector firmly said 'No'.

We sat with our beers in a beautiful garden while the sun set fire to a cloud mass above Mount Kigali, then slipped behind the mountain's purple bulk. Yesterday morning Hector's gardener found four strangled male bodies beside the footpath he uses on the way to work. Said Hector, 'It's only to be expected, it's hap-pening all over the country all the time. We only hear about some incidents by chance. Genocide is like a comet, it has a tail.'

'It might have a shorter tail', said Pius, 'if justice wasn't now a DIY job for ordinary Rwandans.'

Hector concurred. He believes demands for fair trials, for every sort of 'human rights' safeguard, should be seen as irrelevant in post-genocide Rwanda. He asserted, vehemently, that no one is entitled to inhibit the authorities from dealing with the accused in a way that would be good for the mental and emotional health of the whole population. He also observed that 'the survivors' are not only the Tutsi and moderate Hutu who escaped with their lives. Every Rwandan is a survivor – deeply affected, in a variety of ways, by the genocide. Without a public placing of responsibility where it belongs, and appropriate punishments being meted out, both those who killed under duress and the passive witnesses will continue to feel – and will be – at risk. And the bereaved will become more bitter, more angry – and more vengeful.

15 FEBRUARY

This morning I had an odd encounter with a senior civil servant who belongs to that powerful group sometimes described as 'the Ugandan Mafia'. We met in the canteen of his government department, a large rondavel across the street from a skyscraper housing several ministries. Here, at 9 a.m., I was drinking a litre of *amasi* (fermented milk) from a glass beer-tankard while around me half a dozen civil servants enjoyed their first (I presume) Primus of the day. I had an appointment with Gaspard, a young Tutsi who hoped I could help him, and he arrived accompanied by his uncle, Mr B——. A tall slender gentleman, Mr B—— wore an immaculate khaki safari-suit and his shaven head accentuated his Tutsi features.

Twenty minutes later Mr B—— was offering me a twelve-month, multiple entry visa, to enable me to write a travel book to increase Rwanda's revenue from tourism – an offer both touching and absurd. How could Mr B—— think it possible for anyone to collect travel-book material at present? How could he imagine that a description of my experiences in Rwanda in 1997 would encourage tourism? How could I accept this privilege – a considerable privilege – under false pretences? Yet Mr B—— is a highly intelligent man; he graduated (Gaspard told me) from Makerere

University in Kampala with an honours degree in economics and political science. This incident illustrates the limitations of many African leaders, people with talent but unaware of how things tick in the outside world – one reason why they so easily fall prey to corporate predators.

Gaspard is in the sort of trap only too familiar to many of the Poor World's educated young. The BBC's World Service has offered Gaspard a job (he showed me the letter) but it is conditional on his having a telephone. To obtain a telephone in Kigali takes months beyond reckoning and even then costs considerably more than the official installation fee. He cannot get a phone until he gets a steady, comparatively well-paid job that will enable him to borrow enough money to get a phone ... It puzzled me that the nephew of a senior civil servant has this problem – perhaps Mr B—— is not Mafia-tainted?

With an Irish friend I spent a boozy afternoon on the rooftop of the Skyview Hotel, an open-air bar and simple restaurant where I have never seen other *muzungus*. The ascent from the street is daunting: three long, steep and very unsteady flights of metal steps, a Heath Robinson construction with a temporary air though I'm told it's been in place for years.

While waiting for Dee I stood looking over the chest-high parapet, then decided it would be safe – I was alone – to take a few photographs of the city-centre roofscape and the street far below. I had taken two shots when it seemed a riot was starting on the pavement opposite; a group of young men were gesturing violently while shouting angrily. It took me a moment to realize that all this was directed against me and my camera. Hastily I stepped back, out of sight. Perhaps these were ex-*interahamwe* who suspected me of trying to trace killers surreptitiously. I hoped they wouldn't attack me, to seize the camera, as we left; but our session was a long one – so long that neither of us dared to descend the ladder-like stairs. An amused waitress showed us a safer way down, through the building, and we emerged onto another street.

Normally Kigali's climate is blissful; even at noon a cool breeze blows and the mornings and late afternoons are perfect for walking. But today was different: very hot and oppressive, not a breath

of wind, slightly overcast. Then, towards sunset, came forty minutes of torrential tropical rain, blotting out the view across the
valley from John's bungalow and so loud on the tin roof that I
had difficulty hearing the friend who rang to ask if we would like
to eat tapia from Lake Victoria. We decided that we would –
though some of the more sensitive souls here eschew this delicacy,
remembering how long tapia live and what their diet might have
been less than three years ago. Crisp-fried with chilli sauce, tapia
is food for the gods. The fish, served alone, is some eighteen inches long – you don't need another meal for a week.

The Novotel restaurant, popular with expats, is half open-air
but now everyone eats inside; this evening we were the only cur-
few-defying *muzungus* present. A fine building – the interior walls
pleasantly blending wood and brick – it was originally owned by
a leading Tutsi businessman, Landwald Ndasingwa, who was
killed, together with his Canadian wife and two children, on the
first day of the genocide. We had almost finished our meal when
we heard that a Hutu Kigali High Court judge, and three visiting
friends, were murdered this evening as they sat drinking beer on
the judge's verandah. As his wife's car was being admitted to the
forecourt of their home by an askari, three armed men wearing
military uniforms followed it, overpowered the askari, killed the
four men and vanished. Later the World Service reported that this
judge was not involved in the genocide trials – but in fact, as Public Prosecutor, he was deeply involved. He is to be buried in his
home commune twenty miles from Kigali.

16 FEBRUARY

Yesterday the institution in charge of John's project gave him permission, after days of dithering about security, to drive to Mulindi.
I went along for the ride; one can safely bird-watch around the tea
estate. But somehow my mood today was not ornithological. For
hours I walked the nearby hills, rethinking one of my most cherished principles.

All my life I have passionately opposed capital punishment,
yet now I see the execution by the state of the organizers of the
genocide as necessary – though the notion of 'healing through
execution' so offends our recently acquired Western European

sensibilities. I am convinced that the creation of an atmosphere in which reconciliation will be possible requires the judicial killing of the organizers. If the government cannot or will not formally, ceremonially, execute those criminals, then ordinary Rwandans will kill (are killing) the people within reach – most of whom are other ordinary Rwandans. After genocide, there has to be retribution. To me it is not immoral or uncivilized for the state, on behalf of the survivors, to seek vengeance, whereas a world that allows the organizers to evade punishment is frighteningly uncivilized. And it signals to others that if any minority becomes too much of a nuisance there are ways of dealing with the problem while the international community averts its eyes. Most of my friends won't be able to understand why one particular set of circumstances, 'Genocide in Rwanda', should have compelled me to abandon such an important principle – 'Killing is Wrong'. I'll find it impossible to argue coherently about this, to justify making an exception for criminals who may never, personally, have murdered anyone. No doubt some will accuse me of a sort of blood-lust, an impulse coming more from the heart than the head. Yet there is one practical argument in favour of execution as catharsis. Even if the organizers were sentenced to life-imprisonment, the public would believe that their power, wealth and influential friends would soon bring about their release – or 'escape'. Thus the culture of impunity would be seen, by all, to continue to flourish.

17 FEBRUARY

News has just come of the bombing of Bukavu by Zairean government planes – or at least planes operating on behalf of the Zairean government, which isn't quite the same thing. Three bombs were dropped, one falling on the main market, and nine people died; forty are reported seriously wounded. This rather feeble air raid is surely a sign of desperation; Mobutu can have no hope of defeating the so-called 'rebels' on the ground as Kabila gains more and more volunteer recruits. Had my plans not gone agley, I would have been arriving in Bukavu this evening.

In this death-shadowed country my dreams have been extraordinary. According to the experts we all dream every night, but I am rarely aware of having dreamed – which perhaps indicates that I'm insufficiently in touch with my subconscious. However, within a few days of arriving in Rwanda I began to have a remarkable series of vivid dreams, never unpleasant or frightening but always intensely moving – the emotion still with me on awakening. These detailed dreams are about the individuals now dead – the majority long dead – who were the most important, the most beloved people in my life. I am simply recording this experience, I have made no effort to understand it.

Tomorrow morning, very conveniently for me, John is returning to Mulindi and a colleague has kindly offered to drive me to the border crossing.

KABALE, UGANDA, 18 FEBRUARY

Only on stepping out of Rwanda, back into the easy-going friendliness of Uganda, did I realize how unrelaxed I had become among those Thousand Hills. Rwanda has been a scary experience. Not because of the tiresome security problems but because it forces one to confront the evil inherent in us all, as human beings – however humane and compassionate we may seem as untested individuals. The deeds done there I have described as 'inhuman'. But that's escapist talk. Nothing done by humans is inhuman.

At Gatuna I felt liberated – was liberated, free to track on without interference, military or otherwise. John's thoughtfulness enabled me to walk to Kabale; he is homeward bound next week and volunteered to take my mysterious accumulation of books. Mysterious because Kigali is not renowned for its bookshops – yet there, as everywhere, I gradually acquired a heavy load of relevant volumes.

The waiters at the Visitour Hotel welcomed me back warmly and were eager to hear my impressions of Rwanda; all three look at least part-Tutsi. At sunset two young German women arrived, back from four days in Rwanda on the 'gorilla trip'. They had entered via Kisoro, glimpsed gorillas in the distance at a cost of $500, then taken minibus taxis from Ruhengeri to Kabale via Kigali. They were unaware of any security problem anywhere in Rwanda – having just been through what is allegedly the most insecure corner of all for *muzungus*! No expat crossed their path, no Rwandans issued warnings, they had done nothing to attract the attention of the military and were very puzzled to hear about my frustrated plans.

LONDON, 26 FEBRUARY

During my last few days in Kigali I became strangely afflicted by large, itchy, sore bumps. My hands swelled perceptibly, the knuckles disappearing, and my ears, forehead, legs, buttocks and adjacent areas were similarly tormented. At first I vaguely diagnosed 'mosquito bites'; I am fatalistic about mosquitoes and don't take all the proper precautions. Then I realized that in cool Kigali, where one sleeps under a sheet and blanket, mosquitoes don't in fact get to the buttocks – and in no circumstances do they burrow through one's pubic hair. John it was who made the correct diagnosis. Viewing my swollen hands one evening he exclaimed, 'Bedbugs! It's well known they like knuckles.' Without going into details, I complained that my attackers, whatever their species, liked all parts of my anatomy. Then, thinking far back to Dharamsala and Ethiopia – scenes of my closest encounters with bedbugs in the past – I reckoned John was right. (On my left thigh I still have the scar of a bedbug bite that went septic thirty-four years ago.) But how, in Rwanda – where I had been mostly confined to the hygienic homes of John and aid workers – had I become bedbug-bitten?

It took time for the penny to drop. On my way to Rwanda, in that hotel in Mbarara, I had used my sleeping-bag because the sheets were damp ... On the following day I did notice a few sore itchy spots but thought nothing of them. Obviously the bugs had invaded my sleeping-bag then, in a small way, and subsequently proliferated as bugs are wont to do. And by the time I used the sleeping-bag again, staying overnight with Hector, the Mbarara platoon had become a battalion.

Adult bedbugs are relatively easily dealt with, though the corpses give off a singularly disagreeable smell. Bedbug eggs, however, are indestructible by normal means; on my return from Ethiopia I had to have my sleeping-bag fumigated at vast expense. So I left Kigali with a mega-problem: very likely my garments and rucksack also harboured eggs. And I didn't want Rose (forget Rachel and Andrew) to be condemned to life in a bug-infested flat.

This morning, therefore, Rose found her reunion with Nyanya rather puzzling ... Because Nyanya didn't, on arrival at the flat, behave normally. Instead she unpacked on the doorstep before stripping naked inside the communal hall-door. Then her clothes, sleeping-bag and rucksack were quarantined in the back garden by Mummy – who was of course not fazed, being accustomed to travellers' crises. Suddenly Rose saw the funny side of a naked Nyanya – the backside – and repeatedly pinched it, chortling loudly, as we went upstairs.

EPILOGUE

Soon after my departure from Rwanda, expat unease was compounded by an unwholesome political development.

Enter the unsavoury Colonel Alexis Kanyarengwe – Ruhengeri-born, a Hutu Power fanatic in his youth, later a useful ally of Habyarimana during the 1973 coup. In 1980 Kanyarengwe was involved in an abortive attempt to overthrow his friend and had to move house rather rapidly, settling in Tanzania. Ten years later he joined the RPF (then eager to acquire Hutu members, not to be seen as exclusively Tutsi) and became its Secretary-General – a cosmetic post, allowing him little influence. Although appointed Vice Prime Minister – more cosmeticism – in July '94, another year passed before he attained real power, on replacing the sacked Hutu Minister of the Interior, Seth Sendashonga.

Throughout Ruhengeri prefecture Kanyarengwe was seen as the Hutu peasants' protector (*shebuja*) within the RPF, and he soon demonstrated his regional power by recruiting a considerable number of Hutu into the RPA. Then, as the insecurity situation worsened in January and February '97, he found himself in an awkward – not to say potentially lethal – position. On the Ruhengeri hills, hundreds of Hutu, including many members of his own family, were being killed during RPA crackdowns. On 3 March the murders of two RPA soldiers provoked the 'reprisal' deaths of more than 150 Hutu in three communes, and Kanyarengwe realized he must take action. At a public meeting he supported the *préfet*, Ignace Karuhije, who had already condemned the army's indiscriminate violence and demanded the arrest of Major Rugambwa, Commander of Battalion 199. The major was arrested, but soon freed. Then the *préfet* was arrested, reprimanded – and dismissed.

On 27 March Kanyarengwe was compelled to resign as Minister of the Interior, and the Vice Prime Minister pretend-job was scrapped. A cabinet reshuffle followed – and firmly nailed the lid on the coffin of Rwanda's coalition government. (It had never had much life in it.) The five changes, out of eighteen ministries, marked the rejection of Hutu participation in the running of the country. Kanyarengwe was replaced by a nonentity, a Muslim reared in Tanzania and belonging to no political group. Marc Ruganera, the last surviving leader of the Hutu moderates' Parti Social Démocrate, was downgraded from the Ministry of Finance to the newly invented Ministry of Tourism, Mines and Crafts. (Gérard Prunier dryly commented, 'Since there is no tourism and there are no mines, this minister's job is to administer a handful of arts and crafts co-operatives.') As Minister of Finance, Ruganera had persistently queried the unauthorized allocating of vast sums of money to the RPA. His replacement, Jean Birara – Director of the Central Bank under Habyarimana – was an apolitical administrator who had already proved his pliability in the hands of the RPF.

Patrick Mazimpaka, a founding member of the RPF, was also downgraded; a moderate Tutsi who spent his exile in Canada, he lacks an influential support group such as most Tutsi returnees have. His Ministry of Rehabilitation and Social Solidarity (its Orwellian ring slightly startling) was abolished on 28 March, despite the return of over a million refugees only four months previously. Mazimpaka was then given another of those pretend-jobs – 'Minister in the President's Office' – while Rehabilitation and Social Solidarity, now a mere Secretariat d'Etat, was abandoned to Beatrice Sebarware-Panda, whose infamous father is on the ICTR's 'wanted' list. Given her need to counteract this paternity, she was expected to look at things uncritically, through RPF/RPA eyes, and make few demands on behalf of the Hutu returnees.

Two other changes – Bonaventure Niyibizi to the Ministry of Trade and Dr Vincent Biruta to the Ministry of Health – promoted highly qualified but politically inexperienced young Tutsi, unlikely to argue with their elders.

Secrecy enveloped this reshuffle, which was completed within forty-eight hours. Disregarding the Arusha Accords and the Government Convention of 24 December '94, the régime ignored the other political parties – which had never provided more than a 'Government of National Unity' façade behind which the RPF/RPA got on with their own thing. However, as Gérard Prunier observed, 'The fact that they were unceremoniously buried signalled an end to any pretence of a democratic régime in Rwanda. The symmetry between the political promotion of the Army and the disappearance of the political parties has turned Rwanda into a de facto collegial military dictatorship.'

In mid-March Radio Rwanda reported the 'disappearance' from Rubungo of forty-seven ex-FAR officers who had recently returned from Zaire and been placed under the 'protection' of the 42nd Brigade of the RPA. By then it was evident that the RPA had become either an outrageously undisciplined force or a force that was being used to punish Hutu *per se*. One would prefer to see it as the former. But those political developments outlined above suggest that it is more likely to be the latter. Was my initial belief in the sincerity of the RPF's reconciliation crusade naïve? Even in Rwanda (perhaps particularly in Rwanda, where one clutches desperately at every straw of hope), I was predisposed to 'think positive', a trait that rather lessens my value as a commentator on current affairs.

As one ages – snowballing through the decades, collecting more and more friends – this small world gets even smaller. In December '97, at the beginning of a journey through Laos, my hostess in Vientiane was one of the three evacuees from Cyangugu whom I had met ten months earlier in Butare. I didn't at once recognize Sheila, so traumatized had she been on that occasion – immediately after her friends' murders.

For hours we talked about Rwanda, swapping gloomy scraps of information. It seems the grenade that failed to go off in Kigali's bus station, in early February, was of more significance than appeared at the time. It had been planted to frame one Lieutenant

Dr Mugemanshuro, who in due course was arrested and charged with 'attempted terrorism'. The doctor, an ex-FAR returnee, had just found a job with the Pallotin Fathers' Gikondo Health Centre, and this was more than the local Tutsi survivors could stomach. As the months passed educated Hutu returnees found it increasingly dangerous to work in their former professions. Many have taken refuge on the ancestral hills, resigning themselves to a life of subsistence farming. In general, however, ordinary peasants are not seen as 'legitimate targets' by vengeful freelance executioners. But relations between the Hutu returnees and the régime continue to deteriorate. The RPA accuses the returnees of sheltering the militia – and no doubt they do, as anyone would after looking down the barrel of an AK-47 held by a professional killer.

Even the theoretically highest in the land, President Pasteur Bizimungu, cannot insulate himself from the thickening miasma of ethnic animosity. Many outsiders are confused by his being Hutu – surely this means the régime is power-sharing? But of course the misfortunate Bizimungu is no more than a figurehead, all real power being wielded by Paul Kagame, Vice President and Defence Minister, and his formidable following of Uganda returnees, known as 'the Uganda Colonels'. (The Tutsi returnees form three distinct factions, according to their country of exile.) As is usual in Africa, 'followers' are of primary importance on Rwanda's political scene, and Bizimungu – formerly a civil servant and one of the Arusha negotiators, a man widely respected for his integrity – has none. (Perhaps this is one reason for his being appointed President?) He lives in isolation, enduring severe and relentless emotional pressures. Because a Hutu President is seen as a mere public relations gimmick, useful to the Tutsi régime, his children were mocked at school as 'children of the Protector' – the Protector being a brand of condom popular in Kigali. Eventually, unable to withstand daily bullying by Tutsi classmates, they had to be taken away from school and given private tutors. Even the President's Tutsi aides taunt him subtly, sometimes in the presence of distinguished visitors. He has on occasions retaliated physically by slapping or spitting at his tormentors – thus prompting gossip about 'mental instability'. Said I to Sheila, 'If I were him, I'd resign and settle in the Southern Highlands of Tanzania.'

Something baffling and extremely disquieting happened in June '97: the appointment of Boniface Rucagu as *préfet* of Ruhengeri. Rucagu had been arrested and freed three times in the previous two years; at one stage he was number 120 on the list of 2000 Category 1 prisoners. When Parliament challenged his appointment and demanded that he be rearrested President Bizimungu insisted that his inclusion on the list had been 'a mistake' and the Minister of the Interior stated defensively, 'There is no concrete evidence Rucagu committed genocide.' Yet it is common knowledge (documented) that he was a founder-shareholder of Radio Mille Collines and a regular contributor to *Kangura*, in which journal he gleefully predicted the genocide. Videotapes existed showing him in rabble-rousing action at anti-Tutsi meetings in Gitarama. However, when Deus Kagirancza, a Tutsi survivor MP, asked why all this evidence has not been used he was told, 'The Rucagu file has been lost' – whereupon he swiftly pointed out that the witnesses have not been lost. A former *préfet* of Gitarama is still prepared to testify that he saw Rucagu personally murdering six people. And other equally courageous witnesses, men and women, are willing to swear that they heard Rucagu publicly urging peasants to kill Tutsi. For three days Parliament debated the issue, then ordered the administration to sack – and rearrest – Rucagu. Six months later he was still in office.

What goes on here? There is something downright sinister about an alliance between the Tutsi régime and one of the most notorious *génocidaires*, a man who killed with relish and boasted of his part in priming the country for genocide. Did the government hope that, having given the hard-line Ruhengeri Hutu 'one of their own' as *préfet*, some degree of order might replace the region's prevailing near-anarchy? Maybe – but this is no excuse for co-opting one of the leaders of the genocide after colluding in his evasion of the judicial process. Evidently the RPF/RPA are willing actively to promote the culture of impunity if by so doing they can strengthen their own position. At this point I despaired of any of the genocide tribunals or courts, at home or abroad, ever taking their duties seriously.

Sheila's South African partner shared our rage as we recalled his government's shameful decision, in July '97, to resume arms

sales to Rwanda – the feeble excuse being Paul Kagame's assur-
ance that South African military equipment would be used 'only
for the legitimate defence of Rwanda'. Then our conversation was
interrupted (it felt like an eerie coincidence) by the World Service
reporting that on 4 December the Hutu militia had freed all the
prisoners (more than 600) from Bulinga jail, thirty miles north-
west of Kigali.

This feat must have badly shaken the government. Never
before had the militia attacked so close to Kigali – moved so far
from their 'homeland' in the north-west. At least ten people,
including four prison guards, were killed by some 300 militia
armed with guns, machetes and spears. Following the release of
those prisoners, the death-rate among local Tutsi survivors was
said to be rising rapidly.

A few days earlier – continued the BBC – more than a hundred
were freed from a jail near Ruhengeri. And a fortnight before that
some 300 people died when 1200 militia (the RPA's figure) tried to
dynamite their way through the walls of Gisenyi jail and burn
down buildings. Next day they attempted to take control of Gisenyi
airport but were successfully resisted at the cost of eighty lives.

On 11 December the World Service reported a night-time raid
on Mudende camp, fifteen miles from Gisenyi, where 17,000 or
so Tutsi refugees (citizens of Zaire) were being sheltered – but not
protected. During the last raid on Mudende, in August, 148 men,
women and children were murdered. At around 2 a.m. on 10
December, 230 were killed with machetes and about the same
number seriously wounded. Before leaving, the attackers set fire
to 200 tents. No *muzungu* witnessed the attack; every afternoon
at 3.30 the UNHCR staff had to return to Kigali under armed
escort. Next morning the camp-site was deserted and the food
store had been looted.

The World Service added a quote from Madeleine Albright, US
Secretary of State, then visiting Kigali: 'The US pledges to Rwanda
full moral and financial support, the country's future is critical to
the region. We congratulate Rwanda on the remarkable accom-
plishment of repatriating hundreds of thousands of refugees.'

In March '98 I returned from travels in Laos, anxiously sought the latest news of Rwanda, and was appalled. I remembered then my conversation with Pius in Kigali on 11 February '97. What he most dreaded – regular Burundi-type violence – is now happening. It could be argued that the government is no longer in control of Rwanda. Or, if it is, its form of control is little better than (though in style very different from) the Hutu tyranny it set out to replace.

During January Gisenyi became a war zone. A bus carrying forty brewery workers was attacked near the town; when the Hutu and Tutsi refused to separate, the militia murdered everyone. Local people gathered to applaud them, then helped by hacking to death those who tried to escape.

In the Rugerero sector, seventeen died when their bus was set alight.

A few miles from the Rwewere sector, machetes were used to murder nine nuns as they worked in their convent's clinic.

In the Kabilizi sector, an RPA crackdown left more than 500 dead. As no land was available for a mass grave, many bodies were eaten by pigs.

On the night of 3 February hundreds of militia – armed with many machetes and a few guns, some wearing RPA uniforms as disguise – invaded the refugee camp for Zairean Tutsi at Kinigi, near Ruhengeri. Thirty were killed, 350 seriously wounded.

Four days later Reuters quoted 'the governor of Ruhengeri, Mr Boniface Rucagu' (the name made me shudder involuntarily). Said Mr Rucagu, 'This week a large group of militia armed with guns, machetes, axes and clubs raided Jenda settlement, broke into houses and thirty people died on the spot. Three of thirteen wounded later died. The rebels didn't distinguish between Tutsi and Hutu.'

On the same date Paul Cullen, *The Irish Times*' brave and astute Development Correspondent, reported: 'Rwanda is host to a massive array of human rights organisations. Yet the presence of the UN and many NGOs has made little impact on an increasingly bloody conflict. Gisenyi, where there has been shelling and aerial bombardment, can be reached only by plane. As a result, no one knows how many people are dying.'

Some observers within Rwanda were by then convinced that Paul Kagame is no longer 'the Boss', that the civil war in the north-west (its admitted casualties for '97 approximately 600 but probably many more) has given three or four ruthless generals the opportunity to take direct control of that area and indirect control of the whole troubled country. This plausible theory accords with my belief that the pre-invasion RPF/RPA really was idealistic/foolish enough to imagine that it could lead Rwanda into a stable future – that reconciliation was possible. In October 1990, when Fred Rwigyema and Paul Kagame launched their War of Liberation, they could not have imagined what they would be required to cope with, as victors, in July '94. How to govern a country totally devastated by genocide? There are no models to be referred to for guidance. The new régime was dependent on its army for everything: transport, communications, electricity and water supplies, medical care, policing, repairing the infrastructure. Perhaps the rot set in then – the RPA generals acquiring a taste for power while recruiting more and more troops of doubtful quality.

In an article in the *Guardian Weekly* (21 March '98) Victoria Brittain reported the completion of 300 genocide trials during '97, with fifteen acquittals and 100 death sentences passed – but no one, as yet, executed. The 130,000 still in jail 'now see themselves as victims'. Miss Brittain accepted the government's argument that the judicial process must be seen to be fair, however long it takes, and that the annual spending of US$12 million (a third provided by the Red Cross) to keep so many in jail 'while society stabilises' is 'money well spent'. There is a certain ambiguity here. From the régime's point of view, it makes sense to isolate a segment of the population quite likely to rejoin the militia – or at least support them – if released.

Victoria Brittain reproached Mary Robinson (Ireland's former President, now UN High Commissioner for Human Rights) for her criticism of the government's lack of commitment to reconciliation. Miss Brittain saw this as a clear case of 'blaming the victim', and when in Rwanda I might have agreed with her. Now, this seems to me too simplistic a view of an extremely convoluted situation. Yet Mary Robinson's criticism is also too simplistic, for reasons succinctly stated by Gérard Prunier:

The total failure of the International Tribunal to produce anything like a modicum of justice reinforces the complementary attitudes of the two communities. For the Tutsi it is: 'We have our backs to the wall. Unless we maintain absolute control they will finish us next time.' And for the Hutu: 'We only have to wait, numbers will play in our favour and the so-called international community will neither want nor be able to stop us.' It is difficult to see how in such a context governmental control can be exercised except by repression, and national reconciliation is still a very remote prospect indeed.

Unlike Gérard Prunier, the UN Secretary-General, Kofi Annan, claimed to be 'extremely encouraged' by the progress of the International Tribunal. Addressing its UN staff in Arusha he declared, 'For the victims of the genocide we seek and will find justice.' He urged the staff to 'continue their commitment in order to establish a new relationship between Rwanda and the UN and to send a message around the world that impunity can no longer be allowed to go unpunished'. Even by UN-speak standards, this was a notable feat of incoherence.

On 24 March the Registrar of the International Tribunal, Agwu Uiwe Okali, told a press conference:

It is time to put the negative image of the Rwanda Tribunal aside. The Internal Oversight Committee's latest audit report showed improvements in every area since the previous report, when no area was found to work effectively. Thus far, thirty-five persons have been indicted. Twenty-three are in custody in Arusha, the others being held elsewhere including one detained in the US. At present, four trials are ongoing, two in the advanced stage, and judgement on one will be coming down during the first half of the year.

Mr Okali saw this as 'not a bad record, the Yugoslavia Tribunal's process is going no faster'. He added, disarmingly, 'Both tribunals have so far demonstrated how not to conduct tribunals.'

Five weeks later the Security Council approved the addition of a third trial chamber to the Arusha tribunal, at an estimated cost of US$5.5 million for 1998. (How long can a legal gravy-train get?) This move was in response to a request from Laity Kama, the Tribunal President, who had calculated that without three more judges (eleven were already *in situ*) it would take seven years to bring the indicted to trial – and the Tribunal's mandate ends in May 1999.

At Arusha, on 1 May, Jean Kambanda, Rwanda's prime minister during the genocide, pleaded guilty to six charges: genocide, conspiracy to commit genocide, direct and public incitement to commit genocide, complicity in genocide and two charges of crimes against humanity. Kambanda had been held in isolation in a house in Dodoma, Tanzania, since his arrest in July 1997 when he imprudently moved from Zaire to Kenya. His guilty plea raised hopes that he might give evidence against his fellow-accused, thereby lessening the fourteen judges' exhausting workload – and, no doubt, shortening his own sentence.

The fourth anniversary of the genocide prompted President Clinton to apologize to the survivors on behalf of the international community. What is this 'international community'? Am I a member of it? If so, I don't fancy having Bill Clinton as my spokesman. In June '94 he was host to a White House conference on Africa – a conference that kept the genocide off its agenda, so determined was the post-Somalia Clinton Administration to thwart UN 'peace-keeping' missions. In October '93 eighteen American soldiers had been killed in Somalia – a more potent figure, in Washington, than 800,000 Rwandans. Commenting on President Clinton's '98 apology, Lionel Rosenblatt, president of Refugees International, recalled, 'The ball was not only dropped by the US, it was blocked by the US.'

In France, Le Figaro marked the anniversary by revealing certain facts that had been circulating widely, as unconfirmed rumours, during my visit to Rwanda. For some time, various French journalists and academics had been digging deeply into their country's political muck-heap, and Le Figaro reported that the three-man crew of the crashed presidential plane were covert French government employees, ostensibly working for a private air company. Jean-Pierre Minaberry, Jacquy Heraud and Jean-Michel Perrine were decorated posthumously as Chevaliers de la Légion d'Honneur. And, according to one widow, all three civilians were given the military status of 'killed in action'. Le Figaro's Rwanda expert, Patrick de Saint-Exupéry, also discovered that the two missiles used to bring down the plane were Iraqi armaments seized by the French during the Gulf War. Le Monde quoted a Kigali-based French priest who repeated the plausible claim – current since

1994 – that nearby witnesses saw two white men firing those missiles. These, presumably, were mercenaries hired by the genocide leaders who by then wanted Habyarimana out of the way. At that stage it seemed he might allow – albeit very reluctantly – the Arusha Accords to be implemented in full.

On 2 April the independently run Rwanda News Agency reported that on 30 March militiamen knifed to death nine Hutu peasants in three sectors of Nyabikenke commune, in central Rwanda. A resident was quoted: 'The militiamen have their hidden bases in the forest. They no longer target only genocide survivors. These days they more and more kill Hutu they accuse of collaborating with the government.'

Meanwhile, throughout the north-west, well-armed ex-FAR and *interahamwe* fighters were repeatedly engaging the RPA in what can only be described as a civil war. The continuous flow of blood, in Rwanda, Burundi and parts of Kivu Province, inspired the Security Council, on 10 April, to request the Secretary-General 'to reactivate its International Commission of Inquiry into the sale and supply of arms and related material to former Rwandan government forces and militias in the Great Lakes region, contrary to Council Resolution 918 (1994)'. This Commission's mandate requires it to 'identify parties aiding and abetting the illegal sale to, or acquisition of, arms by those forces and militias, and make recommendations on the illegal flow of arms in the region'. In November '96 the Commission's last report to the Security Council recorded an ample flow of arms, from a variety of sources, to the genocidal troops. The nationals of at least two members of the Security Council – France and Britain – were among those sources. There is no record of their governments' having since intervened to close the legal loopholes so adroitly used by arms traders.

In May, during Kofi Annan's tour of eight African countries, an excellent article by Philip Gourevitch in *The New Yorker* revived controversy about General Dallaire's cable of 11 January 1994. (See chapter 4.) At once the international media, already in a retrospective mood about the genocide, fell upon Kofi Annan's ignoring of that momentous cable when he was Under-Secretary-General for Peacekeeping Operations. At the Secretary-General's African press conferences, journalists behaved like delighted terriers with a ripe dug-up chop bone, all the tastier for having been long forgotten. In response to one hostile question, Mr Annan insisted:

The fundamental failure was lack of political will, not lack of information. If it is lack of information that prevents action, that prevents the solution of crises, then I think we would have very few crises in the world today. No one can deny that the world failed Rwanda. But the crucial issue today is not how to apportion blame with the benefit of hindsight. We should be asking how we can ensure that such a tragedy can never happen again.

Another hostile question brought the reply:

My predecessor, Mr Boutros Boutros-Ghali, pushed the member states so hard to give the UN the capacity and the facility to do something in Rwanda and we did not get it. I agree with General Dallaire when he says, 'If I had had 5000 men well trained and equipped I could have saved hundreds of thousands of lives.' That capacity he did not have, not because the capacity did not exist in the world and no government had it or could have provided it, but because the will to provide, the will to act, was not there, and that is the crux of the matter.

When asked why he had refused General Dallaire permission to testify before the Belgian government's Special Commission on Rwanda, Mr Annan replied, 'The explanations were very clear, given in a letter to the Belgian authorities. Based on the privileges and immunities of the UN, we could not lift his immunity to go and address the Belgian government, but Dallaire answered lots of questions in writing.'

One wonders if the General's answers had to pass a UN censor. On 5 February, while I was flying home from Africa, he gave evidence before the Arusha Tribunal and wept openly while recalling, 'Every day we saw people being massacred and yet the world folded its arms.' Before his appearance, judges were warned that he had been forbidden to give evidence about communications between himself and the UN.

During this revival of the cable controversy part of me rejoiced to see the UN's impotence and Washington's callousness re-exposed. But another part sympathized with the wretched Secretary-General, an evidently well-meaning man trapped in a labyrinthine structure incorporating countless agencies not renowned for co-operating during crises. His plaintive cry, 'We can't compel governments to supply troops and funding!' is a grim bottom line, revealing the UN as a toothless purveyor of platitudes. It requests and demands and deplores and condemns and passes resolutions and imposes embargoes that are routinely ignored unless they coincide with US policies and ambitions. Having operated within this structure for more than thirty years, Mr Annan cannot reasonably be expected to show much independence of spirit or originality of thought. Although his desire to reform the UN seems genuine enough, and he is very proud of having reduced its bloated staff by a thousand, the likelihood of his achieving real reforms is remote. If your reforming abilities are outstanding, you don't get to the top of such a venal organization. However, one mustn't become too misty-eyed about poor Kofi Annan. Had he acted promptly on reading the Dallaire cable – checking on the reliability of its information, then twisting Washington's arm by alerting the whole world to what was being planned in Rwanda – would he subsequently have been backed by the Americans as the new Secretary-General of the UN?

On arrival in Rwanda on 7 May, as an uninvited guest Mr Annan had a conciliatory (in his estimation) speech prepared for delivery that afternoon to the National Assembly. As he was about to address the deputies, Anastase Gasana – Rwanda's Foreign Minister, sitting beside him – suddenly launched a bitter attack on the international community's complicity in the exploitation of Rwanda since 1922, first under the League of Nations, then under the UN. Angrily, Mr Gasana demanded compensation from the UN for the genocide survivors. All the deputies loudly cheered his calling on the UN to hold a public inquiry into its failure to prevent the genocide – and to 'pull itself together'.

Touring VIPs are not normally exposed to this sort of treatment, but the visibly shaken Secretary-General quickly 'pulled himself together' and replied, 'I did not come here to get into polemics and I'm sure most of you know the old proverb, "The guest is always a prisoner of the host".' Mr Annan then read his speech:

We must and we do acknowledge that the world failed Rwanda at that time of evil. The international community and the UN could not muster the political will to confront it. The world must deeply repent this failure. Rwanda's tragedy was the world's tragedy. All of us who cared about Rwanda, all of us who witnessed its suffering, fervently wish that we could have prevented the genocide. Looking back now, we see the signs which then were not recognized. Now we know that what we did was not nearly enough – not enough to save Rwanda from itself, not enough to honour the ideals for which the UN exists. We will not deny that, in their greatest hour of need, the world failed the people of Rwanda ... In the face of genocide, there can be no standing aside, no looking away, no neutrality – there are perpetrators, and there are victims. There is evil and there is evil's harvest. Evil in Rwanda was aimed not only at Tutsis. It was aimed at anyone who would stand up or speak out against the murder. Let us remember, therefore, that when the killers began they also sought out Hutus now described as moderate – that is, Hutus who would not kill, Hutus who would not hate. That fact is what gives us hope today and inspires confidence that you will succeed in rebuilding your One Rwanda on which future generations will build a tolerant society, defined by the quality of forgiveness which is inherent in our African heritage.

This disingenuous apology poured oil on the fire of Rwandan rage. As Pius wrote to me afterwards, 'Why was he trying to pass the buck to "the world"? The world wasn't given a chance to act on Dallaire's information. His cable was hushed up.'

Joseph Bideri, the presidential spokesman, described the speech as 'extremely arrogant, insensitive and insulting to the Rwandan people'. Both President Bizimungu and Vice President Kagame refused to attend the dinner given that evening by the government in Mr Annan's honour. His visiting Rwanda was one more UN blunder – minor, yet unhelpful all round. The Secretary-General's advisers should have known that he would certainly 'get into polemics' (if nothing worse) in Kigali. Which is not to condone the Rwandans' discourtesy; their resentment of Mr Annan's pre-genocide passivity could have been expressed as forcefully, with more dignity, by refusing to receive him in their country. But clearly they were glad of this opportunity to punish and humiliate him. 'Genocide is like a comet, it has a tail' – as Hector observed in Kigali.

On the following day, in Kampala, Mr Annan – evidently still smarting – sent a rather childish message to Kigali via his press conference: 'If governments do not want to work with the UN there is a limit to what you can do and there is also a limit to patience. So there may come a time when we have to just cut our losses and focus where we can do useful work, where the governments and people concerned recognize and welcome what we are doing.'

Fourteen months after that walk around the Mulindi hills, during which I painfully came to terms with the appropriateness of the death sentence for *génocidaires*, my volte-face was tested for durability. On 21 April the government announced that forty-eight hours later twenty-two persons convicted of genocide (unnamed as yet) would be publicly executed by firing squad in Kigali, Nyamata, Gikongoro, Cyasemakamba and Murambi. At once pleas for clemency came from the Pope, Tony Blair as President of the EU, Kofi Annan, Mary Robinson, the US government (not normally noted for its squeamishness about capital punishment), Amnesty International and several other human rights groups. These last complained about the *génocidaires* not being given a 'fair hearing', a number of trials having been dealt with 'in a few hours'. Given the peculiar circumstances prevailing in Rwanda, such complaints are nonsensical. As the authors of *Death, Despair and Defiance* note in their concluding chapter, 'Most Rwandans know who is primarily responsible. The organization and implementation of the genocide and extermination of politically moderate Hutu – and the incitement of the population – was too public for there to be any doubt about who should carry the primary responsibility.' For instance, Froduald Karamira – the first major suspect to be tried and one of those executed in Kigali – was described in '94, by a missionary who had fled from the Kabgayi diocese, as

one of the men directly responsible for the massacres in Rwanda. Immediately after the plane crash, every single day, Karamira gave an interview to the RTLM radio and to Radio Rwanda making the most inflammatory statements. Identifying all Tutsi as RPF supporters, he would say that 'there is no way the rebels will find alive any of the people they are claiming as their own'. He would ask villagers to 'clear up' their villages of these Tutsi cockroaches ...

Karamira was an immensely wealthy businessman, by birth a Tutsi from Butare – one of those rare Tutsi who became ultra-fanatical Hutu Power advocates. (Perhaps, in his case, by way of furthering his business interests.) Besides his propaganda work, Karamira supervised the complex network of roadblocks at which thousands of Tutsi were killed in and around Kigali.

The passage of time had not weakened my conviction that for the sake of Rwanda's future collective psychic health it is necessary that those who organized the killing of some 800,000 human beings should themselves be killed. In an odd way this comforted me, seeming to prove that my volte-face was not merely an emotional reaction to being present in post-genocide Rwanda. However, some shocked friends accused me of having allowed myself to be demoralized by the genocide. In their view I am, indirectly, another of its victims, so overwhelmed by its evil that I have regressed to being ruled by a primitive thirst for vengeance. But unexpected oblique support came from a Quaker friend who worked for twenty-five years in East Africa. 'Of course I can't agree with you,' she said. 'All the same, I do see where you're coming from. You empathize with Africans, that's why you feel so strongly these executions are right. Yes, I do know where you're at – and if not a card-carrying Quaker most likely I'd be there with you!'

Usually we debate capital punishment in relation to killings by one or more persons acting as individuals. Murderers can be regarded as abnormal members of society, in some sense sick, possibly capable of being restored to normality, certainly not deserving of cold-blooded execution by the state. However, the organizers of Rwanda's genocide were not abnormal or sick but evil – cool, calculating, unlikely ever to commit a 'conventional' murder, capable of migrating to other countries, post-genocide, and practising their professions as stable, amiable, acceptable members of society. I have read that many concentration camp overseers were equally nice to know: addicted to Bach and Mozart (Wagner wouldn't count), delighting in their rose gardens, kind to their animals, devoted to their families. Truly, genocide is 'something else ...' Therefore I admire the Rwandan government's refusal to be cowed by an international community that on this issue has its moral knickers in a serious twist – first pretending not to notice the genocide, then springing to the defence of those *génocidaires* who were about to receive their just deserts.

The charge of barbarism was applied by most outsiders and some Rwandans to the government's encouragement of the public to attend the executions. In Nyamata, thirty miles south of Kigali, all schools were closed to enable the pupils to attend, if they so wished. The sight of small children being hoisted onto parental shoulders, as the *génocidaires* were being roped to wooden stakes and hooded, must have been deeply disturbing. Yet to me the official attitude made sense; the killings and massacres were also public – very public. Perhaps this is where my 'empathy with Africans' does count. Admittedly, had I been in Rwanda at the time I could not have brought myself to witness those shootings – partly because of an aversion to seeing anyone killed, partly because the executions felt like Rwanda's 'private business'.

In the event, not all that many spectators assembled at any of the five sites. Foreign journalists variously estimated the Kigali crowd; 'between 7000 and 10,000', reckoned Stephen Buckley of *The Washington Post*. Chris Simpson noted: 'Foreign journalists, the only obvious non-Rwandans watching the executions, reported a mood of general hostility against them.' This is unsurprising; naturally they were seen as representatives of the international 'human rights' lobby. Typically, the journalists assumed the banning of cameras and tape-recorders to be a defensive government reaction to outside criticism, an effort to reduce 'bad publicity'. In fact, when Rwanda's law was amended in 1997 to permit *génocidaires* to be publicly executed, the filming or recording of executions by anyone was made illegal. These deaths were not intended as mass entertainment. They had a solemn purpose, far removed from the giving of morbid thrills to TV viewers and newspaper readers.

After the Kigali executions, Cabo Ninyetegeta – an aide to President Bizimungu and himself a Hutu – said, 'We are not sadists. But there is a legacy of political ruthlessness. Justice must be done.'

APPENDIX

The following is the prepared statement of Richard L. McCall, Chief of Staff to the Administrator of the US Agency for International Development, before the House of Representatives Committee on International Relations Subcommittee on International Operations and Human Rights. McCall testified on 5 May 1998.

Mr Chairman, and members of the Subcommittee, I want to express my appreciation for your inviting me to participate in today's hearings on 'Rwanda: Genocide and the Continuing Cycle of Violence'.

I think most experts would agree that the current crisis in the Great Lakes region of Africa began long before the shocking and tragic genocide of 1994. The manner in which the international community reacted to the genocide, before, during, and afterwards, has led to considerable soul-searching among donors and both international and non-governmental relief organizations.

The international community was ill-equipped to deal with the post-Cold War world, particularly the emergence of complex emergencies, many of which have as their underpinning ethnic, religious, cultural or nationalistic roots. This vexing reality has led to several informal meetings comprising donors, international humanitarian organizations, non-governmental organizations and private and voluntary organizations. The first meeting was held in March 1995 at Wilton Park, outside of London. The most recent was held on April 3–4 of this year in Stockholm, Sweden, and was co-hosted by the Swedish Government and Sergio Viera de Mello, the new Under-Secretary-General of the United Nations for Humanitarian Affairs. Some forty representatives of selected donor nations, United Nations agencies, African countries, academics and non-governmental organizations were invited to the Stockholm meeting, not as representatives of their organizations, but as individuals.

In opening the Stockholm seminar Jan Eliason, the Foreign Minister of Sweden, posed the following questions for us to ponder:

1. Have we sufficiently analyzed and adapted to the reality of today's conflicts? The answer is clearly no.

2. Do we have comprehensive answers to these complex conflicts and do those answers reflect the realities on the ground? Once again, the answer is clearly no.

3. Do we look at these conflicts within the totality of all interventions, military, political, humanitarian and economic? Again, the answer is clearly no.

4. Do we have the mechanisms not only to mobilize effective resources, but also to ensure that those resources are used to ameliorate the root causes of conflict? Again, the answer is no.

5. How can we maintain the integrity, let alone apply the principles, of humanitarian law when many actors are non-state actors? That is the challenge we have faced not only in the Great Lakes, but in Bosnia and Somalia as well.

The Stockholm seminar discussions focused on the ongoing crisis in the Great Lakes. A major independent assessment, entitled 'Strategic Humanitarian Coordination in the Great Lakes Region 1996–1997', was prepared in advance for the discussions. That assessment built upon the five-volume multi-donor evaluation of the role of the international community in events leading up to, and during, the Rwanda genocide. The latter evaluation was published in early 1996.

Throughout my prepared statement, I will refer to both the Stockholm assessment and UNHCR's winter of 1997 publication of *Refugees*, the entire issue of which was entitled 'Crisis in the Great Lakes: Anatomy of a Tragedy'.

My purpose is to lay out the concerns that have now crystallized within the international community. Unless political and humanitarian actors learn the lessons of the previous responses to complex emergencies, history will repeat itself, and the opportunity for donor retrospectives will continue in abundance.

In a context where humanitarian assistance has been routinely abused and manipulated, and where repeated mass violations of humanitarian law and human rights are a constant reality, it is critical that well-thought-out policies should inform well-prepared and -executed humanitarian operations. This has not been the state of affairs in the Great Lakes region, where the humanitarian assistance became a valuable resource to be exploited by non-humanitarians for ends most brutal.

While the international community was shocked by the brutality and horror of the genocide in Rwanda, I think few understood the cohesion and the breadth of the political organization behind this killing machine – until it was too late.

There is now consensus that in 1994 the exodus into eastern Zaire of Hutus was largely determined by a concerted effort on the part of the former régime to create a human shield inside the Zairean border with Rwanda. In August 1994, UNHCR organized the first repatriation from Goma. However, as the UNHCR publication pointed out, after the first day of repatriation, the extremists attacked those refugees wanting to return to their homes in Rwanda. The old commune and village structures were reconstituted in Zaire and Tanzania. The camp populations were routinely harassed and killed by the senior officials and *interahamwe* militias, determined to maintain their own political and military control over the refugees. Refugees who stepped out of line by agreeing to repatriate or challenge the old authorities were beaten or killed. Food distribution was effectively controlled by the old guard.

The Stockholm assessment stated that

> the ex-FAR used the refugee camps as a political and military base and to intimidate the refugees into staying in Zaire, where they would continue to serve their essential function as a shield and base for the rearming of ex-FAR. Controversially, some international NGOs also provided relief directly to military camps in nearby Lac Vert under the argument that doing so would limit the extent to which military forces stole from the civilian population. In 1995, the ex-FAR was sufficiently rejuvenated to begin a series of attacks into western Rwanda.

As African Rights documented, the targets of those attacks were genocide survivors and those who could serve as potential witnesses to the genocide, including Hutus.

The empowerment of the *génocidaires* in the Zaire camps had the effect of transferring Rwanda's political tensions throughout the subregion, laying the groundwork for continued warfare in eastern Zaire and the eventual attack on the refugee camps, and ultimately leading to the overthrow of the Mobutu régime.

During the 1994–1996 period, the ex-FAR and *interahamwe*, in collusion with elements of the Zairean army, undertook operations that effectively ethnically cleansed Zairean Tutsis from the Masisi region of Zaire northwest of Goma. Similar efforts directed at the Banyamulenge in South Kivu, and other ethnic groups, proved to be the seminal event precipitating the rebellion led by Laurent Kabila.

Once all-out war broke out, as the Stockholm assessment observed:

It was evident and clear that the military elements among the refugee population were deliberately pushing part of the refugee population ahead of itself to shield itself from the attacks by the RPA/ADFL. These people (meaning the legitimate refugees) became four times victimized – having been forced out of Rwanda by the genocide armies in 1994, and then intimidated, harassed and oppressed by those same armies in Goma-region camps, they were in 1996 again forced to flee as a population shield and many of these people were killed in the ensuing fighting.

The nature of the evil continuing to plague the region cannot be underestimated. Not only are the *génocidaires* committed to finishing what was left undone in 1994, but they are willing to kill and sacrifice thousands of their own people to do so.

Mr Chairman, I appreciate the fact that in previous hearings you, yourself, have covered a lot of this background in your statements. However, with your indulgence, it is important that the various strands of the international community's belated intervention in the Great Lakes be woven together, in an effort to begin finding some answers as to how we deal with complex emergencies in the future.

As the editor of *Refugees* observed about the Great Lakes crisis:

> Genocide. It is perhaps the most chilling word in any language, one so heavily antithetical to basic civilized behavior that individuals, institutions and governments almost automatically refrain from its use even when logic dictates otherwise ...
>
> The sheer number of victims involved in the slaughter has shaped everything that followed, making the Great Lakes very different [from] other humanitarian emergencies.
>
> Should we, the humanitarians, continue to feed camps which were full of, and often controlled by, the *génocidaires*? Should field workers tell the world what they knew of fresh killings in the forests that endangered not only their own lives, but also ongoing efforts to save many tens of thousands still living as refugees? In such extreme circumstances was the principle of 'voluntary repatriation' practical or even possible?

That question – whether the principle of voluntary repatriation was practical or even possible under those circumstances – was and continues to be the crux of the past and present debate surrounding the Great Lakes.

According to the Stockholm assessment, the lack of attention to refugee camp security and the empowerment of the *génocidaires* led to growing violence in the region. 'The festering discontent in 1996–97 confirmed the urgency of specific recommendations to remove barriers to repatriation. The manipulation by belligerent and criminal elements in the refugee camps in eastern Zaire in 1994 was a rerun of problems unaddressed in the Cambodian refugee camps along the Thai border years before.' In other words, we have been there before. Lessons were not learned or heeded, needlessly producing thousands of innocent victims.

Too often the international community provides assistance, but not protection. As one of the participants in the Stockholm seminar observed: 'We deal with the symptoms, not the root causes. We don't understand the culture and history of the country that, of necessity, becomes the object of our political and humanitarian interventions.'

The complexity of any failed state requires a multifaceted response. We must begin redefining accountability. In the past, accountability meant assuring that humanitarian assistance reached those in need. As another participant stated:

> Now accountability includes a realistic assessment of protection we provide or do not provide, security, and the impact on stability. Humanitarian action does have a political impact. For fifty years the UN has worked in watertight compartments. We can no longer afford to do so.

At a minimum, the Great Lakes crisis has led us to acknowledge a number of serious deficiencies. Included are the following:

1. We have to gain an understanding of the on-the-ground reality and adjust to that reality.

2. The quality of the political, economic and social analysis is not good and in many cases is non-existent.

3. The crisis is rarely over once immediate humanitarian needs are met – the challenge is to mitigate the ongoing crisis.

4. Compartmentalization produces inflexibility in the entire system. Complex emergencies by definition require a co-ordinated system-wide approach and talent beyond what the system can produce.

5. Humanitarian law is often violated or compromised from the moment refugee populations are stabilized. As we saw in the Great Lakes, humanitarian operations do have an impact on the dynamics of violence. The intervention was built around violence and tried to accommodate that violence in the hope that other actors would live up to their obligations under humanitarian law.

One of the major lessons learned from the Great Lakes crisis is that humanitarian intervention cannot be separated from the political, military and economic interventions of the international community.

While the *génocidaires* were accorded sanctuary and protection in Zaire under the international humanitarian intervention, a reconstituted UNAMIR inside Rwanda had a very limited mandate – that of protecting the humanitarian operation. In other words, UNAMIR could only protect humanitarian aid workers, not Rwandans. Therefore, the killers from the camps could continue to operate with impunity, with only the RPA standing in their way.

Under humanitarian law, it is the responsibility of the host state to ensure armed elements do not enjoy the status, and with such status the sanctuary and sustenance, accorded legitimate refugees. In the case of the Great Lakes, the Mobutu régime was an ally of the ex-Rwandan government and it was one of the worst-kept secrets that the régime allowed weapons to continue flowing to the ex-FAR and *interahamwe*.

Because of the dilemma posed by the inability to separate the armed and political elements from the refugees, and the belief that it was necessary to maintain the principle of voluntary repatriation, the international effort became viewed by the Rwandan government as aiding and abetting the continued genocide.

Unfortunately, the nature of the international intervention contributed to the institutionalization of violence, rather than breaking the cycle of impunity which gave rise to the genocide in the first place.

During my travels to the region during 1995–1996, in particular, it was apparent that unless the international community came up with a solution to a problem that was increasingly destabilizing the region, the Rwandans ultimately would feel compelled to respond. No one doubted they would, from UNHCR representatives in the field, to many of the NGOs working on the ground. The moral dilemma for the humanitarian workers was becoming an unbearable burden to carry. NGOs, in particular, became more outspoken when I visited the camps in emphasizing that this was a political problem, not a refugee problem, and there was no reason for the camps to continue to be supported.

In the end the question of whether voluntary repatriation was practical and even possible under these circumstances was particularly unrealistic since the legitimate refugees did not have the option of exercising free will in making that choice. Legitimate refugees were controlled by those who needed them and the services provided them to further their own ends.

The Great Lakes crisis also revealed other serious deficiencies in the international system. Of major concern is the seeming inability of donors to collaboratively structure relief and rehabilitation efforts in a way that the root causes of conflict are addressed. This entails focusing resources not within a traditional relief and rehabilitation framework, but in such a manner that effectively ameliorates ethnic, religious or cultural tensions. Often, short-term relief and rehabilitation responses do not reflect strategic analysis or planning that is structured in such a way so as to avoid the next conflict. The international response to Rwanda serves as a classic example of this problem.

We spent hundreds of millions of dollars in meeting the needs of the refugees. Despite donor pledges amounting to hundreds of millions of dollars, disbursement of significant sums of these pledges were agonizingly slow in Rwanda. This problem stems from the various rules and regulations governing individual donor programs. Fast-disbursing resources are available for immediate humanitarian relief and meet rehabilitation needs. Flexible tools to bridge the gap between rehabilitation and traditional development programs are limited, which slows down the disbursal rate considerably.

One of the best analyses of the current situation in Rwanda was recently published by the U.S. Committee for Refugees. In that study, it was pointed out that there are basically five different groups in Rwanda. Those who survived the genocide; those Hutus who remained inside Rwanda after the genocide; those Tutsi refugees who fled Rwanda in 1959 and the early 1960s and returned; the Hutu refugees who returned from the Zaire, Tanzania and Burundi camps; and Tutsis who fled Burundi and Zaire. Each group suffers from the same deprivations, a lack of even minimal health and education services, and economic opportunity. This is creating serious tensions among the five groups, belying the notion that Rwanda's problems are essentially a Tutsi/Hutu problem.

Once again, in recognition of this problem, donors will be meeting later this month with the Government of Rwanda to develop a strategic framework to more effectively address these fundamental problems. There is a growing consensus that reconciliation in Rwanda will occur only when the basic needs of the entire population are met and problems common to all are addressed. There is a recognition on the part of the donor community that we have to do business differently in Rwanda and the region. We have to be much more flexible in the deployment of resources than has been the case in the past.

It has been anticipated that there will be additional follow-up to the Stockholm conference to deal with many of the suggestions of the independent assessment. The assessment is not yet available publicly since it is still undergoing revisions. However, I would like to touch upon some of the suggestions to give the Subcommittee a sense of the issues with which the international community is presently grappling.

First, it is suggested that the Inter-Agency Standing Committee of the United Nations engage authorities from the Democratic Republic of the Congo, Rwanda, Burundi, Uganda and Tanzania to obtain a commitment to providing a framework for consent for humanitarian action in the Great Lakes region. This should be done in collaboration and consultation with the Office for the Coordination of Humanitarian Affairs.

A salient point in relation to this suggestion is as follows:

> Given that a framework for consent is defined by the intersection of political, humanitarian, economic and social interests of authorities in the region, UN offices should routinely engage in multidisciplinary analysis of these aspects of conflict. Authorities in the region and other foreign governments should respect the need for the UN to conduct this analysis insofar as it relates to defining, delimiting and protecting humanitarian space.

Second, the Inter-Agency Standing Committee should define the process whereby, when a framework for consent has collapsed, the system-wide suspension of humanitarian activities and nonintervention are systematically evaluated and employed as rational responses to some aspects of complex emergencies. In this regard it is suggested that conflict impact assessment tools be used to plan humanitarian activities, monitor their ongoing impact, and assess their contribution to sustainable processes of peace-building.

In addition, it is suggested that a deliberate effort be made to 'attract and place individuals with adequate skills and experience to evaluate the political, military, social and humanitarian context of the crisis in the Great Lakes region, placing such staff as key advisers to UN staff responsible for key operational and strategic humanitarian co-ordination decisions in the region.'

Third, the Inter-Agency Standing Committee should work to address the question of how human rights and humanitarian organizations can more effectively work together. Included in this suggestion is a review of the relationship between human rights law and UN agency protection mandates and the need to routinely train UN humanitarian staff in human rights law.

Fourth, the entire UN system working in the Great Lakes region should recognize that unacceptable human tragedies continue in the Great Lakes region. Therefore, measures should be taken to ensure that the primary humanitarian obligation to save lives and reduce human suffering remains a focus of the UN system in the region, while working through such fora as the Secretary-General's Task Force on Relief, Reconstruction and Development to address underlying problems and long-term solutions.

This suggestion calls for a review of the 'appropriateness of the application of the relief-to-development continuum in the region, given the deepening of civil conflict in Rwanda, the continuing conflict in Burundi, and renewed conflict in the DRC'. The need for ongoing humanitarian operations in Rwanda should be recognized, 'and the vital importance of ensuring that humanitarian and development activities in the country are complementary, reinforcing common objectives'.

Fifth, 'UN agencies were not designed to work in close collaboration with one another. The wording of each agency's mandate specifically defines responsibility for what once were nearly unrelated issues; refugees, development, children, etc. The end of the Cold War has brought new and still unresolved challenges to the UN system ... The hard realities of complex emergencies demand that the UN ... conform itself to these challenges and become what it never has been: a system of agencies that cooperate in pursuit of common goals.'

I might add that this problem is not unique to the United Nations. If there is one thing that every Western donor acknowledges, it is the fact that we all suffer in varying degrees from the same compartmentalization within our own systems.

Sixth, the Inter-Agency Standing Committee should seek to strengthen existing mechanisms for strategic co-ordination.

Of particular importance was the suggestion that the need for improved capacities for strategic analysis be recognized, with 'strong links to operational and strategic decisions, and work through the DPA/DPK/OCHA framework to ensure that the IASC has sufficient access to political and strategic analysis of the political and military context and framework of humanitarian issues. An increased emphasis should be placed on interagency training, recognizing that such training will contribute to improved multidimensional planning and the creation of cross-agency networks.'

Seventh, the Inter-Agency Standing Committee should task the Office for Coordination of Humanitarian Affairs to support coordination functions irrespective of where they occur. OCHA should reliably and consistently provide high-quality co-ordination support staff to staff, or when necessary, directly fulfil co-ordination roles.

Eighth, the Inter-Agency Standing Committee should energetically seek to resolve issues of mandate overlaps and gaps, in particular with respect to internally displaced persons.

The assessment concluded with the following observation:

The crisis in the Great Lakes region posed enormous challenges for those tasked to respond to massive, urgent humanitarian needs of suffering populations. Some of the problems faced were unique to the region; many are problems faced by the UN system across the globe. These problems are formidable; the solutions require a high level of inter-agency collaboration and commitment to humanitarian principles. However, learning these lessons, and translating lessons learned into improved structures, procedures, and systems for strategic co-ordination is an essential task of continuing to improve the UN's overall contribution to lessening the humanitarian costs of what is unfortunately likely to be an ongoing feature of international life, complex political crises with tremendously high human costs.

Mr Chairman and members of the Subcommittee, I want to emphasize that those institutions and individuals tasked with meeting the humanitarian needs of legitimate refugees and internally displaced persons have been placed in an untenable position by the nature of the crises to which we are now compelled to respond. The entire system, multilateral, bilateral and non-governmental, has been ill-equipped from both an analytical/strategic and an operational framework to deal with the complexity of failed states. Historically, we have had to respond to the humanitarian needs of those affected by conflict between states. Now, we are being called upon to respond to intra-state conflict.

The fact that we are all undergoing critical self-analysis and reaching a consensus on not only changes that are required in the system, but also the need for close collaboration among all the actors, opens up the real possibility that we can effectively prevent conflict, or at least mitigate its consequences.

However, no amount of analysis is a substitute for action. We all know what are the problems and now it is incumbent on us to begin adjusting our institutional responses accordingly to reflect these acknowledged realities.

Thank you very much and I am ready to take questions now.

GLOSSARY

Akazu the 'inner circle' of government who wielded most power during Habyarimana's presidency

askari East African soldier or policeman, a term now used in France's former colonies to describe a privately employed security guard

Banyamulenge group of Tutsi native to South Kivu, once seen as initiators of Kabila's rebellion; media reports inaccurately used this term to describe all Kabila's troops; Kabila himself is not a Banyamulenge

burgomaster a commune's chief administrative officer, appointed by the central government

cellule a group of ten or so rural households: the smallest unit in a commune

commune a group of thousands of homesteads scattered over adjacent hills

EU European Union

FAR Rwandan armed forces pre-genocide; following the RPA victory in 1994 FAR became an illegal paramilitary force, referred to as 'ex-FAR'

HRFOR Human Rights Field Operation in Rwanda

IMF International Monetary Fund

interahamwe a civilian militia recruited to help implement genocide

indaba a conference or serious debate, usually involving the elders of a community

matatu minibus taxi

MRND Mouvement Révolutionnaire National pour le Développement, founded by President Habyarimana in 1975: the only political party permitted under his rule

MSF Médecins Sans Frontières

muzungu white person

NGO Non-governmental organization, e.g., Concern, Oxfam, Médecins Sans Frontières, Christian Aid

OAU Organization of African Unity

RMC Radio Mille Collines, a private radio station used to incite hatred of the Tutsi

RPA Rwandan Patriotic Army, military branch of RPF

RPF Rwandan Patriotic Front, movement started by Tutsi exiles; victorious in civil war and now dominant in 'government of national unity'

ruga peasant homestead: one or more huts usually enclosed by a fence

SAP Structural Adjustment Programme: a spending restriction placed by the IMF on countries indebted to it

UNHCR United Nations High Commission for Refugees

UNAMIR United Nations Assistance Mission to Rwanda

WFP World Food Programme

umuganda free labour demanded by the state (previously by kings or chiefs) as a form of tax

UNICEF United Nations International Children's Emergency Fund

SELECT
BIBLIOGRAPHY

African Rights. *Rwanda: Death, Despair and Defiance* (rev. ed., London, 1995).

African Rights. *Rwanda not so Innocent: When Women Become Killers* (London, 1995).

Destexhe, Alain. *Rwanda and Genocide in the Twentieth Century* (Pluto Press, London, 1995).

Igwara, Obi (ed.). *Ethnic Hatred: Genocide in Rwanda* (ASEN, London, 1995).

Mang, Christa. *Zaire* (Brandt Publications, Chalfont St Peter, 1991).

Newbery, Catharine. *The Cohesion of Oppression: Clientship and Ethnicity in Rwanda, 1860–1960* (Columbia University Press, 1988).

Prunier, Gérard. *The Rwanda Crisis: History of a Genocide* (Hurst & Co., London, 1995).

Whitman, Jim, and David Pocock (eds). *After Rwanda: The Co-ordination of United Nations Humanitarian Assistance* (Macmillan, London, 1996).

INDEX